THE VIRTUE OF ARISTOTLE'S ETHICS

While Aristotle's account of the happy life continues to receive attention, many of his claims about virtue of character seem so puzzling that modern philosophers have often discarded them, or have reworked them to fit more familiar theories that do not make virtue of character central. In this book, Paula Gottlieb takes a fresh look at Aristotle's claims, particularly the much-maligned doctrine of the mean. She shows how they form a thought-provoking ethic of virtue, one that deserves to be developed and refined. The first part of the book addresses the nature of virtue and the virtues, illuminated by the doctrine of the mean. Building on the conclusions of this analysis, the second part explains the mentality of the good person and the type of society that will allow such a person to flourish.

Paula Gottlieb is Professor of Philosophy and Affiliate Professor of Classics at the University of Wisconsin–Madison. She was educated at Oxford and Cornell. The author of an analysis and commentary on Aristotle's *Nicomachean Ethics* I and II for project Archelogos, she has received fellowships from the Center for Hellenic Studies, Washington, DC, and the Institute for Research in the Humanities at the University of Wisconsin–Madison.

THE VIRTUE OF ARISTOTLE'S ETHICS

Paula Gottlieb

University of Wisconsin–Madison

CAMBRIDGE
UNIVERSITY PRESS

CAMBRIDGE UNIVERSITY PRESS
Cambridge, New York, Melbourne, Madrid, Cape Town, Singapore, São Paulo, Delhi

Cambridge University Press
32 Avenue of the Americas, New York, NY 10013–2473, USA

www.cambridge.org
Information on this title: www.cambridge.org/9780521761765

First published 2009

Printed in the United States of America

A catalog record for this publication is available from the British Library.

Library of Congress Cataloging in Publication data
Gottlieb, Paula, 1958–
    The virtue of Aristotle's ethics / Paula Gottlieb.
        p. cm
    Includes bibliographical references and index.
    ISBN 978-0-521-76176-5 (hardback)
    1. Aristotle.   2. Ethics.   3. Virtue.   4. Virtues.   5. Character.   6. Aristotle.
    Nicomachean ethics.   I.   Title.
    B491.E7G68 2009
    171′.3–dc22   2008043683

ISBN 978-0-521-76176-5 hardback

To Sybil and Bernard

Contents

Preface and Acknowledgments

In his ethical works, Aristotle presents an extraordinarily nuanced and insightful account of the different aspects of the good human being and the good human being's life. Yet many of Aristotle's claims about ethical virtue seem so puzzling that modern philosophers have often discarded them, or reworked them to fit more familiar modern theories that do not make ethical virtue central. My aim in this book is to re-examine Aristotle's puzzling claims, especially the much-maligned doctrine of the mean, showing how together they form a thought-provoking ethic of virtue, one that deserves to be developed and refined. Aristotle's *Nicomachean Ethics*, the most important of his ethical treatises, appeals to anyone interested in ethical character and thought, including undergraduates, graduates, specialists in ancient Greek philosophy, and modern virtue ethicists. I should be pleased if this book does the same.

There is a fine line between a work on Aristotle's ethics and a work on Aristotelian Ethics, the former being more closely tied to Aristotle's texts, the latter going into new territory, inspired by Aristotle's ideas. While I have approached Aristotle's texts from a less familiar perspective, bringing out elements in his philosophy that have not received their due, and considering them in the light of ancient and modern debates,[1] I have refrained from venturing too far from his original views. The exception is Chapter 4, where I consider possible virtues that Aristotle himself does not consider, but, even there, I keep comments on the particular virtues short and to the point.

[1] See the discussion of philosophical scholarship in Section 4 of the Introduction.

The passage of more than two thousand years has yielded a wealth of scholarship about Aristotle's work, and the last thirty years has seen burgeoning interest in Aristotle's ethics, with new books and articles published every year. While I should like to be able to address every line of thought in detail, I have had to be selective. I have addressed the views of particular philosophers at length where those views clearly advanced my general argument, or were crucial in showing how I wished to change the terms of reference of a particular debate. Otherwise, I have relegated references, extra qualifications, and further more-detailed scholarly philosophical comments to footnotes.

Different readers respond to different styles of writing. Some like frequent summaries and recapitulations; others want to read an uninterrupted flow. For the first type of reader, I have provided summaries and a table of contents that allows one to see at a glance the main points of each chapter. The second type of reader may skip the table of contents and summaries.

The select bibliography is very select. It is intended mainly to give references to specific secondary literature cited in the text, although other influential works have been included as well. For a recent comprehensive bibliography, see Lockwood 2005. Translating Aristotle is difficult. Although some of my interpretations of the texts may be original, the translations are quite conservative so as to be intelligible in the light of available translations and past scholarly literature. Here, I am indebted to Ross and Irwin.[2]

I first encountered Aristotle's *Nicomachean Ethics* in the gap year between high school and university more than thirty years ago. Since then, I have benefited from discussions of Aristotle's ethics with teachers, colleagues, and students. I have received many challenging questions about my interpretation of Aristotle from specialists in ancient philosophy, modern philosophers, classicists, and other professors in the Humanities, and have incorporated many of their suggestions into the text. Although I criticize various lines of thought in my book, I have learnt a great deal from their proponents. My book has also been improved by the rigorous scrutiny and generous suggestions of anonymous readers of earlier versions of particular chapters and of the whole work.

[2] Ross 1923 and Irwin 1985 and revised version, 1999.

Some of the central ideas of my book stem from 1992–3, when I had the opportunity to take up a fellowship at the Center for Hellenic Studies in Washington, DC, to study the unity of the Aristotelian virtues. A Sabbatical leave for 1997–8, awarded by the Graduate School of the University of Wisconsin–Madison, allowed me to crystallize Aristotle's distinctive ethic of virtue as the general theme of my book, and to compose a detailed outline of the chapters and further work to be done. I am grateful to the Institute for Research in the Humanities in Madison for a fellowship to continue work on my book in the fall of 2001, and the Graduate School of the University of Wisconsin–Madison for several summer grants.

My earliest debts are to my teachers at Oxford and Cornell, especially Jean Austin, Michael Woods, and Terry Irwin. The present work on Aristotle's ethics is part of a continuing attempt to answer the difficult questions they posed many years ago. Thanks also to Julia Annas, David Charles, Gail Fine, David Lyons, and Nick Sturgeon for their support.

More recently, I have benefited from discussions with colleagues and numerous tutorials with students at the University of Wisconsin–Madison. I should like to thank Terry Penner for invaluable, but sceptical, comments on various chapters of the book; Claudia Card for helpful conversations and comments; Russ Shafer-Landau and Elliott Sober for generously commenting on particular chapters; Noël Carroll, Berent Enç, Dan Hausman, and Leora Weitzman for helpful discussion of the general project; and Bill Hay and Lester Hunt for bibliographic help.

Thanks also to the following for questions and objections: Marty Barrett, Scott Berman, Jim Butler, Mike Byrd, Andy Coan, Monica Cowart, Ellery Eells, Ted Everett, Malcolm Forster, Jean Goodwin, Chris Johnson, Stephan Johnson, Pat Kain, Joanna King, Pam Knoll, Silvia Montiglio, Cora Lee Mooney neé Kleinhenz, Pat Mooney, Kate Norlock, Tasia Persson, Naomi Reshotko, Sheri Ross, Andrew Ruis, Ben Sachs, Fran Schrag, LaVerne Shelton, Alan Sidelle, Ivan Soll, Denny Stampe, Josh Thurow, Rimas Uzgiris, Andrea Veltman, Mark Vieaux, Shawn Wanta, Shawn Welnak, Ajume Hassan Wingo, Keith Yandell, and Dave Yount. Special thanks to Terry Penner, Ruth Saunders, and "the Greeks" for making sure that I kept Socrates in mind. Also, thanks to visiting "Greeks" Giovanni Giorgini, Rachana Kamtekar, John Longeway, and Christopher Rowe, for discussing my early work.

An earlier version of Chapter 2 was published as "Aristotle's 'Nameless' Virtues" in *Apeiron* 27.1, March 1994, 1–15. I should like to thank Academic Printing and Publishing for allowing me to reprint it here. A revised version of "Are the Virtues Remedial?" in *Journal of Value Inquiry* 35, 2001, 343–54, is printed here as Chapter 3 with kind permission of Springer Science and Business Media. I should also like to thank Koninklijke Brill NV for allowing me to publish a revised version of "Aristotle on Dividing the Soul and Uniting the Virtues" in *Phronesis* 39.3, 1994, 275–90, as Chapter 5. I thank Blackwell for allowing me to use material from "The Practical Syllogism", published in *Blackwell's Guide to Aristotle's Ethics*, ed. Richard Kraut, 2006, 218–33, for Chapter 8.

Over the past years, I have presented fledgling parts of my book in many places. An earlier version of Chapter 1 was presented at Georgia State University and at the University of Georgia in March 2001. A shorter version was presented at the annual meeting of the Central American Philosophical Association in May 2001. I should like to thank May Sim, the commentator, for her very helpful remarks. I should also like to thank those who raised questions in Georgia, especially Edward Halper, Steve Strange, Beth Preston, and David Weberman. Thanks also to Howard Curzer for helpful written comments on my paper, and to Lesley Brown for answering a question about her view.

Special thanks to Terry Penner, Constance Meinwald, and Nancy Sherman for very helpful discussion and criticisms of the original draft of Chapter 2. I have also benefited from the comments of Claudia Card, Berent Enç, Mark Munn, Roger Shiner, Elliott Sober, Jan Van Ophuijsen, Leora Weitzman, and Keith Yandell.

Ancestral versions of Chapter 3 were presented to "the Greeks" in Madison and at the Chicago Workshop in Ancient Philosophy, 1996, and at the University of St. Andrew's, 1998. Many thanks to the following for a host of helpful questions and suggestions: in Chicago, Constance Meinwald, Richard Kraut, Ken Alprin, Elizabeth Asmis, Ian Mueller, Nathan Nicol, Meredith Williams, Michael Williams, and Edyta Imai; in Madison, Terry Penner, Ruth Saunders, William Courtenay, Christopher Rowe, and Leora Weitzman; and in Scotland, Neil Cooper, Bonnie Kent, Paul Markwick, and Leslie Stevenson. Thanks also to Dale Jaquette and, most recently, to Russ Shafer-Landau for written comments.

An earlier presentation that included some ideas from Chapter 4 was given to the Institute for Research in the Humanities at the University of Wisconsin–Madison in the fall of 2001. Thanks to the following for their questions: Sally Banes, Paul Boyer, Phillip Harth, David Hillman, Robert Kingdon, Ullrich Langer, Mike Shank, David Woodward, and especially Claudia Card, Noël Carroll, and John Longeway.

Special thanks to the following for helpful criticisms and suggestions on the topic of Chapter 5: Terry Penner, Constance Meinwald, Jan M. Van Ophuijsen, Claudia Card, Leora Weitzman, and Terry Irwin. I should also like to thank Nancy Sherman and Alphonso Gómez-Lobo for helpful conversations, and Robert W. Sharples for detailed written comments and helpful discussion.

A version of Chapter 6 was presented at an invited session at the Pacific meeting of the American Philosophical Association, 2004. Thanks especially to Susan Sauvé Meyer and Christopher Rowe, the commentators, for their helpful criticism and encouragement. Thanks also to Adrian Moore, David Charles, Paolo Crivelli, Lindsay Judson, and Ben Morison for questions in Oxford, and Terry Penner and Mark Lovas for generous written comments.

While working on the topic of Chapter 7, I benefited from commenting on John Kultgen's paper on civic courage at the annual meeting of the Central States Philosophical Association 2002, and from the Kantian objections of Christine Korsgaard. Thanks also to Jim Butler and Tony Chu, and to Terry Penner for helpful, though sceptical, discussion.

The first version of Chapter 8 was presented at a conference on *Nicomachean Ethics* VI at the Virginia Polytechnic Institute and State University, 1997, the latest at the Berlin workshop on the practical syllogism, 2007. I should like to thank the following for detailed comments on earlier versions of this chapter: Norman Dahl, Mark Gifford, R. J. Hankinson, Rachana Kamtekar, John Longeway, Terry Penner, Ruth Saunders, Elliott Sober, and Leora Weitzman. Special thanks to Richard Kraut for a host of helpful suggestions.

I have benefited from discussing the issues raised in Sections 1–5 of Chapter 9 with Terry Penner, Leora Weitzman, David Hillman, and members of the Department of Philosophy at the University of

Milwaukee, especially Margaret Atherton, Mark Kaplan, William Wainwright, Robert Schwartz, Eric Shank, Joan Weiner, and also Gene Fendt and Mark Kucsewski. Thanks also to those who attended a colloquium at the Department of Philosophy at the University of Edinburgh, especially Alexander Bird, Neil Cooper, Robin Smith, Dory Scaltsas, and Paolo Crivelli. I should also like to thank Terry Irwin for helpful discussion of *Nicomachean Ethics* I 4. I am grateful to Ted Everett, Malcolm Forster, Bernard Gottlieb, Terry Penner, Ruth Saunders, LaVerne Shelton, Elliott Sober, Leora Weitzman, and also G. Anagnostopoulos, Lloyd Gerson, Mark Gifford, V. A. Goutorov, Sergei Karpyuk, Fred Miller, Richard Pianka, R. Purtill, P. Schollmeier, E. W. Schütrumpf, I. G. Tchernychov, and J. Wilcox for questions about Sections 5 and 6 of Chapter 10, which were originally presented at the sixth international conference of the International Association for Greek Philosophy, on *Aristotle's Political Philosophy*. Thanks also to Cora Lee Kleinhenz, Andrew Ruis, and Shawn Welnak for helpful discussion. Most recently, I have benefited from written comments on the whole chapter by Claudia Card and Josiah Ober.

Many thanks to Susan Sauvé Meyer and an anonymous referee, whose comments on details of chapters and on the general themes of the entire work have led to numerous improvements.

I continue to benefit from the help and encouragement of the Publishing Director for the Humanities at Cambridge University Press, Beatrice Rehl.

Finally, I should like to thank Henry, with love.

Paula Gottlieb
University of Wisconsin–Madison

Abbreviations

Abbreviations for Aristotle's works are as follows:

A Post.	*Analytica Posteriora*
A Pr.	*Analytica Priora*
de An.	*de Anima*
EE	*Ethica Eudemia*
EN	*Ethica Nicomachea*
Fr.	*Fragmenta*
HA	*Historia Animalium*
MA	*de Motu Animalium*
MM	*Magna Moralia*
Mem.	*de Memoria*
Metaph.	*Metaphysica*
Ph.	*Physica*
Pol.	*Politica*
Rh.	*Rhetorica*
SE	*Sophistici Elenchi*
Sens.	*de Sensu*
Top.	*Topica*

Aristotle's works are cited by book, chapter and Bekker page, and column and line numbers. Plato's works are cited by dialogue, Stephanus pages, and columns. *CAG* refers to *Commentaria in Aristotelem Graeca*, edita consilio et auctoritate Academiae Litterarum Regiae Borussicae: Berolini typis et impensis Georgii Reimeri, vols. 19–20, 1889. Abbreviations for other works are included in the Select Bibliography.

Introduction

1. THE GENERAL THEME AND THE MAIN ARGUMENT OF THE BOOK

The main theme of the book is virtue of character, or, in Aristotelian terms, ethical virtue.[1] My main argument is that Aristotle's puzzling claims about ethical virtue, especially the elusive doctrine of the mean, together form a distinctive ethic of virtue that is well worth pursuing. Hence the title "The Virtue of Aristotle's Ethics".

In treating Aristotle first and foremost as a virtue ethicist, I approach Aristotle from a different angle from other commentators. For example, I pay close attention to those parts of Aristotle's theory that are often denigrated or neglected, such as Aristotle's doctrine of the mean and the nameless virtues, showing how closely they are related to other important parts of his theory. Again, while others take Aristotle's "function argument" and his views on happiness as their point of departure,[2] I discuss these matters instead as they emerge in the context of Aristotle's controversial views about virtue.[3]

The book is divided into two parts. In Part I, I examine various controversial claims that Aristotle makes about ethical virtue, especially

---

[1] Like Aristotle, I often use the term "virtue" alone, when it is clear from the context that ethical virtue is meant.

[2] For example, Irwin 1980, Kraut 1989, N. White 2002, and Richardson Lear 2004.

[3] For example, my discussions of types of goods and the function argument from *EN* I, and of happiness in *EN* X, are embedded in Ch. 7 (Sections 1–3), Ch. 3 (Sections 3 and 5), and Ch. 10 (Section 2).

his view that ethical virtues are in a mean, a doctrine that permeates his ethical theory. I argue that the nameless virtues, long-neglected but comprising half of Aristotle's ethical virtues, are important, both from a philosophical and from a practical point of view. I also argue that the virtues are not essentially remedial, for example, they do not remedy defects in human nature. I argue that both the doctrine of the mean and the non-remedial view of the virtues are required to show that Aristotle's list of ethical virtues is of substantive theoretical interest, especially when compared with some modern candidates for virtue. Finally, I show that Aristotle's rationale for the claim that it is impossible to have one ethical virtue fully without having all the rest contains a deep insight into the type of thoughtfulness and motivation required for ethical virtue.

In Part II, I examine various aspects of the ethical reasoning that informs Aristotelian ethical virtue, and show how Aristotle applies the different theses discussed in Part I. I argue that Aristotle's discussion of moral dilemmas is more humane than modern and indeed ancient analyses permit, due to the doctrine of the mean. I also argue that Aristotle's controversial practical syllogism is best understood in connection with his view that practical wisdom requires full ethical virtue and conversely. Continuing the account of practical wisdom, I raise a puzzle about how much the good person and the student of ethics need to know. I also explain why the combined partial practical wisdom of those in a democracy should have good results.

I argue that attention to particular ethical virtues can explain recalcitrant aspects of Aristotle's more abstract account, for example, his discussions of bravery and friendship illuminate his view of the good human being's motivation, and the nameless virtue of truthfulness contributes to an understanding of Aristotelian practical wisdom as distinct from a technical skill. The good person must not only keep to the mean, but must know his own abilities, in order to act correctly.

Aristotle says that his inquiry is "a sort of politics". I conclude with a discussion of the appropriate society for the Aristotelian virtues, arguing that various passages about the polis and happiness are less puzzling when understood against the backdrop of the arguments about ethical virtue presented in earlier chapters.

2. INTERLOCKING THEMES AND THESES

My point of departure is Aristotle's much-maligned doctrine of the mean. Immanuel Kant thought that it was false and Bertrand Russell dismissed it as "true, but uninteresting".[4] I argue that, when properly understood, it is both interesting and true, and I distinguish three different aspects of the doctrine that make this the case. First, virtue, like health, is in equilibrium and is produced and preserved by avoiding extremes. The good person, having a balanced disposition, will have the correct emotions on the correct occasions and act accordingly. Second, virtue is in a mean relative to us. Third, each virtue is in a mean between two vices, one of excess and one of deficiency. I examine and analyse each of these claims in detail.

While it may be tempting to explain other themes in the book as stemming from the doctrine of the mean, the different themes and theses of the book cannot simply be deduced from any one thesis; rather, they are mutually supporting and interlocking. First, as I explain, the doctrine of the mean contributes to Aristotle's account of the nameless virtues. Second, the doctrine of the mean shows that there are appropriate and inappropriate ways to experience the emotions, but that the emotions themselves are neutral, a point that supports the conclusion that the ethical virtues are not remedial. I argue that ethical virtues are not there to remedy defects, emotional or otherwise, contrary to what recent interpreters suggest.[5] Again, I argue that paying attention to the doctrine of the mean shows how Aristotle generates his list of ethical virtues in a more complicated and plausible way than has previously been thought. In addition, I argue that Aristotle's view about the unity of the virtues complements his view of ethical virtue in equilibrium.

The doctrine of the mean also supports and is bolstered by many of the conclusions of Part II of the book. The doctrine of the mean underwrites Aristotle's approach to situations where difficult decisions have to be made, it partly accounts for the importance of the minor premiss

---

[4] Kant *DOV* XIII, 163; Russell 1930, ch. 16. See too Williams 1985, 36.

[5] For example, Foot 1978 and Korsgaard 1986.

of the practical syllogism, and it contributes to Aristotle's explanation of how democracy can succeed. The medical analogy, first introduced to explain the first aspect of the doctrine of the mean, also helps solve the problem about how much the good person needs to know.

Aristotle is often contrasted with Plato for not being interested in providing a response to the immoralist. Surprisingly, on my interpretation, the third aspect of the doctrine of the mean helps provide a response to just such a person. Finally, I argue that the interconnected theses of the unity of the virtues and their non-remedial nature both resurface in the explanation of the appropriate societal setting for Aristotle's ethical virtues, and that the nameless virtues play an especially important role in Aristotle's account of happiness.

According to Aristotle, ethical virtue and practical wisdom are intimately connected, a related theme that runs throughout my book. Aristotle says that ethical virtue is defined in some way by the person with practical wisdom, and that a person cannot have one ethical virtue fully without having all the rest. Ethical virtue requires practical wisdom and practical wisdom requires ethical virtue. I argue that Aristotle's rationale for the fact that the ethical virtues are united is that ethical virtue "involves reason" (*meta logou*) and is not merely "in accordance with reason" (*kata logon*), and I give an interpretation of the distinction that has broader ramifications. I argue that the idea that ethical virtue "involves reason" is also behind Aristotle's explanation of how the good person is motivated to act "for the sake of the fine". Most important, I show that Aristotle's thesis that practical wisdom requires ethical virtue casts new light on his controversial practical syllogism, with ethical virtue at the heart of the discussion.

3. ARISTOTLE AND VIRTUE ETHICS

The term "virtue ethics" was introduced in the 1960s to refer to an ethical approach that not only makes virtue of character primary but also marks a distinctive and superior alternative to prevailing Utilitarian and Kantian approaches. Briefly, while Utilitarians are interested in the goodness of states of affairs or the consequences that flow from particular actions, and Kantians concentrate on duties and goodness of motives, the virtue ethicist is interested in goodness of character.

The original proponents of virtue ethics took Aristotle's work to be a prime example of their own approach. However, more recently, Aristotelian scholars have been taking a different tack, comparing Aristotle's views with Kant's,[6] and even neo-Aristotelian proponents of virtue ethics have abandoned key facets of Aristotle's own view, such as the doctrine of the mean, and the view that the ethical virtues are not remedial, following Kant.[7]

It should come as no surprise that the features of Aristotle's view on which I focus are the ones most neglected and misunderstood, because they are the ones least congenial to modern thinking, especially of the Kantian and Utilitarian sort. In paying close attention to these features, I am at the very same time paying close attention to Aristotle's ethic of virtue. My aim is not to examine Utilitarianism or Kantian theory or modern virtue ethics in detail, but to give a fair and sympathetic account of what I take to be those features of Aristotle's own view that might serve to characterize an ethic of virtue for the future, although the project of developing such an approach lies beyond the scope of this book.

As Julia Annas explains in one of her books on ancient Greek and Hellenistic ethics:

> All serious discussion of moral thinking would benefit from recognizing, and giving due attention to the element in our moral thinking which is concerned with virtue and character. But after decades of neglect this is a difficult task to carry out. Reflection on ancient ethical theory may make it easier for us to do this; for we need to study theories which make these notions primary in order to recover a proper understanding of them.[8]

---

[6] For example, the majority of contributors to Engstrom and Whiting 1996 and Sherman 1997. I do not mean to suggest that this trend is universal.

[7] See Foot 1978 and Hursthouse 1999.

[8] Annas 1993, 455. Unlike Annas's treatment of ancient virtue ethics, my book and its conclusions are restricted to Aristotle. Others in the non-Kantian tradition of Aristotelian interpretation include Wiggins 1975–6 and Nussbaum 1986.

4. PHILOSOPHICAL METHOD AND SOLVING PUZZLES

My discussion is based on a careful reading of the texts. My main text is Aristotle's *Nicomachean Ethics*, but I shall also discuss some of the *Eudemian Ethics* and passages from other works that help to illuminate the central text. Since almost all interpretation of Aristotelian texts is controversial, there is no such thing as pure exegesis in the following pages. In order to understand what Aristotle is saying, it is also neces-sary to take his views seriously, even and especially when they appear inimical to modern thought, and to consider what is plausible and true in his thinking, in the context of both ancient and modern debates. For example, it is fruitful to consider whether Aristotle thinks that the ethical virtues are remedial, or whether there are moral dilemmas as described by modern thinkers, especially when modern philosophers attribute to Aristotle their own views. According to Aristotle himself, everyone has something to contribute to the truth, so it is reasonable to see what Aristotle can contribute to current debates, just as it is rea-sonable for Aristotle to see what Socrates, for example, can contribute to debate in Aristotle's day.[9] This is also the method of modern philo-sophical scholarship.[10]

Aristotle thinks that the best way to become clear about a partic-ular subject matter is by going through the puzzles (e.g., *EN* VII 1 1145b1–7). In his *Metaphysics*, he even devotes a whole book to puz-zles and difficulties about metaphysics. Following Aristotle's lead, and in order to become clearer about Aristotelian ethical virtue, I address different puzzling questions about Aristotle's ethics in each chapter of

---

[9] Aristotle treats the Socrates of the early Platonic dialogues as the historical Socrates, and distinguishes Socrates' views from those presented in later Platonic dialogues (*Metaphysics* I 6, XIII 4, 9–10, *Nicomachean Ethics* IV 7 1127b22–6, VI 13 1144b14–21, VII 2 1145b22–7, *Eudemian Ethics* I 5 1216b2–11, *Sophistici Elenchi* I 34 183b6–8). An influential group of modern philosophers doubt Aristotle's account, for example, Kahn 1996 and Annas 1999. For the opposing view, see, for example, Vlastos 1991 and Penner 1992a. I side with Aristotle, but the debate does not affect anything I have to say about Aristotle's ethics.

[10] See Charles 1984, ix–x who coins the term and defends the method, and Irwin 1986a who argues that the method is long-standing.

my book.[11] What does Aristotle mean by the claim that virtue is "in a mean relative to us"? What is the point of having triads of virtue and vices (Chapter 1)? What are the nameless virtues, why are they included among the ethical virtues, and why are they nameless (Chapter 2)? Do the ethical virtues presuppose that human beings are naturally good or bad or neither? Are the virtues remedial (Chapter 3)? What is the rationale for Aristotle's claim that it is not possible to have one ethical virtue fully without having all the rest (Chapter 4)? How does Aristotle generate the ethical virtues on his list? Why does he include the ethical virtues he does, and not include other dispositions that have been considered virtues (Chapter 5)? Given his views about the doctrine of the mean and the unity of the virtues, what does Aristotle have to say about moral dilemmas, an important topic in ancient and modern thought (Chapter 6)? How can Aristotle coherently hold that we can be motivated by some good both for its own sake and for the sake of something else? Can Aristotle explain how we can care for a friend for his or her own sake (Chapter 7)? How does the nameless virtue of truthfulness help explain the difference between practical wisdom and technical skill? How can there be such a thing as a *practical* syllogism and how does it relate to Aristotle's account of ethical virtue (Chapter 8)? How much does the good person have to know (Chapter 9)? How should we understand Aristotle's claim that his inquiry in the *Nicomachean Ethics* is "a sort of Politics", that is, what sort of polis would be suitable for Aristotle's ethical virtues, and would that polis be democratic in any way? Can we make sense of Aristotle's ranking of different happy lives in *Nicomachean Ethics* X (Chapter 10)?

5. SYNOPSIS OF CHAPTERS

Chapter 1 marks the beginning of a lengthy argument to re-evaluate Aristotle's doctrine of the mean. I argue that although the doctrine is not a decision procedure, nor, as Kant thought, a doctrine of moderation, it has substantive content: it combines a doctrine of equilibrium,

---

[11] The reader may find Rorty 1980 useful for the source of some of these puzzles.

a sophisticated view of the particulars of the situation, and a triadic taxonomy of different good and bad mentalities.

I explain how Aristotle introduces his doctrine of the mean by analogy with medicine and dietetics. Next, I distinguish three aspects of the doctrine of the mean. First, the virtuous person has a balanced disposition that allows him to have the correct emotions and to act accordingly on the correct occasions and so forth – Aristotle's doctrine of equilibrium. Second, virtue is in a mean "relative to us". I argue that the debate about how this is to be understood needs to be reformulated so as to see precisely which factors about the agent need to be taken into account, whether these factors are relevant in all cases, and whether the same factors are at play in ethical decisions affecting ourselves and others. I examine particular Aristotelian virtues, including a "large-scale" virtue and some nameless virtues, to show that the "relativity to us" at issue is not necessarily invariant across all cases. It is not just that what the correct thing is to do varies from situation to situation, according to Aristotle, but there are factors relative to which certain things are right and wrong – facts about the agent, including the agent's abilities, or information about who the agent is – that also vary from situation to situation. I argue that Aristotle is therefore misapplying his own theory when he thinks that being a woman or a slave are *always* relevant factors, when they may vary, just as in medicine being a woman is a crucial factor in treating heart disease, but not in treating a broken ankle.

Third, Aristotle claims that each virtue comes between two vices. An oft-repeated criticism of Aristotle's view is that one can find more than two vices to flank particular virtues, for example, the virtue of bravery. In fact, one can find more than two vices for any Aristotelian virtue, but I argue that there is still a point to the triadic system, because it highlights three importantly different mentalities, as can be gleaned from Aristotle's account of self-love and a puzzling passage about practical wisdom itself being in a mean in the *Eudemian Ethics*. A practical consequence of abandoning Aristotle's triadic framework is that one may mistake one of the true vices for the virtue. An example of this problem also appears in the next chapter.

In Chapter 2, I continue to discuss the application of the doctrine of the mean, turning now to the much-neglected nameless virtues, which comprise half the virtues on Aristotle's list. The main argument, continued in Chapter 4, is that Aristotle is not merely accepting contemporary views, nor is he ignoring his theoretical commitment to the doctrine of the mean, when it comes to discussing particular virtues. Aristotle's triadic account of virtue and vices, the third aspect of his doctrine of the mean, helps solve a problem about the proper (nameless) virtue in the sphere of small honours. In addition, Aristotle is right to claim that certain "questionable mean dispositions" in *Eudemian Ethics* are full-blown nameless ethical virtues in his *Nicomachean Ethics*. Finally, I argue that there are positive reasons for including the nameless virtues in the roster of virtues, not least for the maintenance of a democratic society, a point to be elaborated in Chapter 10.

Given the nature of the nameless virtues, it is implausible to think that the Aristotelian virtues are essentially remedial. In fact, it is a central thesis of his ethic of virtue that they are not. In Chapter 3, I address the view of some modern ethicists, a virtue ethicist and a Kantian, who enlist Aristotle in arguing for the opposite view that the main role of the virtues is to remedy defects in human nature and in the world. The remedial view is supposedly linked with the idea that if human beings were perfect, or if they lived in a perfect world, for example, "the isles of the blessed", there would be no need for the ethical virtues.

I argue that Aristotle's discussions of gods, humans, and the isles of the blessed do not support the remedial view. I argue that the idea of corrective virtues is antithetical to the first aspect of the doctrine of the mean. I argue that it is also antithetical to the correct way of understanding the function of a human being in Aristotle's famous function argument. Finally, I make some suggestions about the origin of remedial views, including the traditional interpretation of Kant, and why such views should be rejected.

Aristotle's list of ethical virtues is interesting both for what it includes and what it omits. In Chapter 4, I address the question of how Aristotle generates his list of ethical virtues. I consider various different suggestions about how Aristotle derives his list, including some discussed in earlier chapters, and I argue that, to give a complete explanation, we need to refer to the different aspects of Aristotle's doctrine of the mean, as explained in earlier chapters. I also discuss various possible particular virtues, popular in modern times and among modern philosophers, applying Aristotle's doctrine of the mean and related theses. My main aim is to show that Aristotle's doctrine of the mean is far from vacuous when considered from this less familiar perspective.

I argue that the resulting Aristotelian list is quite controversial. He omits perseverance, endurance, faith, piety, and hope and sympathy *tout court* from his list. *Pace* Bentham and others, he does make room for charity and benevolence. While he rejects asceticism, meekness, self-sacrifice, and self-control as virtues, he also accepts the "social virtues" despite Kant's deprecating remarks on the subject. Aristotle rejects pusillanimity as a virtue, contrary to a modern Utilitarian, and his triadic view rules out the virtues approved of by the followers of Ayn Rand. Aristotelian justice is the odd one out, but equity is more important. Finally, I argue that one might extend Aristotle's view to include green virtues, and, most important, the nameless virtue of tolerance.

In Chapter 5, I examine Aristotle's controversial thesis that it is impossible to have one ethical virtue fully without having all the rest. The thesis is compatible with the doctrine of the mean, but Aristotle supports it using his innovative distinction between "involving reason" and "being in accordance with reason", a distinction that we will revisit in later chapters. Aristotle introduces his thesis about the unity of the virtues in the context of Socrates' view, but Socrates' view differs from Aristotle's because, according to Aristotle, Socrates did not divide the psyche into a rational and non-rational part. The problem for Aristotle is then how to reintegrate the psyche and the ethical virtues. The solution is to be found in Aristotle's new distinction. On my interpretation, the good person's disposition *involves* reason and is not merely *accompanied* by reason as other commentators suggest, and it takes more for ethical virtue to involve reason than it does for a skill to involve reason. I return to this point in Chapter 8. The good person's emotions are fully integrated with his reason. When this occurs, the good person has all the ethical virtues, because incorrect thinking or emotions in any one sphere may undermine the correct thinking or emotions in any other. Since the emotions and reason have to be integrated in order to have ethical virtue, temperament and cleverness alone are not sufficient for ethical virtue, so it is not possible to have one ethical virtue without the rest.

In sum, I argue that Aristotle's thesis underwrites the common-sense view that the good person is someone of integrity. It also supports the first aspect of the doctrine of the mean, because, if the good person is always in equilibrium, such a person needs to have all of the ethical virtues in order to confront all eventualities in life without falling out of kilter. In order to remain balanced, such a person will need to have their emotions and reason going hand in hand.

Aristotle's thesis about the unity of the virtues leads us to expect that the good person is free of inner conflict and regret, and that there are no conflicts within or between the different virtues. It is therefore unclear how Aristotle can deal with cases of either "dirty hands" or tragic dilemmas, where supposedly even the good agent is faced with conflicting demands and does something shameful that stains her character in some way. It has been argued that there are examples of such cases in Greek tragedy and also that Aristotle's example of the tyrant, in his discussion of voluntary action in *Nicomachean Ethics* III, is meant to be a case of dirty hands. According to the modern analysis, when the tyrant asks someone to do something shameful in order to save his family from death, his victim ought to save his family, but in so doing, does something somehow wrong that occasions a special type of regret. In Chapter 6, I argue that Aristotle does not in fact subscribe to the modern analysis of such dilemmas, but that this makes his account more, rather than less, sophisticated and humane than modern alternatives.

First, I present the modern analysis of cases of dirty hands and also tragic dilemmas like Sophie's choice in more detail. Next, I consider whether the Aristotelian agent has the special type of regret required by the modern analysis. I argue that Aristotle does give an account of regret, but not the special type of regret in question. I go on to discuss the thorny problem of "mixed actions", and what Aristotle means by saying that the action of throwing cargo overboard in a storm, for example, is voluntary, but involuntary without qualification. I argue that what counts most are the particular circumstances and stakes involved, as is consistent with the second aspect of Aristotle's doctrine of the mean. I then address the supposed relationship between Aristotle's account of mixed actions and moral dilemmas as analysed by modern philosophers. I argue that there are two main differences: there is no regret in Aristotelian mixed actions that detracts from the agent's good character and the structure of Aristotelian decision-making is antithetical to the modern analysis of moral dilemmas. Aristotle does not see the problems as what to choose *instead of what*, but what to choose *at the price of what*, so he does not analyse the dilemma as consisting of two competing options – do one shameful thing (leaving your family to die) or do another shameful thing (whatever the tyrant wants). Therefore, what the agent does *in the situation* is not vicious or involuntary. At this point, I raise the question whether we should have accepted the modern view that the right thing to do is obviously to help the tyrant. I argue that the answer is that we need far more detail about the situation, just as the second aspect of the doctrine of the mean requires.

Finally, I discuss what Aristotle might say about tragic dilemmas. The upshot is that, according to Aristotle, the agent's character in such a case will not be marred for life, although, plausibly, given that happiness requires external goods including friends and family, she will not be happy. Therefore, contrary to those who accept the modern analysis of tragic dilemmas, Aristotle's view of life is optimistic and humane, and presupposes a coherent view of the world and the perceptions of those in it. Aristotle's view about moral dilemmas applies his doctrine of the mean, and is also at odds with the traditional view of Kant, as one would expect for an ethic of virtue.

In Chapter 7, I argue that Aristotle's claims that the virtuous person acts "for the sake of the fine" and cares for her friend for the friend's own sake, are best understood as theses within an ethic of virtue, further elucidating the way in which ethical virtue "involves reason", as explained in Chapter 5. Commentators, especially Kantians, have been puzzled by Aristotle's view that one can choose something both for its own sake and for the sake of something else. For example, one can choose to do a brave action both for its own sake and for the sake of happiness. I first show how Aristotle's view is plausible by comparing it with Plato's views. Next, I discuss and raise difficulties for Kantian and Utilitarian interpretations of Aristotle's view. Choosing x for its own sake and for the sake of y makes sense taken at face value, provided that y does not undermine one's choosing x in the first place. I argue that cases of mock bravery, where choosing x for the sake of y does undermine the initial choice, support this interpretation, and Aristotle's account of cases of mock bravery elucidates the incorrect, and therefore, the correct motivation on the part of the good person. "Civic bravery", one of the mock forms of bravery, turns out to be comparable with the civic disposition that Aristotle attributes to the warmongering Spartans, discussed further in Chapter 10. Here, I argue against a Kantian interpretation of Aristotle's account of civic virtue in *Eudemian Ethics* VIII 3. Value is objective and is not conferred by the good person's motivation.

Finally, I raise the question how the good person is motivated to care for his friend for the friend's own sake. Commentators have taken Aristotle to mean that if x and y are friends of good character, x cares for y simply because y has a good character, where good character is a repeatable general property, and they have chided and praised Aristotle accordingly. Aristotle's example of mother and child is telling. Contrary to the commentators in question, Aristotle does not think that one cares for a friend merely derivatively from the friend's general character, and he is right not to do so. A good friend needs to be someone of stable character and integrity, as explained in Aristotle's doctrine of the mean and his thesis about the unity of the virtues, in order to be cared for for himself. The Kantian interpretation of Aristotelian friendship and motivation fails to capture the humanity of Aristotle's view.

Chapter 8 completes the argument of Chapter 5 that practical wisdom requires ethical virtue, and conversely, and shows the way in which ethical virtue is at the heart of Aristotelian practical reasoning, a view that is probably most controversial from a modern standpoint and least congenial to Utilitarians and Kantians. I begin with the problem about how to distinguish practical wisdom and technical skill, arguing that the solution comes from Aristotle's views about the virtues, especially the nameless virtue of truthfulness. There remains a further problem about whether Aristotle is begging the question when he says that the difference between practical wisdom and technical skill is that the first requires the ethical virtues, whereas the second does not. As we saw in Chapter 4, it is impossible to have the ethical virtues fully without having practical wisdom and it is impossible to have practical wisdom without having the ethical virtues fully. This raises the question of how exactly practical wisdom requires ethical virtue. I therefore formulate the type of reasoning, represented by the practical syllogism, that explains how this is the case, showing that there can indeed be pieces of reason that are *practical*. I argue that the practical syllogism is analogous to the theoretical syllogism, and that the middle term of the theoretical syllogism, the part that explains why and how the conclusion follows from the premisses, is matched by the first part of the minor premiss of the practical syllogism that says, for example, "I am a generous human being". This part of the minor premiss licenses the move from major premiss to conclusion (action), explains why the agent acts as he does, and the indexical "I" shows how the reasoning is practical. I consider various objections to my interpretation, relating to the middle term, the ethical agent, and deliberation. Finally, I explain the role of the practical syllogism in motivation, as described in Chapter 7, and in justification, and argue that the enkratic, akratic, and learner are not using the practical syllogism, although they may be aspiring to do so. In sum, I argue that the practical syllogism represents the ethical thought of the good person. Practical wisdom and ethical virtue are inseparable.

In Chapters 5 and 8, I argued in different ways that practical wisdom and ethical virtue go hand in hand. However, the aspects of practical wisdom discussed so far have been fairly minimal, so one might think that the person with practical wisdom needs to know a lot more than I have so far discussed. Therefore, in Chapter 9, I discuss the puzzling question of how much it is necessary to know in order to be an Aristotelian good person, and what the good student needs to know in order to study ethics.

Aristotle compares the good person with the healthy person and with the physician. The analogies point in different directions, because a healthy person need not know much about health, whereas a physician needs to know a good deal about health and maybe other scientific disciplines as well. I argue that, despite first appearances, the analogy between the good person and the healthy person is not supposed to show that the good person is merely instinctively good, without any knowledge, because one cannot be good, according to Aristotle, unless one has practical wisdom, as we have seen in Chapters 5 and 8, and practical wisdom involves some general knowledge. Nor is the analogy between the good person and the physician supposed to show that the good person must know as much as Plato's guardians. Turning to the good person's knowledge of psychology, I argue that the good person does need to know some general principles, some human psychology, and, at least implicitly, some more general theses like the doctrine of the mean. However, I argue that even if the good person's knowledge is ultimately based on and uses conclusions from Aristotelian metaphysics, the good person need not be a metaphysician to be good, any more than a physician need be a geometer.

If all this is so, how much will one need to know in order to be a good student of ethics, and what will the student learn from reading Aristotle's *Nicomachean Ethics*? The upshot of an examination of different views and interpretations of the texts is that the *Nicomachean Ethics* is useful, even for the person who already has ethical virtue and practical wisdom, because it is to ethics as a Hippocratic treatise describing different medical conditions and the like is to medicine. It is also useful, given the taxonomy of different mentalities implicit in the third aspect of the doctrine of the mean, in showing what is wrong with the immoralist's life. Finally, Aristotle's use of medical analogies allows him to stake out a position between the early Utilitarians and Kant. Aristotle is firmly in the tradition of virtue ethics.

Since Aristotle's *Nicomachean Ethics* is framed by political questions, in Chapter 10, I address the question of what sort of society or polis would be appropriate for the Aristotelian ethical virtues, and draw on many of the arguments about ethical virtue presented in earlier chapters. First, I consider why political society is needed, according to Aristotle's *Politics*, and how, *contra* Hobbes, the genesis and justification for the polis stem from Aristotle's objective view of the good for human beings *and* his view that the virtues are not remedial. Next, I consider the type of happiness that the polis aims at, and the point of rating different types of happiness in *Nicomachean Ethics* X, since at first sight this ranking seems to be at odds with the second aspect of the doctrine of the mean. Here, I argue that the nameless virtues play an important role in the ranking. I also explain how justice applies in the polis, and, the type of polis most suitable for the virtues of the *Nicomachean Ethics*. Finally, I argue that Aristotle's important defence of collective decision-making in such a polis, in *Politics* III 11, surprisingly is bolstered by Aristotle's theses about the unity of the virtues and the doctrine of the mean.

I conclude with a brief discussion about Aristotle's distinctive ethic of virtue and some speculation about its future development.

PART I

ETHICAL VIRTUE

1   Virtue in the Mean

The aim of this chapter is to re-evaluate a central but much-maligned thesis in Aristotle's *Nicomachean Ethics*, the doctrine of the mean. The doctrine of the mean is a prominent thesis in Aristotle's account of virtue, and it enables other aspects of Aristotle's ethics to be understood from a new perspective, as we shall see in the chapters to come. Aristotle's doctrine of the mean has had a bad press, from being dubbed the "Goldilocks theory of Ethics" to receiving Bernard Williams's intended epitaph that the doctrine is "better forgotten".[1] Most of the unkind comments are based on construing the doctrine of the mean as a decision procedure, and a useless one at that. I wish to examine some aspects of the doctrine that show it in a different light, but that involves solving some long-standing puzzles in the interpretation of the doctrine itself, with special reference to how the doctrine applies to particular ethical virtues.

I argue that Aristotle's doctrine of the mean has the following three aspects. First, virtue, like health, is in equilibrium and is produced and preserved by avoiding extremes and hitting the mean; it is self-sustaining. Second, virtue is in a mean "relative to us". Third, each virtue is in a mean between two vices, one of excess and one of deficiency.

Aristotle himself says that his account is "true, but not at all clear" (*EN* VI 1138b26), and, at first sight, there are certainly many unclarities. First, it is unclear what Aristotle's *positive* account of the mean "relative to us" is. If each virtue comes between two vices, one of excess and one of deficiency, must the doctrine of the mean be a doctrine of moderation – a view that Kant, among others, attributed to Aristotle

[1] Williams 1985, 36.

and thought was clearly false (*DOV*, 163)? Furthermore, if each virtue and flanking vices are to be placed on one continuum, what should be said about those virtues that seem to intersect more than one continuum? Finally, if Aristotle's account is not a doctrine of moderation, what is it instead; and if each virtue can intersect many continua, what is the point of Aristotle's lists of *triads* of virtue and vices? As we shall see, the answers to these questions are connected, but I begin with the medical analogy Aristotle uses to introduce his view, and then consider the three aspects of the doctrine of the mean one by one.

1. A MEDICAL ANALOGY AND THREE ASPECTS OF THE DOCTRINE OF THE MEAN

Aristotle first introduces his doctrine of the mean by way of an analogy with medicine: a person is healthy when his bodily functions are in equilibrium. They can be thrown out of equilibrium in various ways. For example, too much or too little food and drink ruins one's health. Similarly, too much or too little exercise ruins one's strength, whereas the proportionate amount both produces and preserves it (*EN* II 1104a12–18). A similar point is made in the Hippocratic writings (*De Vet. Med.* 9). What the correct amount is is not explained until a few chapters further along where Aristotle says that it is "the intermediate that is relative to us" and gives another example from medical dietetics:

> If, for instance, ten are many and two are few, people take six as intermediate in the object, since it exceeds [two] and is exceeded [by ten] by an equal amount [four]. This is what is intermediate according to arithmetical proportion. But the intermediate that is relative to us must not be taken so. For if ten pounds [of food], for example, are a lot to eat and two a little, the trainer will not [necessarily] prescribe six, because this might be either a little or a lot for the person who is to take it. It [six pounds] would be a little for Milo but a lot for someone beginning gymnastics ... (*EN* II 6 1106a33–1106b4)

Six pounds would hardly be enough to keep up the strength of Milo, who was reputed to have eaten a whole joint of beef at one sitting,[2] and

---

[2] See Aquinas citing Solinus 314, 105.

it would be overwhelming to someone who lacked Milo's bulk. The correct amount, then, is not what is "intermediate in the object", the arithmetical mean, but what is "relative to us".

Virtue, like health and strength, is also "in a mean relative to us" (*EN* II 6 1106b36–1107a1). Aristotle does not describe the mean in the object, but goes straight to describing the mean relative to us: one must do and feel the right things at the right time, in the right way, and for the right reasons (*EN* II 6 1106b21–7).[3] Aristotle describes this, again using medical terminology, as the idea that virtue is *stochastikē* of the intermediate (*EN* II 6 1106b28). The medical term *stochastikē* is in turn derived from a term in archery, referring to hitting the target.[4] In other words, virtue hits the mean. While this is the way to hit on the right action, it is presumably also the way to create or, once created, to preserve one's virtue, and thus to keep oneself in equilibrium.[5] But psychological equilibrium manifests itself via different dispositions. Here again, Aristotle takes over the term *hexis* (disposition) from the medical writers and applies it to the ethical virtues.[6]

Indeed, the idea of relativity can be found in the chapters surrounding the famous chapter 9 of the Hippocratic writing *On Ancient Medicine*. There, the author explains that "no-one would have even sought for medicine, if the same ways of life had suited both the sick and those in health" (chapter 5). The author goes on to explain medicine as a development of the art of dietetics (chapter 7). What food is good for healthy human beings is different from what is good for the sick. In fact, the author points out, a healthy human being's diet would be as bad for someone who is ill as a wild animals' diet would be for a healthy human being (chapter 8). However, good diet is not only relative to members of different species and different for the healthy and for the sick, but

---

[3] As Kosman argues against Joachim, "It is with respect to how one feels *and not simply* how one acts in light of one's feelings that one is said to be virtuous" (Kosman 1980, 109, my emphasis).

[4] Interestingly, an analogy from archery is also used in the Confucian doctrine of the mean. See Yu 2002.

[5] On Aristotle's application of the notion of the mean to states of character and also to particular responses, see Broadie 1991, 96–101.

[6] See Jaeger 1957, 58. On medical analogies, see also Lloyd 1968 and Hutchinson 1988.

the author makes it clear that different dietary habits may be good for different *healthy* people. For example, some people have an adverse reaction if they miss lunch; others have an adverse reaction if they have lunch (chapter 11). Similarly, cheese is good for some people and bad for others (chapter 20). While Aristotle clearly endorses the view that what is good for one species may be bad for another (*EN* VI on fish), as we shall see below, it is controversial whether Aristotle thinks that all of these types of relativity hold when it comes to virtue.

Finally, according to Aristotle, each virtue is in a mean between two vices, one of excess and one of deficiency.

2. THE FIRST ASPECT: EQUILIBRIUM INSTEAD OF MODERATION

It is tempting to describe Aristotle's doctrine of the mean as a doctrine of moderation. This is the view that Kant attributed to Aristotle and thought was clearly false (*DOV*, 163).[7] In his search for the genus of virtue, Aristotle comments, "Dispositions (*hexeis*) are [those things] according to which we are well or badly off in relation to the emotions. For example, with respect to being angry, we are badly disposed if [we feel anger] violently or slackly, and well disposed if [we feel anger] *mesōs*. And the same goes for the other emotions" (*EN* II 5 1105b25–8).

The term *mesōs* literally means "meanly". Ross translates it "moderately", which may seem reasonable in the context. However, Aristotle's full discussion of the virtue shows that Ross is incorrect:

> The one who is angry at the right things and towards the right people, and also in the right way, at the right time, and for the right length of time, is praised ... The deficiency ... is blamed. For those who are not angered by

[7] When Kant complains, "Let good management, for instance, consist in the *mean* between two vices, prodigality and avarice: as a virtue, it cannot be represented as arising either from a gradual diminution of prodigality (by saving) or from an increase of spending on the miser's part – as if these two vices, moving in opposite directions, met in good management" (*DOV* 163, tr. Gregor), he is right, but only because he is misconstruing Aristotle's doctrine of the mean as a doctrine of moderation.

the right things, or in the right way, or at the right times, or towards the right people, all seem to be foolish ... and ... slavish ... The excess arises in all these ways, in anger toward the wrong people, at the wrong times, more than is right, more hastily than is right and for a longer time – but they are not all found in the same person. (*EN* IV 5 1125b31–1126a11)

Having the virtue "meanly" means being angry at the right time, in the right way, and so forth; it does not mean being moderately angry all the time.[8] On some occasions, it may be appropriate to be very angry; on other occasions, it may not be appropriate to be angry at all. What is wrong with those on the extremes is that they are undiscriminating. Therefore, they do not have anger in the ways they should, or they have anger in the ways they should not.

Aristotle's doctrine of the mean includes an account of equilibrium, not of moderation.

An analogy may be helpful here. Imagine an old-fashioned pair of scales.[9] The empty scales consist of a pivot and a cross-bar with two pans. If the pivot is in the correct place, and the cross-bar is balanced on it, the scales are in equilibrium. Then, when an amount to be weighed is placed in one of the pans, the amount needed to balance it in the other pan will be the correct amount. The scales will work correctly.

The virtuous human being is analogous to the empty scales that are correctly balanced. When something happens, the virtuous human being, who is properly balanced, will respond and act in the correct way. The human being who lacks a balanced disposition will not have the right emotions and act correctly in the right situation, just as unbalanced scales will not correctly react to the weight in the pan. The analogy is between the virtuous human being and the correctly balanced empty scales. A correctly balanced pair of empty scales will correctly weigh what is in one of the empty pans. A human being, correctly balanced, will correctly react to and act on the situation at hand.[10]

---

[8] Cf. Burnet 1900, 92 and Urmson 1973.

[9] I owe the simile to N. Kretzmann.

[10] It is no part of the analogy that the good person "weighs his options" or "balances the alternatives" or "sifts quantitative information". As I explain in later chapters, that is not the way that Aristotelian practical reasoning

Aristotle himself uses musical terminology, describing the person who has the virtue of mildness as being disposed meanly and not violently or slackly. The terms "violently" and "slackly" come from music and invoke a musical analogy. Imagine a lyre. If its strings are too lax, when the lyre is played, they will be flat. If its strings are tuned too tightly, by contrast, they will be sharp. When the strings are correctly tuned, the right notes will sound when the strings are plucked. Just as too much food or too little ruins one's health, so over-tuning strings or under-tuning them ruins the correct tone. A virtuous human being is like a well-tuned instrument; not too tightly wound that he reacts badly to particular situations, nor too lax that he fails to have the right emotions and act appropriately.[11] Again, this is just an analogy. The virtuous human being does not literally have internal strings any more than he weighs quantities in pans. Nevertheless, the analogies capture the harmonious and balanced disposition of the good human being in a way that alternative language cannot.

Since virtue is in equilibrium, a human being becomes virtuous by reaching equilibrium, and, once she achieves equilibrium, virtue is self-sustaining. According to Aristotle, as we saw earlier, health and strength are analogous to virtue. Hence, becoming and remaining healthy and strong is analogous to becoming and remaining virtuous. Therefore, to take the case of courage, if one fears and flees everything and withstands nothing, one will become cowardly; whereas if one generally fears nothing but advances towards everything, one will become rash (EN II 2 1104a20–2). Similarly, too much or too little physical pleasure will prevent one from becoming or being temperate. Aristotle explains that the extremes are destructive, whereas courage and temperance are preserved by the mean (EN II 2 1104a25–7). Strength, according to Aristotle, arises from eating a lot of food and undergoing many labours, and the strong person is best equipped to do these things. Similarly, by getting used to disdain what is fearful and to hold our ground, we become courageous, and once we are courageous, we are most able to stand our ground (EN II 2 1104a30–b1).

works. The analogy is between the virtuous person and empty scales. When each is in equilibrium, they work correctly.

[11] See Long 1991. Thanks to Long for asking me if there was a precursor to the Stoic view of the "harmonics of virtue" in Aristotle.

Imagine a lyre with several strings. If one of the strings in the lyre is out of tune, the other strings will sound out of tune also. Or imagine that the pivot of a pair of scales balances a wheel with spokes (each spoke belonging to a bar with a pan at each end), and one of the bars is out of kilter. In that case, the whole of the scales will be out of kilter also. Now imagine that each string represents an ethical virtue, or that each bar with two pans represents a virtue in the wheel. As we shall see in Chapter 5, this is how Aristotle seems to imagine the ethical virtues. Aristotle does not believe that one can have one disposition in equilibrium while our other dispositions are not. One cannot have any one ethical virtue fully unless one has all the rest.

3. THE SECOND ASPECT: THE MEAN IS "RELATIVE TO US"

According to Aristotle, since the good human being, with her dispositions in equilibrium, will feel and act in the right way, at the right time, and so on, the correct thing to do will vary according to circumstances. The fact that murder is always wrong is no counterexample to this theory. The term "murder" is only given to killing in the wrong situations, at the wrong time, and so on. There is no mean, excess, and deficiency of murder. To think that there is, is to think that an unjust, cowardly, or intemperate action also admits of a mean, excess, or deficiency. As Aristotle himself explains, the terms "unjust", "cowardly", and "intemperate" already denote actions that do not fit the mean (*EN* II 6 1107a9–17). Conversely, temperate action is always right, but what counts as a temperate action in particular circumstances is not easy to ascertain and is "relative to us".

What more Aristotle means by the claim that virtue is "in a mean relative to us" is a matter of controversy. Commentators are generally agreed that the relativity in question is not relativity to whatever the agent happens to think, but they disagree over what the relativity entails. Losin has argued that the relativity in question includes relativity to one's temperament. He says, "Our emotional constitutions provide us with a set of ... complicating factors which can cause us to miss the mark, and will do so if we do not compensate for them" (1987, 337). Presumably, for example, if I know that I am temperamentally apt to get very angry in certain circumstances, I should prepare myself in advance in order to hit the mean. Leighton 1992 (cf. 1995) has argued that the relativity in question includes relativity to one's capacities, activities, stage of development, and station in life.

Lesley Brown 1997 argues that these types of relativity are not at issue in Aristotle's *Nicomachean Ethics*. First, she argues that the passages that Losin relies on for his claim that the doctrine of the mean is relative to temperament are passages concerning what to do in order to become virtuous, not how things are when one has achieved a virtuous disposition, and so are irrelevant. (On my account, they would be relevant to attaining equilibrium in the first place.) Second, Brown argues that not everything Aristotle says about women, men, slaves, rulers, and subjects in the *Politics* (e.g., *Pol.* I 13 1260a28–33) should be read back into the *Ethics*. So, in Aristotle's ethics, we do not need to accept Aristotle's comments that temperance, courage, and the like are different for men and women, and that women should keep quiet, unlike men.[12] In any case, she adds, it is not clear that these people have a different susceptibility to the passions. Third, although this only appears in a footnote of her paper, Brown takes issue with J. L. Ackrill's view that "relative[ly] to us" entails that "what is best for him [the agent] to do depends on his circumstances, *powers, etc.*".[13] According to Brown, virtue is in a mean not relative to different agents, but relative to us as human beings. On her interpretation of Aristotle, virtue is in no sense "agent-relativist".

Brown's conclusion rests on a novel reading of Aristotle's discussion of Milo and the beginning athlete, a passage that I quoted earlier in this chapter. Commentators have traditionally concluded from this passage that virtue is in a mean relative to the individual agent. Brown argues that the relativity in question is not relativity to the agent, because it is Milo and the beginning athletes who require different diets, not the trainer who is the agent making the decision.

[12] Here, Aristotle quotes Gorgias against Socrates, clearly with Plato's *Meno* in mind. In the *Meno*, Meno claims that there is a different virtue for men, women, every station of life, and so on. Socrates disagrees.

[13] Ackrill 1973, 248 quoted by Brown 1997, 82, my emphasis.

Even if Brown's arguments against Losin, Leighton, and Ackrill were to succeed, her novel reading of Milo and the beginner does not settle matters but raises new questions. First, if relativity to the agent is ruled out, is relativity to those affected by a decision what is at stake? If so, is Aristotle implying that beginners and full-fledged virtuous adults are to be treated differently, when he suggests that Milo and the beginner require different treatment? Is virtue relative to *others'* stage in life? If stage in life is to be counted as a circumstance and not something relative to the individual, the question arises of what the difference is between a circumstance and something relative to the individual? In short, what factors are relevant to moral decision-making?[14] If virtue is relative to human beings *in these circumstances*, what are the relevant circumstances? These questions raise even more problems. Factors that are relevant in some circumstances may be irrelevant in others. For example, to take another medical analogy, being a man or woman may be irrelevant in the treatment of a broken ankle, but of great relevance in diagnosing a heart attack, where the symptoms differ between women and men.

To clarify the issues, we need to know: (a) if there are any special factors about the agent that need to be taken into account, apart from the agent's mere humanity; (b) if so, whether these factors are relevant in all cases; and (c) whether the same factors are at play in moral decisions affecting ourselves and others. In the following section, I consider whether Aristotle himself says anything of help in his own account of the particular virtues of character.

3.1. Particular Virtues and Particular Factors

Aristotle says that he must apply his general account to the particular cases, since particular accounts are truer (*EN* II 7 1107a28–33). The case of generosity is the clearest. Generosity, according to Aristotle, is relative to the means of the giver. He writes, "in speaking of generosity we refer to generosity that fits one's property. For what is generous does not depend on the quantity of what is given, but on the disposition of

---

[14] This last sentence summarizes the preceding questions. The questions will be addressed, with the help of the Aristotelian ethical virtues, in the following sections.

the giver, which gives in accordance with one's property. Hence nothing prevents one who gives less [than another] from being more generous, if he gives from fewer resources" (*EN* IV 1 1120b7–11). At the very least, then, generosity is relative to the means of *the agent*. For example, what would be generous for you would be stingy for Bill Gates.

In discussing magnificence, generosity on a large scale, Aristotle notes that "large scale is relative to something (*pros ti*); for the expenses of a war-ship captain and a leader of a delegation are not the same. Hence what is fitting is also relative to oneself (*pros auton*), the circumstances and the purpose (*kai en hō(i) kai peri ho*)" (*EN* IV 2 1122a24–6). Aristotle summarizes his discussion as follows, "in all cases, as we have said, we fix the right amount by reference to the agent – by who he is and what resources he has (*pros ton prattonta anapheretai to tis ōn kai tinōn huparchontōn*); for the amounts must be worthy of these, fitting the producer as well as the product" (*EN* IV 2 1122b23–6). Here, then, the status of the agent is relevant, but it is the political office held that makes particular actions appropriate or not. Wealthy individuals and individuals holding special political offices are expected to do particular actions with respect to public philanthropy. These actions, though, are restricted to certain spheres. Wealthy individuals receive no special dispensations in the sphere of temperance or bravery or anywhere else. Their status is only relevant in the spheres of generosity and magnificence.

In his account of the nameless virtue of friendliness, Aristotle shows that different actions may be relevant for different people. He explains how the friendly person will take a different attitude to someone with a reputation for worth than to just anyone, and to someone he knows better than to someone he knows less well, and so on. Presumably, the point is not that one should be less pleasant to those one knows less well, or to those who have a lesser reputation for worth, but that different actions are appropriate in order to be pleasant to each. Virtue, then, appears also to be relative to individuals other than the agent, and characteristics that would be irrelevant in the agent become relevant if they belong to other people.

There is one virtue that one might expect to be relative to others but that Aristotle seems to conclude is not. That is the nameless virtue of "wit", a virtue that concerns both telling and listening to jokes. At the beginning of Aristotle's discussion of wit, he says that the company one is in makes a difference (EN IV 8), and he also discusses the feelings of the target of a joke. (Aristotle seems to assume that all jokes have victims, or perhaps his virtue of wit only applies to those jokes that do.) Aristotle's comments here suggest that the virtue of wit is relative to other people. Later on, however, Aristotle decides that the sensibilities of the hearer are too vague to define, and so the speaker should decide what to say on the basis of what he, being a good person, is willingly to listen to himself. Wit, then, turns out to be relative to the good person, not to the hearers or victims.

So far, what Aristotle says about the particular ethical virtues in his *Nicomachean Ethics* shows that information about the circumstances of the agent *and* the circumstances of others involved in the agent's actions can be relevant to ethical decision-making. However, what Aristotle says about the agent is compatible both with the view that "relative to us" means "relative to us as human beings" and with the view that it means simply "relative to the agent". The two parties to the debate can simply describe the situations in different terms. For the agent-relativist, presumably, magnificence would be relative to the agent because his status is at issue. For the non agent-relativist, magnificence would be relative to a human being *in the relevant circumstances*, that is, where one is an ambassador or whatever.

Denying the existence of agent-relativity may be harder in the case of the virtues of truthfulness and magnanimity, to which I now turn. Aristotle describes truthfulness as being a virtue that has to do with one's own abilities. The truthful person "acknowledges the qualities he has without belittling or exaggerating" (EN IV 7 1127a25–6). Aristotle describes some of those who have the vice of boastfulness as pretending to be wise seers or physicians when they are not (EN IV 7 1127b20). Presumably, the truthful person, if a physician, will be aware of her abilities, and her speech will reflect this correctly. The virtue of truthfulness, then, will be relative to the abilities of the agent.

The case of magnanimity makes the issue of self-knowledge even clearer, although here it is one's worth and not just one's particular abilities that is at issue. Aristotle describes magnanimity as the "crowning virtue" (EN IV 3 1124a1–2), and, indeed, Aristotle's description of the magnanimous individual is a description of a person who has all the ethical virtues. Aristotle first explains that the person with the ethical virtue of magnanimity "seems to be the one who thinks himself worthy of great things and is really worthy of them" (*EN* IV 3 1123b1–2). Someone who thinks he is worthy of great things when he is not has the vice of excess, vanity. Someone who thinks he is worthy of less than he is has the vice of deficiency, pusillanimity. Of the pusillanimous person, Aristotle comments, "Indeed, he would seem not to know himself; for if he did, he would aim at the things he is worthy of, since they are goods" (*EN* IV 3 1125a21–3). As for vain people, they "are foolish and do not know themselves" (*EN* IV 3 1125a27–8). The clear implication is that what vicious people are deficient in is self-knowledge, while this is what the virtuous human being has. Virtue seems to be relative to the agent's knowledge of himself. As for those who have the vices, Aristotle says, "The pusillanimous person is deficient both in relation to himself and in relation to the magnanimous person's worth, while the vain person makes claims that are excessive for himself, but not for the magnanimous person" (*EN* IV 3 1123b24–6).

Is relativity to one's abilities (and worth) generalizable to the other virtues, or, as in the case of being especially wealthy or of high office, is it limited to one or two spheres? I wish to suggest that it does make sense to pay attention to one's own abilities when the other virtues are in play as well. To take just one example, if Henry is a good swimmer, he will be acting bravely if he dives in to rescue a fellow soldier in the heat of battle. If he does not know how to swim, diving in will be rash.[15] In this respect, then, the mean is relative to individual agents and not just to us as human beings. Good people will have to know their own particular abilities, since virtue is relative to them. (Here, I do not mean to suggest that self-knowledge is sufficient for virtue.)

---

[15] Halper thinks that the same skills are necessary for all in order to be virtuous in the first place. For example, all soldiers should be able to swim. See also Halper 1999. Although some basic skills may be required, I do not believe that Aristotle thinks that any *particular* skills are necessary in order to be virtuous. This does not mean that the virtuous should not bother to develop the skills they have.

3.2. A New Approach to the Debate about Relativity

In my introductory remarks about the debate between agent-relativists and non-agent-relativists, I raised three questions: (a) whether there are any special factors about the agent that need to be taken into account, apart from the agent's mere humanity; (b) whether, if so, these factors are relevant in all cases; and (c) whether the same factors are at play in moral decisions affecting ourselves and others. From my discussion of particular virtues, the answer to question (a) is "yes". The following factors about the agent need to be taken into account: the agent's wealth and political status, his own abilities, and his virtue. The answer to question (b) is more complicated. While wealth and political status are relevant in generosity and magnificence, it is not clear that they are relevant in all the ethical virtues. Similarly, while some abilities may be relevant on all occasions, others may only be relevant regarding some virtues or on some occasions. The answer therefore depends on what the abilities are. For (c), we need to extrapolate from Aristotle's discussion. Presumably, wealth and status may sometimes be relevant in making ethical decisions that affect others, for example, wealth in deciding what would be a suitable present for the person who has everything, and the abilities of others might be relevant in deciding what to do oneself and how to treat others. In his later discussion of friendship, Aristotle says that it may be finer to let someone else do the fine action than to do it oneself (*EN* IX 9 1169a32–4). It is reasonable to suppose that Aristotle's idea is not that I am doing a fine thing if I let you do the brave action while I sit back and watch, but that in a situation where you have the ability to do it better than I, for example, if you can swim better than I can, it would be finer for me to give you the opportunity rather than make the attempt myself.

So far then, the way in which virtue is "relative to us" has turned out to be a more complicated matter than the parties to the debate have realized, since the relativity to us is not necessarily invariant across all cases. It is not just that what the right thing is to do varies from situation to situation but that there are factors relative to which certain things are right or wrong that also vary from situation to situation. Relativity to one's abilities and self-knowledge are difficult to classify as mere circumstances. As we shall see in the following section, practical wisdom may include these in its very operation.

However, if the more complicated account of Aristotle's views is correct, Aristotle's doctrine of the mean precludes him from making his egregious comments about women and slaves for the following reason. If being a woman or slave is a particular fact about someone, on the lines of Aristotle's discussion in his *Nicomachean Ethics*, it ought to be relevant on some occasions and not on others. But it is always relevant according to the account in the *Politics* and the *Nicomachean Ethics* (*Pol.* I 13 1260a28–33; *EN* VIII 12 1162a25–7), which means that Aristotle is misapplying his own theory. Being a woman and being a slave may certainly be relevant factors in some instances of moral reasoning, but they should not be invariantly relevant factors. Consider as a parallel the medical example I gave previously. Being a woman is a crucial factor in being treated for heart disease but not in being treated for a broken ankle.

4. THE THIRD ASPECT: ARISTOTELIAN TRIADS

Since Aristotle says that each virtue is in a mean between two vices, the virtues and vices constitute a set of triads. A major criticism of Aristotle's doctrine of the mean is that one can generate more than two vices for each virtue, because it is not clear that each virtue is confined to only one continuum. For example, the virtue of courage concerns both fear and confidence, so one can construct more vices than two since it is possible to have too much fear and too little confidence, too little confidence and too little fear, too much fear and too much confidence, and too little fear and too little confidence.[16] This problem, if it is a problem, is ubiquitous. It not only applies to other virtues where there are two continua, for example, generosity (which concerns giving and receiving) and wit (which involves telling and listening to jokes), but one can construct extra vices even when there is only one emotion or type of action at issue, since, according to Aristotle, one must do the right thing at the right time, in the right way, for the right goal, to the

---

[16] According to Stewart 1892, 212, Michelet was the first to notice this problem. It is fully explored by Pears 1980.

right person, and so forth, and each of these parameters can be made to generate new continua.[17]

In one respect, the existence of extra vices should cause no concern. After all, it is enough to dispute the dyadic view – that vice is opposed to virtue and that's that – to point to more than one vice in relation to each virtue, and to show that there can be two opposing vices, one of which is not a virtue. Certainly, it should not matter to Aristotle if there are more vices than two, since, if virtue is a state of character in equilibrium, as I have argued that the medical analogies show, there should be as many vices as there are ways to be out of equilibrium. Indeed, this state of affairs would be in line with the Pythagorean view that Aristotle alludes to with apparent approval: that good is limited but bad unlimited (*EN* II 6 1106b29–30). Nevertheless, it would be helpful to find a rationale for picking out two main vices per virtue, and it would be interesting to know whether there is any unity among the two sets of vices that Aristotle picks out as there is among the virtues.[18]

I wish to suggest that Aristotle does indeed provide material for a psychological profile of the person who has the excesses and the person who has the deficiencies. In his discussion of friendship (*EN* IX 8), Aristotle wants to claim that the good person loves his friend just as he loves himself, but here he must address an objection based on the commonly held view that self-love is bad. Aristotle responds by distinguishing two types of self-lover: one good, the other bad. The good self-lover loves his understanding. In gratifying his understanding, he competes to do what is fine, which will result in everyone being better off.[19] By contrast, the bad self-lover goes after as much money and as many honours and physical pleasures for himself as possible, but more of these goods for one person means less for another, so competition here does not benefit everyone. By indiscriminately gratifying their appetites

---

[17] See Losin 1987, Stocker 1990, 129–64, and cf. *EN* IV 5 1125b31–1126a11 above. For a critique of the presuppositions of the problem, see Hursthouse 1980–1.

[18] Thanks to Ted Everett for pressing the question about unity among the vices.

[19] As I mentioned earlier, if there is an opportunity for more than one person to shine, the person who has the best non-ethical skills should be chosen. Also, as Kraut 1989, 124 suggests, the virtuous person will create greater opportunities for virtuous activity.

and feelings, that is, non-rational part of the soul, bad self-lovers will harm both themselves and their neighbours (*EN* IX 8 1169a14–15). Aristotle concludes that the good person is a (true) self-lover, whereas the vicious person is not.

Aristotle's description of the bad self-lover provides a general account of the mentality of a person who will display many of the excesses on Aristotle's list of triads. If it is implicit that the good self-lover, having the correct reasoning, will also have the right feelings at the right time, and so on, Aristotle's description of the good self-lover gives an account of the mentality and attitude of a person who has all the virtues. There is no mention of the mentality of the person who has the vices of deficiency, presumably because it would be hard to describe the mentality of such a person as a species of self-*love*.[20]

According to the *Eudemian Ethics*, such a person would be ingenuous. There, Aristotle describes practical wisdom (*phronēsis*), as a mean between ingenuousness (*euētheia*) and unscrupulousness (*panourgia*) (*EE* II 3 1221a12, 1221a36–8). The person with practical wisdom, the good self-lover of *EN* IX, takes advantages of the right opportunities; the person who is unscrupulous, the bad self-lover, takes more than his fair share of goods; and the person who is ingenuous takes less.

The passage is controversial. Michael Woods says, "it is hard to believe that, at any stage of his thought, Aristotle held that the doctrine of the mean was applicable to intellectual virtues as well as virtues of character. Although the unworldly [ingenuous] man may lack the intelligence with which the practically wise man is properly endowed, that is surely not something with which it is possible to be over-endowed; hence there is no symmetry in the characteristics of the unscrupulous and unworldly man *vis-à-vis* the man of practical wisdom".[21] Woods therefore excises the offending trio from the text.

Woods's criticism is unfounded. He describes the unscrupulous person as having too much of the intelligence that the good person has. This is similar to Kant's mistake of thinking that the person with the

---

[20] Whether it is particularly selfish, for example, to renounce all of one's physical and emotional needs for an ideal is an issue that is beyond the scope of this book.

[21] Woods 1992, 106.

vice of excess has too much of what the good person has.[22] In the case of practical wisdom, Aristotle explains what the more and the less refer to as follows: "The unscrupulous person is after advantage (*pleonektikos*) in every way and from every source, the unworldly not even from the right source" (*EE* II 3 1221a36–8). The person with practical wisdom, then, will take advantage of the right opportunities, in the right way, and so on. One might of course wonder what sort of knowledge is involved here. Following on from my discussion about magnanimity and self-knowledge, it seems that the type of knowledge needed here is not just general knowledge about what is good or bad for human beings, as in the definition of practical wisdom, but also self-knowledge. However, practical wisdom is not a matter of having neither too much nor too little self-knowledge. Rather, in order to take advantage of the right things, the good person must neither underestimate nor overestimate his own abilities and worth. So, *contra* Woods, there is a symmetry in the characteristics of the unscrupulous and unworldly man *vis-à-vis* practical wisdom after all. The structure of the triad is exactly the same as the others.

We now have two psychological profiles for vicious people. One links together the vices of excess, and the other links together the vices of deficiency. According to the *Eudemian Ethics*, as we saw, the person with practical wisdom takes advantages of the right opportunities, while the person who is unscrupulous takes more than his fair share of goods, and the person who is unworldly takes less. Furthermore, the person with practical wisdom has the right view of his own abilities and worth, whereas the unscrupulous person will overestimate his abilities, and the unworldly person will underestimate his. The coward, the pusillanimous person, the inirascible person, and the person who is indifferent to honour all underestimate their own worth and abilities. The rash person, the vain person, the irascible person, the person who loves honour too much, and the buffoon all overestimate their own worth and abilities.

The match is not perfect. We perhaps need to flip some of the excesses and deficiencies for Aristotle's lists of excesses and deficiencies to line up. The flatterer (flattery being the excess relating to friendliness) would

[22] Kant *DOV*, 163.

appear to go with the above-mentioned deficiencies. Also, the boaster, as described by Aristotle, may not necessarily overestimate his abilities; he may simply be lying about them. Nevertheless, there is now clearly a point in Aristotle's listing *two* vices in the sphere of each virtue. The point has to do with human psychology.

The list of triads also has a practical application. Aristotle comments, "the brave person appears rash in comparison with the coward. Similarly, the temperate person appears intemperate in comparison with the insensible person, and the generous person appears wasteful in comparison with the ungenerous person and ungenerous in comparison with the wasteful person. For this reason the people at the extremes push out the intermediate person, and the coward calls the brave person rash and the rash person calls him a coward, and analogously with the rest" (*EN* II 8 1108b19–26). The passage is reminiscent of Thucydides's famous description of the Corcyraean revolution in his *History of the Peloponnesian war* (III.82.4). Closer to home, though, those who argue that the traits that Aristotle would call excesses are really virtues, often mention the traits that Aristotle would call deficiencies in order to support their view, and vice versa.[23] Taking a dyadic view, they do not see the virtue in between. Perhaps Aristotle would say that it is a necessary condition for being virtuous to see the triadic structure of virtues and vices. I take up the question of exactly what the good person needs to know in Chapter 9.

5. REASSESSING THE DOCTRINE OF THE MEAN

It might be thought that if the doctrine of the mean is indeed a doctrine of equilibrium and not a doctrine of moderation, then it has the fatal flaw of being unable to provide a decision procedure for action, a necessity for real life. This criticism is lurking behind complaints that the doctrine of the mean is unhelpful, or true but uninteresting. Taken one way, the criticism misses Aristotle's point. The correct thing to do, according to the second aspect of the doctrine of the mean, is not a "mean in the object", not something that can be worked out using a

[23] See, e.g., the virtues of selfishness, discussed in Ch. 4.

mathematical algorithm in some mechanical fashion. So if this is what the detractors are asking for, Aristotle is saying that it cannot be had. Taken another way, the criticism is a challenge to show what of interest flows from Aristotle's doctrine and what substantive consequences the doctrine has. I have argued here that the doctrine of the mean has several substantive consequences: it is a doctrine of equilibrium, not moderation; it embraces a very sophisticated view of the particulars of the situation; and it embodies a triadic taxonomy of different mentalities. In the following chapters, I show how the different aspects of the doctrine of the mean permeate other aspects of Aristotle's view and have important consequences for his ethics as a whole.

2   Nameless Virtues

In the previous chapter, I argued that Aristotle's doctrine of the mean is a substantive thesis, and that the substance is to be found in places that have been overlooked. In this chapter, I show how the third aspect of Aristotle's doctrine of the mean, his triadic account of virtue and vices, contributes to his account of the nameless virtues, and I argue that J. L. Ackrill is therefore wrong to claim that "[i]nsofar as Aristotle's accounts of particular virtues embody a particular moral outlook (and that is, perhaps, not far), this is due rather to his acquiescence in the vocabulary and outlook of his time than to his theoretical commitment to 'the doctrine of the mean'", a widely held modern view.[1] I argue that the nameless virtues are no less important than their named companions, and that if Aristotle is right about the existence of the nameless virtues, his doctrine of the mean will have resulted in some important discoveries.[2] I also argue that the very existence of nameless virtues in

[1] Ackrill 1973, 22. See also 24, "Aristotle clearly aligns himself with conventional values and takes them for granted". See too Bernard Williams, who complains that the doctrine of the mean is "one of the most celebrated and least useful parts of his [Aristotle's] system" and "is better forgotten" (Williams 1985, 36). On the supposedly purely parochial nature of Aristotle's views, see most recently Vlastos 1991, N. Cooper 1989, 193, Urmson 1988, 62, and Crisp 2000, xvii–xviii. The charge is an old one. See, e.g., Stewart 1892, 352. None of the above-mentioned authors discuss Aristotle's nameless virtues. Ackrill does not translate *Nicomachean Ethics* IV in which they appear.

[2] It might be objected that the nameless virtues are inherent in ancient Greek life but are unimportant and therefore nameless. My answer to this objection has two parts. First, I do not mean to claim that, once articulated, the nameless virtues look unfamiliar. If that were so, Aristotle's introduction of the

Aristotle's discussion casts doubt on the idea that Aristotle is simply reporting contemporary views. This marks the beginning of an argument, continued in Chapter 4, that Aristotle's account of the ethical virtues depends on his doctrine of the mean and is more innovative than has previously been thought.

In Section 1, I explain which virtues are nameless and what their namelessness consists in. In the next two sections, I explain how the nameless virtues are controversial even within the Aristotelian corpus itself, and yet why there is no reason to exclude them from Aristotle's list of virtues. In Section 2, I explain how Aristotle's introduction of the nameless virtue concerning small honours in the *Nicomachean Ethics* (a) solves a problem in the *Eudemian Ethics* that arises because the virtue is not recognized there, and (b) explains why there is confusion about what the virtue is in the sphere of small honours. As I show, both the problem and the confusion arise from failing to apply the triadic aspect of Aristotle's doctrine of the mean in the proper way. In Section 3, I explain why Aristotle thinks that three of the nameless virtues do not count as virtues in his *Eudemian Ethics*, and why he is wrong to do so. In Section 4, I give some positive reasons for including the nameless virtues in the roster of virtues, to be elaborated in the following chapters, and I show how the nameless virtues transcend the parochial Greek culture of the fourth century BCE. In the concluding section, I suggest some further implications of taking the nameless virtues seriously, which will be further explored in the remaining chapters of the book.

1. THE NAMELESSNESS OF THE NAMELESS VIRTUES

There are five virtues that Aristotle says are nameless in his *Nicomachean Ethics* (*EN* II 7). These are the virtues concerning small honours, *praotēs* (mildness), *alētheia* (truthfulness), *eutrapelia* or *epidexiotēs* (wit), and

---

nameless virtues would appear *ad hoc*. All I am claiming is that there is nothing to parrot before Aristotle's articulation of the nameless virtues. Second, my discussion of these virtues throughout my book shows that they are no mere details.

philia (friendliness).[3] Since Aristotle refers to all of these virtues by name, except for the first, the namelessness of the virtues clearly calls for some explanation. The explanation involves not only the terms that Aristotle uses to describe his virtues, but also the novelty and hence controversial nature of the virtues themselves.

First, in their ordinary usage, the terms Aristotle uses to describe the virtues, and also the terms available for modern commentators to use to translate them, do not capture exactly what Aristotle has in mind. For example, Aristotle himself explains that the term *praotēs* ("mildness") inclines towards the deficiency rather than accurately referring to the mean: "Mildness is a mean with respect to anger. Since the mean is nameless, and the extremes almost so too, we put mildness in the mean, though it inclines towards the deficiency, which is nameless" (*EN* IV 5 1125b26–9).[4]

Interestingly, the latin term "mansuetudo" used by Aquinas and the English translation "mildness" (or "gentleness" and "gentle temper"), not to mention the French term "placidité", have the same unwelcome connotations.[5]

Again, Aristotle says that he will use the Greek word for friendship, *philia*, for the nameless virtue between flattery and quarrelsomeness, because this virtue most resembles friendship, although there is an important difference between the two. Friendship requires a special feeling for the person one is friendly with; friendliness does not (*EN* IV 6 1126b19–28). Indeed, Liddell and Scott cite only Aristotle as using the term *philia* with the sense of "friendliness" or "amiability" (1996, p. 1934). Even the English term "friendliness" is inaccurate. To be a friendly person, according to Aristotle, is not to be indiscriminately friendly, but to accept and to object to the right things in the right way (*EN* IV 6 1126b16–17).

---

[3] The translations are by Irwin 1985. I discuss them below. Ackrill 1973, Joachim 1978, and Ross 1923 all translate the first four as follows: "ambition", "good temper", "truthfulness", and "ready wit".

[4] Aquinas makes Aristotle's linguistic point more explicit in his commentary: "The name meekness (*mansuetudo*) is taken to signify a mean, although the word implies a lack of anger" (*CANE*, lecture 13).

[5] Rackham 1935 translates "gentleness". Woods's (1992) translation is "gentle temper". Gauthier and Jolif 1958 prefer "placidité". They also consider "la douceur" (vol. 2, pars 1, 301).

There are also difficulties in finding adequate English expressions for the other nameless virtues. The translation "wit" and "ready wit", like the Greek terms *eutrapelia* and *epidexiotēs*, conjure up mental dexterity and imply that the person with this virtue will know or be able to make up many good jokes and be good at delivering them. In fact, the point of the virtue of wit is rather to enable its possessor to be sensitive to his audience and to know when a particular joke would be appropriate to make, and also to appreciate, and when not (*EN* IV 8 1128a9–33).

Finally, the term "truthfulness" as a translation for *alētheia* is similarly misleading. It is apt to imply that the truthful person will simply tell the truth on all occasions. Aristotle's account of the virtue he calls *alētheia* is more subtle. His truthful person is one who is truthful about his own possessions, beliefs, and abilities, and who gives out the right amount of information on the right occasions. Aristotle is often thought to restrict truth-telling to explicit statements about oneself, but this is a misunderstanding of his position, since whenever one expresses an opinion, one is indirectly making a claim about one's own abilities, especially the ability to back up the opinion one is expressing.[6]

Not only must the Aristotelian virtuous person's statements truthfully reflect her views of herself, but her assessment of herself must also be right. The term "sincerity" (Rackham's translation) is therefore too narrow, since those who have the vices of boastfulness or self-deprecation may also be quite sincere in their assessment of themselves; they may just be wrong about their abilities.

Aristotle is therefore justified in calling his virtues "nameless" because the Greek terms that exist, just like their modern translations, do not exactly fit the virtues he means to describe.[7] Furthermore, as might be expected, none of Aristotle's nameless virtues are treated as central by his ancient Greek predecessors and contemporaries.

[6] I am grateful to Jean Goodwin and Patrick Mooney for helpful discussion of this point.
[7] One might object that this is true of Aristotle's named virtues too. If so, Aristotle is even more innovative than I am suggesting here. See Ch. 4.

The idea of there being four central virtues seems to have been popular in Plato's time, although not everyone treated the same virtues as central. Significantly, none of Aristotle's nameless virtues appear among the cardinal virtues of Plato's *Republic*, which are wisdom (*sophia*), bravery (*andreia*), temperance (*sōphrosunē*), and justice (*dikaiosunē*) (e.g., *Republic* IV 427E). Nor do Aristotle's nameless virtues appear in any of the other extant lists of four.[8]

Plato also mentions generosity (*eleutheriotēs*) and magnificence (*megaloprepeia*), two more of Aristotle's *named* virtues, prominently in his *Republic* (*Republic* III 402C cf. *Republic* VII 536a and VI 487A). The nearest Plato comes to discussing Aristotle's nameless virtues is in his discussion of the good philosophical student. Such a person, he says, will be, among other things, "gracious, a friend and kin to truth" (*eucharis, philos kai suggenēs alētheias*) (*Republic* VI 487A).[9]

Even if, as appears unlikely from the context, Plato were groping towards the Aristotelian virtues of friendliness and truthfulness with his mention of graciousness and truth, he is clearly discussing the *temperament* of the student, rather than his or her full-blown virtues. True, Plato says that his guardian must be mild (*Republic* II 375C–E), but again, he seems to have temperament in mind, for he worries about how such a person can be both mild and high-spirited. The quality of being mild has a broader sense in Plato's *Republic* than it does in

---

[8] For example, Pindar mentions four main virtues in *Nemean Odes* 3, 70ff, but not by name. Aeschylus describes Amphiaraus as "a temperate, just, courageous and pious man" (*Septem contra Thebas* 610). (On the translation "courageous", connoting military valour, for "*agathos*" see Creed 1973, 217.) Isocrates lists courage, wisdom, piety, and temperance as the four main virtues in *Helen* 31, but in *Evagoras*, like Plato, he substitutes justice for piety. Plato may have taken his particular four virtues from the Pythagoreans. On this, see Ferguson 1958, especially ch. 3. For more on the historical background, see North 1966, especially chs. 3–5.

[9] In a later work, Plato gives a similar list for the qualities of the young person who will be ruler, but the phrase quoted above is conspicuously absent (*Laws* IV 709E–10A). Xenophon praises Agesilaus for *to euchari*, his graciousness (*Agesilaus* VIII), but this is broader than any one of Aristotle's nameless virtues; it seems to be a mixture of Aristotelian friendliness, truthfulness, and magnanimity. Interestingly, in Dover 1974, "friendliness" only appears as a synonym for *philanthrōpia* (201–5). *Alētheia* does not appear at all.

Aristotle's ethics. That it means "quietness" or even "passivity" and is not necessarily a virtue is clear from the passage where Plato notes that convicted criminals in a democracy display this property (*Republic* VIII 558A).[10] Interestingly, Aristotle himself lists mildness among the *emotions* in *de Anima* (*de An.* I 1 403a17). Indeed, whether Aristotle's nameless virtues are true virtues or merely a matter of temperament is an important question, which I address below.

However, it is not necessary to go very far afield to appreciate the novelty of Aristotle's nameless virtues, since whether or not the nameless virtues are virtues is controversial even within the Aristotelian corpus itself. In his extant early works, Aristotle only mentions Plato's cardinal virtues: wisdom, bravery, temperance, and justice (*Fr.* 5 and 12 (*Protrepticus*); *Top.* I 16 108a1–3). In a passage in *Rhetoric*, Aristotle lists a host of virtues but includes only one nameless virtue, here named as "mildness" (*Rh.* I 9 1366b1–3).[11] Interestingly, the passage seems to predate Aristotle's doctrine of the mean, or perhaps it merely reflects ordinary usage, since only one vice is mentioned for each virtue (*Rh.* I 9 1366b3–20).

The most startling discrepancy, however, is between the *Nicomachean Ethics* and the *Eudemian Ethics*. Four of the five nameless virtues of *Nicomachean Ethics* do not appear as virtues in *Eudemian Ethics*. In *Eudemian Ethics*, the virtue concerning small honours is not mentioned at all, and friendliness, truthfulness, and wit are said not to be virtues but

---

[10] Plato's mention of *praotēs* as passivity is not unique. North has an interesting discussion of the connection between *praotēs* (and *metriotēs*) in Isocrates (e.g., *Nicocles* 49) and the political ideal of *sōphrosunē* which here connotes the quiet behaviour and obedience of subjects (North, 147). Isocrates comes nearest to describing contemporary examples of the vices associated with the nameless means in *Areopagiticus* 47–54. The testimony of Theophrastus is inconclusive. His *Characters* is a satire describing *vices*, not virtues. Sometimes his named vices match Aristotle's and sometimes they do not, but when they do, Theophrastus may just be following his teacher, Aristotle.

[11] Here the manuscripts differ. I am using Kassel's text, which relies on a manuscript that includes mildness. Ross, the editor of the Oxford Classical Text, follows the one manuscript that does not mention this virtue. His reading, if accepted, would only strengthen my claim that the nameless virtues are controversial within the Aristotelian corpus itself.

emotional means (*mesotētes ... pathētikai*) instead (*EE* III 7 1233b17–19).[12]
I shall discuss these controversial virtues in more detail below.

2. THE VIRTUE CONCERNING SMALL HONOURS AND THE DOCTRINE OF THE MEAN

In Aristotle's *Nicomachean Ethics*, the pair of virtues, generosity
(*eleutheriotēs*) and generosity on a grand scale, magnificence (*megalopre-peia*), are matched by two virtues concerned with honour, the nameless
virtue concerned with small honours and a virtue concerned with hon-
our on a grand scale, magnanimity (*megalopsuchia*). Although Aristotle
discusses both members of the first pair of virtues in his *Eudemian Ethics*,
he only mentions one member of the second pair, magnanimity. I wish
to suggest that there is a problem arising in Aristotle's discussion of
magnanimity in *Eudemian Ethics* that would be solved by the discovery
of a new and distinct virtue.

In his *Eudemian Ethics*, Aristotle argues that magnanimity is a mean
state by first describing the different attitudes one might have towards
honours. He describes four characters: the person who is worthy of great
things and who thinks himself so worthy; the person who is worthy
of great things but who does not think himself so worthy; the person
who is worthy of small things and who thinks himself so worthy; and
the person who is worthy of small things but who thinks that he is
worthy of great ones. By a process of elimination using the schema of
his doctrine of the mean, Aristotle concludes that magnanimity is a
virtue between the two vices of pusillanimity (*mikropsuchia*) and vanity
(*chaunotēs*). According to Aristotle, the magnanimous person, the person who is worthy of great honours and who thinks himself so worthy,
comes between the person who is worthy of great honours but does not
think that he is, and the person who is not worthy of great honours but
who thinks that he is (*EE* III 5 1233a11–17).

So far so good. However, this leaves out the person who neither is nor
thinks himself worthy of great things (*EE* III 5 1232b32–4). There does

----

[12] The *Magna Moralia* follows the *Eudemian Ethics* in omitting the virtue concerning small honours, but the author leaves it an open question whether friendliness, truthfulness, and wit are virtues or not (*MM* I 32 1193a37–9).

not appear to be a niche for such a person in Aristotle's schema.[13] If this person were also vicious, Aristotle would be left with a tetrad, rather than a triad, of virtue and vices. Aristotle notes that one might think such a person the opposite of the magnanimous person but that this would be wrong, for such a person is not blameworthy. Moreover, he is like the magnanimous person in so far as he has the correct view of his own worth (*EE* III 5 1233a19–24). Aristotle is at pains to point out that such a person is not to be identified with the pusillanimous person. Were great goods to become available to the pusillanimous person, he would not accept them, whereas the fourth sort of person would. This leaves a problem, for it is unclear what virtue the fourth character exhibits. Enter the virtue concerning small honours in the *Nicomachean Ethics*.[14]

In the *Nicomachean Ethics*, Aristotle introduces the virtue concerning small honours after a discussion of the virtue that is especially concerned with great honours, magnanimity. The two form a pair to match the pair of generosity and magnificence. Aristotle says:

> there would also seem to be a virtue concerned with honour whose relation to magnanimity seems similar to the relation of generosity to magnificence.[15]

[13] Aristotle's example of the resident alien shows that the person left out may be unworthy not because he is unfit for great honours, but because he is unqualified to receive them in his present situation. See also the Appendix.

[14] True, in his discussion of magnanimity in *Nicomachean Ethics*, Aristotle describes the character who is worthy of small things and thinks himself so worthy as *sōphrōn* (*EN* IV 3 1123b5–6). Since Aristotle has just argued at length that *sōphrosunē* is temperance restricted to physical pleasures (*EN* III 10), *sōphrōn* here must have the ordinary Greek meaning of "sensible" rather than its specialized Aristotelian sense. Therefore, the question of which virtue such a person exhibits remains open. (Interestingly, in Aristotle's actual discussion of the nameless virtue concerning small honours, Aristotle notes that "we praise the person who is indifferent to honour as measured and *sōphrōn*" (*EN* IV 4 1125b11–14). Here again, Aristotle is giving the ordinary Greek usage of *sōphrōn* rather than his own. "We" refers to those ordinary ancient Greeks whom Aristotle is about to criticize.)

[15] One might object that the parallel breaks down because although the magnificent person will also be generous, the magnanimous person will not also have the virtue concerning small honours because Aristotle says that the magnanimous person will disdain such honours. The objection fails if Aristotle thinks of magnanimity as concerned with honours on a large scale, such as being asked to endow the arts, and of the companion virtue as concerned with honours on a

> For it abstains, just as generosity does, from anything great but forms the
> right attitude in us on medium and small matters; and just as the taking
> and giving of money admits of a mean, an excess and a deficiency, so also we
> can desire honour more or less than is right, and we can desire it from the
> right sources and in the right way. (*EN* IV 4 1125b1–8, tr. Irwin)

Aristotle claims that there is a nameless mean between two vices: an
excess, *philotimia* (love of honour), and a deficiency, *aphilotimia* (indifference to honour). However, because the mean has no name, people
are misled into thinking that the vices are the virtues. Aristotle says,
"But when the mean has no name, the extremes look like rivals for it, as
though it were unclaimed" (*EN* IV 4 1125b17–8, tr. Irwin). Aristotle
explains that sometimes people praise the honour-lover as if he were
the virtuous person. At other times, they praise the indifferent person
as exhibiting the virtue. The introduction of the nameless virtue helps
explain the apparent inconsistency in people's thinking on the topic.
Aristotle dispels the confusion as follows:

> When compared with love of honour, it [sc. the nameless virtue] appears as
> indifference to honour; when compared with indifference, it appears as love
> of honour; and when compared with both, it appears in a way as both. This
> would seem to be true of the other virtues too; but in this case the extreme
> people appear to be opposed [only to each other] because the intermediate
> person has no name. (*EN* IV 4 1125b21–5, tr. Irwin)

It is the doctrine of the mean that shows that the virtue in any sphere
should come between (at least) two vices. This is what allows Aristotle to
explain that there is a virtue where people had not noticed one before.

3. THE "QUESTIONABLE MEAN-DISPOSITIONS"

In his *Eudemian Ethics*, Aristotle argues that three of the *Nicomachean
Ethics*' nameless virtues, *philia* (friendliness), *alētheia* (truthfulness), and

---

more mundane scale, such as being given the appropriate respect in conversation
by someone one admires. The honours the magnanimous person will disdain, by
contrast, will be inappropriate small ones, such as being asked to chair a commit-
tee for deciding the colour of the decorations at a neighbourhood celebration.

eutrapelia (wit) are among six conditions that are not to be classified as virtues (*EE* III 7).[16] The other three, which are not classified as virtues in *Nicomachean Ethics* either, are *nemesis* (righteous indignation), *aidōs* (shame), and *semnotēs* (dignity).[17] In both ethical works, Aristotle argues that virtue is a *hexis* (a settled disposition) and not a *pathos* (emotion) in a mean involving rational choice (*EN* II 5–6; *EE* II 2–3). In his *Eudemian Ethics*, Aristotle explains that none of the above conditions "are virtues, nor are the opposing states vices, because they do not involve *prohairesis* (rational choice). They are all in the classification of the emotions, for each one is an emotion" (*EE* III 7 1234a25–7). In his *Nicomachean Ethics*, Aristotle holds the opposite view; the three nameless virtues have the status of full virtues.

Aristotle's identification of the nameless virtues with emotions in *Eudemian Ethics* is puzzling.[18] All three states involve powers of reasoning and discrimination. Even wit, which might seem the least promising in this regard, involves such powers. It is often thought that Aristotle approves innuendo over out-and-out abuse just as a matter of taste. A more likely explanation is that innuendo involves more reasoning than out-and-out abuse, and it also requires and invites mental agility in response, whereas the latter does not. There is therefore no reason to deny these virtues their due.

Still, the question remains why Aristotle classifies these virtues as "emotional … means" in his *Eudemian Ethics*. The idea that they just *are*

[16] Although the virtues in question are nameless and, as I have explained, the names Aristotle assigns to them do not quite fit, I shall continue to use Aristotle's names because this is less cumbersome than giving a description of each virtue whenever it is discussed.

[17] On *nemesis* and *aidōs*, see *EN* II 7 1108a30–b6, and for more on why *aidōs* is not a virtue, *EN* IV 9 1128b10–33. *Semnotēs* is not mentioned at all. For more on these conditions, see Ch. 5.

[18] Even Fortenbaugh 1968, who argues that the account in *Eudemian Ethics* is the correct one, concedes that none of the nameless virtues are clearly associated with any particular emotion, except for wit, which Fortenbaugh associates with the aesthetic emotion of "finding something laughable" (216), but such an emotion, if it exists, is not mentioned by Aristotle himself. For general criticism of the presuppositions of Fortenbaugh's view, see Sorabji 1973–4, 210–11. Fortenbaugh himself appears to have changed his mind about the nameless virtues by the time he wrote his book (Fortenbaugh 1975, 90–1).

emotions will not hold up, although emotions proper are to be found in the triads of the other conditions that do not count as full-blown virtues in either work.[19] Envy and shame, for example, just are emotions, according to Aristotle; they are not settled states in virtue of which we experience emotions on particular occasions in particular ways. The problem is why Aristotle should even entertain the thought that wit and friendliness are emotions like these. I suggest that Aristotle was worried that wit, truthfulness, and friendliness are matters of temperament rather than virtue.[20] In fact, the way in which these conditions are described in *Eudemian Ethics* might lend support to the idea that someone temperamentally friendly or temperamentally blunt would do just as well as the virtuous person in *Nicomachean Ethics*. In his *Nicomachean Ethics*, Aristotle sees that these virtues are no more matters of sheer temperament than are any of the others. It appears, then, that the *Nicomachean Ethics* contains the superior account.

4. INCLUDING THE NAMELESS VIRTUES

In the previous sections, I argued that despite recognizing the controversial nature of the nameless virtues as virtues, Aristotle provides no conclusive reason not to consider them virtues. I now wish to consider the positive reasons for extending the list of virtues to include them.

At the beginning of *Nicomachean Ethics*, Aristotle presents an important argument relating human happiness and the virtues to human nature (*EN* I 7). Happiness consists in carrying out distinctively human activity well, that is, in accordance with virtue (and it also requires the wherewithal to do so). Therefore, it is reasonable to expect the particular virtues to allow their possessors to make good use of their specifically human attributes and hence to flourish as human beings. All the ethical virtues involve reasoning, a central human activity, but they each pick up on other particular aspects of human nature as well. The nameless virtues are no exception. Mildness concerns the emotion of anger. The virtue concerning small honours concerns the desire for approval

---

[19] I discuss the distinction between natural and full virtue in Ch. 5.

[20] See also, e.g., *Eudemian Ethics* II 2 1220b16 on various temperaments.

or respect on a small scale. The three other nameless virtues concern speech and the sense of humour (besides action), which are also special characteristics of human animals according to Aristotle.[21]

The nameless virtues specifically concern human relationships and community, both the ways in which the agent should present himself and treat other people, and the ways in which he should accept their treatment of him. These virtues therefore deal with a most important aspect of human nature, the social. As Aristotle points out, "human beings are political animals, tending by nature to live together" (*EN* IX 9 1169b18–19 cf. *EN* I 7 1097b11). I shall elaborate on the importance of the nameless virtues for a democratic society in Chapter 10.

The nameless virtues are just as important as their named companions, not only because they relate to important aspects of human activity, but also because they are necessary for any human community to exist as a community. They provide necessary conditions for a human community to flourish and are part of that flourishing itself. I shall expand on this point in the following chapter on non-remedial virtues. Although the *expression* of the nameless virtues may differ from place to place, they themselves are not particular to any place or time, or even, despite Aristotle's occasional comments to the contrary, class and gender. In the case of the nameless virtues, it is particularly clear that they transcend the parochial Greek culture of the fourth century BCE.

One might object that the exercise of the nameless virtues is made redundant by the exercise of the named virtues, especially, for example, justice. The objection fails, but not because the nameless virtues only concern private life whereas the named virtues concern life in the public sphere.[22] Rather, it fails because if one lacks the virtue of mildness,

---

[21] On the relation to speech and language, see *Pol.* I 2 1253a9–18 and *Top.* I 4 102a20–2; on laughter, see *PA* III 10 673a8 and 673a28.

[22] Gauthier and Jolif 1958 (vol II, pars 1, 304–5) argue that truthfulness, friendliness, and wit concern life in society where this excludes public life and business, which they claim is the province of justice. This restriction on the scope of the nameless virtues is unwarranted. The nameless virtues are useful, indeed especially useful, for human relationships in the public sphere, for example for the diplomat who is negotiating a treaty or for the advertiser selling wares. True, Aristotle denies that *alētheia* covers contracts (*EN* IV 7 1127a33–4), which are the province of justice, but Aristotle need not be contrasting the

for example, one will also lack the presence of mind to be just, and similarly with the other virtues. In other words, the objection fails in the face of Aristotle's claim that one cannot have any one virtue fully unless one has all the rest (*EN* VI [=*EE* V] 13 1144b30–1145a2), a thesis I explain in Chapter 5.

Admittedly, Aristotle's thesis about the unity of the virtues comes in a book common to both the *Nicomachean Ethics* and the *Eudemian Ethics* where, as we have seen, some of the nameless virtues do not count as full-blown virtues. However, it is only in the *Eudemian Ethics* that Aristotle suggests that the nameless virtue of truthfulness will contribute to the virtue of practical wisdom (*phronēsis*), an intellectual virtue that is essential to all the ethical virtues (*EE* III 7 1234a33–4). Hence, a nameless virtue would appear to be central to Aristotle's system, as I explain further in Chapter 8.

5. TAKING THE NAMELESS VIRTUES SERIOUSLY

Despite their lack of interest in the nameless virtues as such, modern commentators often treat mildness as the *paradigm* of an Aristotelian mean at work. Not only is the virtue nameless, but it is the only virtue whose associated vices are both called nameless by Aristotle as well (*EN* II 7 1108a6). Perhaps this is an indication of the way in which the nameless virtues provide special insight into Aristotle's views on the nature of the virtues. Indeed, an examination of the nameless virtues brings out the significance of Aristotle's innovative triadic view of the virtues and vices embodied in his doctrine of the mean. As Aristotle himself says, "It is a good idea to examine the nameless virtues *as well as the others*. For if we discuss particular aspects of character one at a time, we will acquire a better knowledge of them; and if we survey the virtues and see that in each case the virtue is a mean, we will have greater trust that the virtues are means" (*EN* IV 7 1127a15–17).

> public sphere with the private. Rather, he is contrasting what is covered by the laws of the city and what is not. Virtuous conduct in abiding by a contract is the province of law. Virtuous conduct in entering into the contract in the first place is not. Both types of conduct are in the public sphere.

In Chapter 4, I continue the argument that the doctrine of the mean helps generate Aristotle's list of ethical virtues, and I revisit some of the nameless virtues in the context of modern suggestions about what the ethical virtues are. In Chapter 8, I show how the virtue of truthfulness has a pivotal role to play in Aristotle's ethics, and, in Chapter 10, I show how the nameless virtues are key in Aristotle's ranking of different happy lives. Although the nameless virtues are nameless, they are an important part of Aristotle's ethic of virtue, and should not be consigned to anonymity.

3 The Non-remedial Nature of the Virtues

It is often thought that what is distinctive about ethical virtues[1] is that they are meant to remedy certain defects, either in human nature or in the world, or both.[2] These views are supposedly linked with the idea that if human beings were perfect, or if they lived in a perfect world, there would be no need for ethical virtues. In this chapter, I argue that Aristotle's ethical virtues are not *essentially* remedial. This is especially clear in the case of the nameless virtues I discussed in the previous chapter, but remedial interpretations are also at odds with aspects of Aristotle's doctrine of the mean, discussed in Chapter 1, and his famous function argument. The view that Aristotelian ethical virtues are not essentially remedial is therefore an important thesis in Aristotle's ethic of virtue. It contributes to Aristotle's account of particular virtues, to be explained in Chapter 4, and it also supports Aristotle's humanism, to be further elaborated in Chapter 6.

Modern proponents of remedial views often trace their position back to Aristotle. For example, Philippa Foot in "Virtues and Vices" says that the "virtues should be seen as correctives" and she suggests that Aristotle would agree.[3] Christine Korsgaard in an influential paper, "Aristotle and Kant on the Source of Value",[4] argues that, according to

---

[1] I mean to be discussing *ethical* virtues throughout. (Aristotle distinguishes ethical and intellectual virtues, e.g., *EN* VI 1 1138b35–1139a1.)

[2] I leave aside a third way in which the ethical virtues may be supposed to be remedial, remedying non-ideal social conditions created by human beings. This view, attributed to Marx, is discussed in Nussbaum 1988, 43.

[3] Foot 1978, 10 and 8.

[4] Korsgaard 1986. Her paper is cited with approval by, e.g., Lawrence, 1993, 3.

Aristotle, the ethical virtues only have conditional value. In Korsgaard's words:

> One can center one's life around, say, justice in fighting for oppressed people or courage in the military life or political and practical wisdom in making laws for the city. For an individual such an activity is a final good, for the virtuous person does these things for their own sake. But this sort of life of the moral virtues is conditional in a particular way, namely, on something's being wrong or imperfect. Engaging in politics is choiceworthy because there are injustices to be put right, and being a soldier is choiceworthy because there are wars to be fought, and being a doctor is choiceworthy because illness is a recurrent flaw in human life and so on. But it would be better if life did not have these limitations and defects.[5]

Korsgaard bases her account on passages in Aristotle's *Nicomachean Ethics* X 7 and 8.

I therefore begin by examining Foot and Korsgaard's arguments at greater length to try to nail down what their remedial views are (and to show that I am not merely attacking straw positions) and why they are antithetical to Aristotle's approach (Sections 1 and 2). I then discuss various passages in Aristotle about gods, humans, and the isles of the blessed that seem closest to these remedial views, but which, I argue, need not and should not be read as supporting such views (Sections 3 and 4). Finally, I argue that Aristotle's way of understanding the concept of function in his famous function argument is inimical to a remedial view (Section 5), and I make some suggestions about the origin of remedial views and why such views should be rejected (Section 6).

1. CORRECTIVE VIRTUES VERSUS THE DOCTRINE OF THE MEAN

In "Virtues and Vices",[6] Philippa Foot sets out what she considers to be distinctive about the ethical virtues. First, ethical virtues in general

---

[5] Korsgaard 1986, 494.
[6] Foot 1978.

are characteristics that are beneficial to the agent and to others. Second, unlike characteristics such as health and strength, ethical virtues must relate to an agent's intentions or will.[7] Third, ethical virtues are corrective. Each virtue, Foot explains, stands "at a point at which there is some temptation to be resisted or some deficiency of motivation to be made good". Enlisting Aristotle, she continues, "As Aristotle put it, virtues are about what is difficult for men". Foot explains her point as follows:

> And now, going back to the idea of virtues as correctives one may say that it is only because fear and the desire for pleasure often operate as temptations that courage and temperance exist as virtues at all. As things are we often want to run away not only where that is the right thing to do but also where we should stand firm; and we want pleasure not only where we should seek pleasure but also where we should not. If human nature had been different there would have been no need for a corrective disposition in the first place, as fear and pleasure would have been good guides to conduct throughout life.

Here she quotes Aquinas, who said that the passions may incite us to something against reason "and so we need a curb, which we name *temperance*" [Aquinas *Summa Theologica*, 1a2ae Q.61 a.3.].[8]

The quotation from Aquinas is significant. Aristotle has dropped out of the picture, and not surprisingly, because it is clearly not Aristotle's view that the virtuous person is overcoming any recalcitrant desires when he acts virtuously. On the contrary, for Aristotle, someone who acts rightly in the face of recalcitrant desires would count as enkratic or self-controlled, rather than virtuous (*EN* VII 7 1150a32–1150b1). As we shall see in Chapter 4, Aristotle also distinguishes virtue from endurance. In Aristotle's considered view, endurance is not a virtue. It is not listed as such in the *Nicomachean Ethics*, and, in *Nicomachean Ethics* VII (a common book), it is put on a par with self-control. Aristotelian virtues, then, do not seem to be corrective in the way in which Foot proposes. According to Aristotle, we do not have a particular virtue if we suffer from those

---

[7] By contrast, in Aristotle's view, one can voluntarily become ill, e.g., *EN* III 5 1114a15–16.

[8] Quotations are from Foot 1978, 8 and 9. The emphasis is Foot's.

particular temptations and difficulties that Foot describes. Foot modifies her position accordingly. She concludes, "I have argued that the virtues can be seen as correctives in relation to human nature in general but not that each virtue must present a difficulty to each and every man".[9] For example, courage is a virtue because "men in general find it hard to face great dangers or evils, and even small ones".[10]

This new suggestion is even more puzzling. Why should the fact that most people find it difficult to face great dangers, if it is true, show that this is a general defect in human nature that needs to be corrected, or that courage is the way of correcting this defect? Certainly Aristotle would allow that fear is part of human nature, and that people need to train their fear for the good in order to have courage, but this does not show that excessive, or for that matter deficient, fear is a general defect in human nature, nor that courage is the way to correct it. According to Aristotle's doctrine of the mean, there is a right and at least two wrong ways to have fear, but this does not mean that fear is an inherent defect in human nature. Compare training someone to dance.[11] A teacher trains a pupil to make the right movements, but this does not entail that the teacher corrects inherently wrong posture on the part of the student. Nor is the student necessarily correcting any defects when he or she practises alone. Similarly, a vine lacks an inherent direction but can be trained to grow up a trellis.[12] By analogy, training an emotion to go in the right direction is one thing, correcting something inherently bad in human nature is another.[13]

---

[9] Foot 1978, 11.

[10] Foot 1978, 10.

[11] I owe the analogy to Constance Meinwald.

[12] The argument here may suggest that both virtue and vice are the result of socialization. It might be objected that someone outside society is less likely to be virtuous. Hence, vice would seem to be innate. However, Aristotle thinks that the polis exists by nature, and that the person outside society is either bad (*phaulos*) or greater than a human being (*Politics* I 1253a1–4). For further discussion, see Ch. 10 Section 1. In the *Eudemian Ethics*, Aristotle goes as far as to claim that humans naturally wish for the good and, only if corrupted, will they wish for what is bad (*EE* II X 1227a28–31).

[13] Yes, children may feel fear or confidence in the wrong way, but that does not show that fear and confidence are bad in themselves and need correcting.

According to Aristotle, the emotions in themselves are neutral.[14] It is whether the emotions are exercised for good or ill that makes a person good or bad, as is implicit in the first aspect of the doctrine of the mean, explained in Chapter 1. Even hatred may be properly or improperly directed. Aristotle explains ethical virtue as a good disposition in relation to the emotions (*EN* II 1105b25–6). The ethically virtuous person is someone who has the right emotions and acts correctly in all circumstances. As Aristotle says, the ethical virtues do not come by nature, but nor are they contrary to nature (*EN* II 1 1103a23–4). If people had naturally bad tendencies that had to be overcome, the ethical virtues would be contrary to nature. Of course, this does not preclude some people being born with a tendency in one direction or another, but what is a bad tendency in one circumstance may be a good tendency in another, given Aristotle's doctrine of the mean.[15] According to Aristotle, we must get to know our own natural tendencies so that we can adjust for them accordingly (*EN* II 9 1109b1–5). However, it does not follow that the essential point of the ethical virtues is to correct such tendencies. Indeed, adjusting for our natural tendencies is called a "second-best tack" to hitting the mean directly (*EN* II 9 1109a34–5).[16]

Perhaps Foot's point is just that we cannot make sense of the virtue of courage unless most people do not have it. Hence, if most people did not lack courage, courage would not be the virtue it is. But why should most people have to lack courage? Suppose only half the population did, or a quarter? Perhaps Foot would say that at least some people have to lack courage for courage to be a virtue. However, this is to commit what Marcus Singer calls "the polarity fallacy", that is, the fallacy of supposing that it follows that, if we can only understand one term if we understand its opposite, then an instance of the one cannot exist unless an instance of the other does.[17]

---

[14] Of the emotions listed in *EN* II 5, envy is the exception, but it may have the same root as emulation. Spite perhaps results from wrongly directed joy and pain. It has an anomalous role in the *Nicomachean Ethics*. See, e.g., *EN* II 7.

[15] See Urmson 1973. For a discussion of Aristotle's distinction between natural and full virtue, see Ch. 5.

[16] True, in *Politics* III 16 1287a30–2, Aristotle says that appetite and emotion corrupt the best of men, but the first line of chapter 17 shows that he does not accept everything in the arguments of the previous chapter.

[17] Singer 1990–1.

It may be true that virtue implies the possibility of vice, but that is a far cry from the claim that virtue actually *corrects* something deficient in human nature. According to Aristotle, virtue and vice come by habituation. Virtue does not correct vice, since Aristotle does not think that human beings are inherently vicious. Whatever the truth in Foot's claim, it turns out not to have the substantive ramifications of the remedial view. If Foot's claim is that virtue corrects a flaw in human nature, or that virtue corrects a bad tendency, the claim is substantive but not Aristotelian. If her claim is that to understand virtue we must understand vice, or that virtue implies the possibility of vice, what she is claiming is fine, but it is no longer a remedial view, so her account no longer poses a threat to the non-remedial understanding of Aristotle's view.

2. CONDITIONAL VALUE AND NAMELESS VIRTUES

Let us turn to the view of Christine Korsgaard, which is broader than Foot's.[18] In her view, the ethical virtues are there to remedy flaws in human nature and in the world. According to Korsgaard, the exercise of ethical virtue has conditional value in two ways. First, it is not something that makes human life worthy of choice. As Korsgaard says, "Certainly, one would not choose a human life or choose to be a human being in order to keep one's promises and to exercise temperance".[19] The value of exercising ethical virtue depends on contemplation, the exercise of the intellectual virtue of wisdom, which has unconditional value and thus makes human life worthwhile. Second, exercising ethical virtue is supposed to be conditional on something being wrong or imperfect. Korsgaard seems to connect the two points, arguing that what has unconditional value is what does not depend on anything being wrong or imperfect. If exercising ethical virtue only has conditional value, then (a) its value depends on the value of something that has unconditional value, and (or because?) (b) it depends on something being wrong or imperfect. For present purposes, I shall concentrate on Korsgaard's arguments for (b).

---

[18] Korsgaard 1986, esp. 492–5.
[19] Korsgaard 1986, 495.

Korsgaard holds that the morally virtuous activity of a political life aims at establishing the conditions for a good life, and so cannot be the good life itself. She uses the following analogy: "The doctor cures people so that they may have the health that makes a good life possible. Imagine that the *only* good life is the life of the doctor. Then if the doctor were successful and everyone were healthy, there would be no point to life".[20] However, the analogy suggests the opposite conclusion. If everyone were healthy, we would still need doctors to tell us what to do to keep that way. Similarly, a politician may be setting up conditions to make it easier for people to continue acting virtuously. Since ethical virtue is self-sustaining, according to Aristotle, there is no reason why its aim should not be to promote itself. When one politician goes, others are needed to continue the good work. It is unclear from Korsgaard's discussion whether she has in mind the person who first wrote the constitution of a city, or the person who legislates once it is set up. Assuming that both act with ethical virtue, the point holds in either case.

Even if we were to suppose that ethically virtuous political activity was aimed at something other than itself, it would not follow that it was not choiceworthy for its own sake, according to Aristotle. In Aristotle's view, there are three classes of goods: goods choiceworthy only for the sake of something else; goods choiceworthy for their own sake and for the sake of something else; and goods choiceworthy for their own sake and not for the sake of anything else (*EN* I 7 1097a25–b6).[21] Korsgaard leaves out goods of the second kind.

Korsgaard suggests that such political activity is conditional: "Engaging in politics is choiceworthy because there are injustices to be put right, and being a soldier is choiceworthy because there are wars to be fought, and being a doctor is choiceworthy because illness is a recurrent flaw in human life and so on. But it would be better if life did not have these limitations and defects".[22] We have already seen that engaging in politics might be choiceworthy not only to rectify injustices, but also to sustain any just practices that may already obtain or to prevent

[20] Korsgaard 1986, 494.

[21] I discuss the trichotomy in Ch. 7.

[22] Korsgaard 1986, 494.

injustice. Similarly, one might choose to be a soldier to deter aggression, or to be a doctor to ensure that illness did not recur in human life.

Suppose, though, that war, injustice, and illness were wiped out. Interestingly, Korsgaard argues that the people would still need "everyday justice to keep promises and contracts and to return services". They will need the so-called nameless virtues of wit and friendliness as well as temperance. Here, Korsgaard switches tack, arguing that one would not choose life in order to keep promises, and so on (the other way in which the virtues are supposed to be conditional on her account). She continues, "Aristotle therefore looks for an activity that would make life worth living even if life had no defects and limitations to overcome". The limitations, it turns out, are human "needs, fears, or bad appetites".[23] Presumably, the idea is that if humans did not need each other's company, they would not need wit and friendliness, and if they did not have bad appetites, they would not need temperance.

However, as Aristotle explains, humans are political, not solitary animals. Unlike gods, their well-being is not self-confined (e.g., *EE* VII 12 1245b18). The fact that human beings need each other's company is not a flaw. As for bad appetites, Korsgaard's argument has collapsed into Foot's, and so the same objections apply. According to Aristotle, human appetites are not inherently bad; they merely need to be trained in the right direction in accordance with the doctrine of the mean. There is nothing wrong and defective here.[24]

So far, I have been examining Korsgaard's argument on its own terms. I should now like to consider the passages in Aristotle that prompt her interpretation.

3. GODS AND HUMANS

The two main passages addressed by Korsgaard are *Nicomachean Ethics* X 7 1177b4–26 and X 8 1178b7–22. In Book X, Aristotle returns to the question of what happiness, "the human good", is. In Book I, he set out various formal constraints on what is to count as happiness, and he

[23] Korsgaard 1986, 495.
[24] See also the criticisms of Korsgaard's view by Stocker 1990, 63–4.

argues that happiness is carrying out the distinctive function of human beings in accordance with the most complete or most final virtue in a full life. In the course of the *Nicomachean Ethics*, Aristotle describes a host of ethical virtues and two main intellectual virtues: practical wisdom or *phronēsis*, which requires and is required by all of the ethical virtues; and wisdom or *sophia*. There are, therefore, three candidates for a happy life: a life in accordance with practical wisdom (and all the ethical virtues); a life in accordance with wisdom; and a life in accordance with both. In Book I, Aristotle criticized some lives on the grounds that they were more suitable for non-human animals or for plants than for adult human beings. In Book X chapter 6, Aristotle uses similar considerations to show that happiness is an activity, not a state, and that it is not a life of mere amusement. Happiness is not what is fit for a plant or for a child.

We might therefore expect Aristotle to continue his search in Book X chapters 7 and 8 by considering what is most suitable for human beings. Instead, surprisingly,[25] he discusses the idea that human beings have a godlike element, the intellect, and that we should therefore consider the traditional view that "the gods more than anyone are blessed and happy" in order to see what activity makes the gods happy, and what mere mortals have in common with them.

Aristotle presents an argument to show that the contemplative life appears to be superior to the life of political activity and perhaps ethical virtue (*EN* X 7 1177b4–26) if we pay attention to the idea that happiness is in time of leisure.[26] He writes:

> Happiness seems to be found in leisure, since we accept trouble so that we can be at leisure, and fight wars so that we can be at peace. Now the virtues concerned with action have their activities in politics or war, and actions here seem to require trouble.

[25] Perhaps not so surprisingly, since the entire passage may be merely aporetic, as appears from *EN* X 8 cited below.

[26] It is not my intention to enter the debate about whether happiness consists merely in contemplation or also or only in ethical virtue at this juncture. As will emerge in Ch. 10, though, I think that there is an important puzzle to be solved before this debate even gets off the ground, and I argue for a different way of understanding Aristotle's discussion in *EN* X.

This seems completely true for actions in war, since no one chooses to fight a war, and no one continues it, for the sake of fighting a war; for someone would have to be a complete murderer if he made his friends his enemies so that there could be battles and killings.

But the actions of the politician require trouble also. Beyond political activities themselves these actions seek positions of power and honours; or at least they seek happiness for the politician himself and for his fellow-citizens, which is something different from political science (*politikē*) itself, and clearly is sought on the assumption that it is different.

Hence among actions expressing the virtues those in politics and war are pre-eminently great; but they require trouble, aim at some [further] end, and are choiceworthy for something other than themselves.

But the activity of understanding, it seems, is superior in excellence because it is the activity of study; aims at no end beyond itself; has its own proper pleasure, which increases the activity; and is self-sufficient, leisured and unwearied, as far [as these are possible] for a human being. And whatever else is ascribed to the happy person is evidently found in connection with this activity.

Hence a human being's complete happiness will be this activity, if it receives a complete span of life, since nothing incomplete is proper to happiness.[27]

The following considerations may cast doubt on whether this passage really supports any remedial view. Certainly, we may fight wars to be at peace, but are we brave in order to have peace? This is unclear. It might promote peace sooner if all the soldiers on one side ran away. Presumably, being brave requires a just war aimed at a just peace. Arriving at a just peace might require diplomacy, which depends for its success on the nameless virtues more than on the bravery of individual soldiers. However, it is not essential to the nameless virtues that they be used to stop wars. Moreover, it is odd that Aristotle says that political action aims at power and honours, since elsewhere he views these as mistaken aims, the aims of people who lack ethical virtue (*EN* I 5 1095b22–30; *EE* I 5 1216a23–7). Finally, Aristotle says that political activity may aim at happiness for the politician and the people,

---

[27] Translations of Aristotle's *Nicomachean Ethics* are by Irwin 1985.

which is different from *politikē* (*EN* X 7 1177b14–15). If *politikē* is political science, Aristotle's point is irrelevant. If it is action according to the intellectual virtue of practical wisdom (*politikē* being an adjective qualifying the good activity above), it is not clear why the politician cannot be promoting more of the same. If what he is promoting is contemplation, the argument begs the question.

The argument fails to show that actions of ethical virtue are aimed at something other than themselves. If the argument were successful, it would not follow that the aim of ethical virtue is merely to correct things that have gone wrong in the world. If one thing is for the sake of something else, it does not follow that it must be meant to correct some defect. For example, if I walk through the park to visit a friend, it does not follow that the walk corrects any defect. It is unclear how seriously Aristotle takes the argument, at least as far as it pertains to humans, for he goes on to dispute its conclusion about the self-sufficiency of contemplation; he points out that what is self-sufficient for gods will not be for human beings. For example, humans need external goods (*EN* X 8 1178b33–5) and things needed for a human life (*EN* X 8 1178b2–5).

Another argument (*EN* X 8 1178b7–22) is based on the idea that what the gods enjoy is complete happiness. This argument is also unusual, since the gods in question are neither the traditional Greek gods, who exhibit all kinds of vices, nor Aristotle's god who is splendidly alone.[28] In addition, as we saw above, Aristotle elsewhere disputes the appropriateness of any analogy between god and humans (*EN* VIII 7 1159a5–12 cf. *EE* VII 12 1245b12–19).

Aristotle explains that we traditionally suppose that the gods are happy. However, the gods do not do any actions that require virtue, and they are not asleep. As a result, there is only one thing left that they can be doing that makes them happy; they must be contemplating. Hence, happiness must be contemplation.

In the midst of the argument, Aristotle asks a series of rhetorical questions: "[W]hat sorts of actions ought we to ascribe to them? Just actions?

---

[28] Even if Aristotle means to be referring to his own god who contemplates, he also relies on the premiss that the gods are happy, a premiss that comes from popular opinion. But this may make matters worse. For example, as Bostock wryly observes, "One may well doubt whether these two premises can be held jointly" (Bostock 2000, 198).

Surely they will appear ridiculous making contracts, returning deposits and so on. Brave actions? Do they endure what's frightening and endure dangers because it is fine? Generous actions? Whom will they give to? And surely it would be absurd for them to have currency or anything like that", culminating in "What would their temperate actions be? Surely it is vulgar praise to say that they do not have base appetites" (*EN* X 1178b10–16). T. H. Irwin explains, "The gods do not suffer from the human limitations that make virtues of character necessary and praiseworthy for human beings. There is no point in praising them for not having base appetites, as we would praise the temperate person; for the gods were never in danger of having them, and did not need to train themselves".[29]

However, it is not necessary to hang the entire baggage of a remedial view on Aristotle's last question. We need not suppose that human beings are limited if they need virtues of character. One could just as well conclude that the gods are limited because they lack good appetites or because they lack human needs. Strangely, Aristotle here seems to be forgetting his doctrine of the mean. For human beings, lack of appetites, though rare, is a vice, *anaesthēsia* (II 8 1109a2–5). Surely the gods are not vicious if they lack appetites. When Aristotle describes happiness for the gods, then, he need not be claiming that human beings are defective insofar as they are not gods. He need not be saying that we would be better off if we were gods.[30] Nor is he saying that there is no point in being born a human being because we are not gods. Instead, Aristotle is grappling with the problem of what counts as happiness for creatures that, while human, have a divine element in them. He is not arguing that, since they are not wholly divine, they are therefore defective.

4. THE ISLES OF THE BLESSED

Let us now turn to two passages in Aristotle that, though not mentioned by Korsgaard herself, may at first sight appear to clinch the case for the remedial view. The first passage is in Aristotle's *Politics* and the other is from his *Protrepticus*.

[29] Irwin 1985, 381.

[30] See, e.g, *EN* VIII 7 1159a5–11, where Aristotle says that friends should not wish a friend to be a god.

In Aristotle's *Politics* VII 15, Aristotle explains how the best city-state and the best individual have the same priorities. As peace should be the aim of war, so leisure should be the goal of occupation, and not the other way round; war should not be the aim of peace, nor occupation the goal of leisure. Aristotle, therefore, chides the Spartans for gearing their city-state for war, and for promoting bravery at the expense of the other ethical virtues. He says that bravery and endurance are needed for occupation, and philosophy is needed for leisure (*Pol.* VII 15 1334a22–3). Temperance and justice are required in both times, and especially in time of peace and leisure.

Several points are worthy of note. First, the four virtues are Plato's cardinal virtues. Second, there is no mention of any of Aristotle's nameless virtues. Third, endurance is not clearly a virtue, as we have seen. Nevertheless, the comment that temperance and justice are required in times of business *and leisure*, the time when one would be thinking, suggests that they cannot be remedial in the way in which Korsgaard suggests. Although the earlier passages we considered were compatible with, although they did not require, the remedial view, this passage suggests a stronger claim. The ethical virtues cannot be essentially remedial, because they would still be needed when things were going right.

In the following passage, Aristotle explains that temperance and justice are especially needed in peacetime because prosperity "is more apt to make men overbearing (*hubristas*). A special degree of justice and temperance is therefore required in those who appear to be faring exceptionally well and enjoying all that the world accounts to be happiness, like the denizens of 'the happy isles' of which poets sing; and the greater the leisure which these men are able to use, when they are set among an abundance of blessings, the greater too will be their need of wisdom, as well as of temperance and justice" (*Pol.* VII 15 1334a27–34).[31]

We could think that this passage supports Foot's view, since temperance and justice are required because of *hubris*. However, Aristotle does not say that human beings are naturally overbearing, only that prosperity tends to make them so. One might object that the virtues are

[31] The translation is by Barker 1946.

needed to correct this tendency. However, a passage in the *Protrepticus*[32] suggests that we need not read the passage as supporting any remedial view. There, Aristotle quotes the proverb that "surfeit breeds hubris", but he is making the point that vice has worse consequences in times of prosperity than in other circumstances. Bad people can do a good deal more harm if they have lots of good things like wealth and strength than if they do not. That is why virtue becomes especially important. There need be no suggestion that virtue is needed to correct anything.

There are two accounts of Aristotle's remarks from the *Proptrepticus*: Iamblichus *Protrepticus* 9 and Augustine's record of Cicero's comments in *De Trinitate* 14.9.12.[33] In Augustine's record of Cicero's comments, Cicero asks what use eloquence will be in the isles of the blessed when there are no trials or law-courts, or what need there will be even of the virtues themselves. There will be no need for fortitude when there is no labour or danger. He goes further than the passage in the *Politics*, saying that there is "no need for justice when there is nothing belonging to anyone else to be sought, no need for temperance when there are no passions, nor prudence when there is no choice between goods and bads".

In Iamblichus's account, Aristotle distinguishes things that are necessary from goods in themselves, and says that, in the isles of the blessed, we will not need anything except philosophy. However, Aristotle's strategy, as it emerges from Iamblichus's account, is quite the reverse from what is needed to support Korsgaard's view. Aristotle appears to be addressing someone who thinks that things are worthwhile only if they are useful, that is, for something else, and he tries to argue that philosophy is worthwhile even if it is not for the sake of anything else. His aim is not to downgrade things that are good for the sake of other things (and he does not specify what these are), but to show that it is also possible to be good and not be for the sake of anything else. Philosophy does not fit the standard for goodness for the rest. The central point is not that the virtues are useless on the isles of the blessed but that philosophy is good there, and the fact that philosophy is good there is supposed to help explain why philosophy is good.

[32] *Fr.* 3 cf. Düring 1961, fragment 4.
[33] *Fr.* 12 cf. Düring 1961, fragments 42–4.

Previous commentators have been partisan. Werner Jaeger argued that Cicero has got it right and Iamblichus has not.[34] Ingemar Düring disagreed, suggesting that Cicero knew the passage from the *Politics* and the *Protrepticus*, and added in some local Roman flavour. In Düring's words, "It is all mixed up".[35] But there is merely a difference in emphasis in the two accounts. Even if we accept Cicero's report, we need not accept a remedial reading. Even if there is no need for ethical virtues on the isles of blessed, it does not follow that it is part of the essential nature of the ethical virtues to correct bad things in ordinary life. Cicero need be saying no more than that if there is no opportunity for vice, then there is no opportunity for virtue. If we also accept Iamblichus's account, however, Aristotle's account is clearly inimical to the remedial way of thinking.

5. THE FUNCTION ARGUMENT

At the beginning of the *Nicomachean Ethics*, Aristotle says that while everyone agrees that the highest good is happiness, there is disagreement over what happiness is. In order to clarify what happiness is, Aristotle presents his famous argument concerning the function (*ergon*) of human beings (*EN* I 7 1097b24–1098a18). In broad outline, the argument runs as follows:

(1) An F's good (literally, its well) depends on its function (*ergon*), if it has one.

An F's good is exercising-its-*ergon* (*en-erg-eia*) well.

(2) Human beings have a function.

(3) The human function is activity (*energeia*) of the soul in accordance with or not without reason.

By (1), (4) The human good (happiness, doing well) depends on the human function.

(5) The function of an F is the same in kind as the function of an excellent F.

[34] Jaeger 1923, 73.
[35] Düring 1961, 211.

> So (6) The human good (happiness) is activity of the soul (in accordance with or not without reason) (done) well, that is, in accordance with virtue, or, if there is more than one virtue, in accordance with the best and most complete/final virtue, and not just for a short time.[36]

Very briefly, Aristotle argues for (1) by induction, using examples of flautists, sculptors, and artisans in general. Similarly, for (5) he relies on the example of a harpist. He argues for (2) with a series of questions, asking whether it is reasonable to think that a carpenter and a tanner have functions, while a human being does not, or if a hand, eye, and foot have functions whereas a human being does not. The argument for (3) relies on Aristotle's distinction between capacity and activity and on Aristotelian psychology. Aristotle divides the human psyche into three parts: (a) the rational part; (b) the appetitive part, shared with other animals, comprising feelings, appetites, and sense-perception; and (c) the nutritive part, shared with plants and containing capacities for nutrition, growth, and reproduction (*EN* I 13 1102a32–1102b2). Since the human function is what is distinctive of human beings, by a process of elimination it must involve a certain complexity of thought that non-human animals (and, of course, plants) lack.

As emerges later, there are two main virtues of thought: wisdom (*sophia*), the virtue of theoretical reasoning: and practical wisdom (*phronēsis*), the virtue of practical reasoning, both belonging to the rational part of the psyche (*EN* VI 1 1139a5–15). Ethical virtues are dispositions of the appetitive part, but they require and are required by practical wisdom. The conclusion of the function argument is therefore unclear. If Aristotle is saying that happiness is in accordance with the *most final* virtue, we might conclude that happiness is simply the exercise of theoretical thought, in accord with the virtue of wisdom. On the other hand, if Aristotle is claiming that happiness is in accord with the *most complete* virtue, we might conclude that happiness covers a range of activities, involving wisdom, practical wisdom, and the ethical

---

[36] Aristotle means a long stretch of time, but not necessarily a whole lifetime. See *EN* I 10 1101a9–14.

virtues too.[37] I shall return to this issue in Chapter 10 and I shall address the relationship between particular virtues and the human function at the beginning of Chapter 4.

The details of the argument are controversial,[38] but for present purposes, I wish to concentrate on the argument for premiss (5). I shall argue that Aristotle includes that piece of argument to counteract an assumption about what a function is that is presented by Thrasymachus in an earlier function argument set out at the end of Plato's *Republic* I (*Republic* I 352D–354A). The argument there runs as follows:

(1) There is such a thing as the function of an F, e.g., of a horse.

(2) The function of an F is that which (a) one can do only with it, or (b) best with it.

   [So (a) the function of an eye is to see, (b) of a pruning-knife to prune etc.]

(3) Each thing to which a function is assigned also has a virtue that enables it to perform its function well, and an opposing vice. [For example, sight is the virtue of the eye, and blindness the vice.]

   By (1) and (2), (4) The soul has a function: taking care of things, ruling and deliberating, and living.

   By (3), (5) It has a virtue and will only function well if it has its peculiar virtue.

---

[37] Hardie 1967 first raised the problem, arguing that Aristotle is confused and inconsistent in Books I and X of the *Nicomachean Ethics*. Controversy rages even over the interpretation of Book I. For example, Kenny 1978, Kraut 1989, and Reeve 1992 take the exclusive view. Gauthier and Jolif 1958, Ackrill 1974, Irwin, e.g., 1985a, Devereux 1981, Keyt 1983, Whiting 1986, Cooper 1987, and Roche 1988 take the inclusive view. Others, e.g., N. White 1988, Broadie 1991, and Lawrence 1997 argue that happiness is the *focus* of the best life, but the focal interpretation by itself does not solve the controversy, because one can dispute what that focus contains. N. White 1988 argues that the focus is simply contemplation. Lawrence 1997, 73 argues that the focus has more than one component. Kraut 1989 and Curzer 1991 think that the happy life aims at contemplation but includes ethical activity too, and Richardson Lear 2004 argues that while contemplation is the final end, virtuous activity is important and choiceworthy because it mimics contemplation.

[38] For a more detailed analysis of the argument, comments, and bibliography, see Gottlieb 2001a.

(6) Justice (earlier agreed) is its peculiar virtue.

(7) A just soul and just human being will live well, an unjust one badly.

(8) Anyone who lives well is blessed and happy. Anyone who does not is the opposite.

(9) It profits no-one to be unhappy.

So (10) Injustice is never more profitable than justice.

Aristotle makes some important innovations. He allows for a non-rational part of the human psyche, and, as a biologist, he arrives at the human function by considering human faculties in the light of the specific faculties of animals and plants. But the most important Aristotelian clarification, relating to the question of remedial virtues, involves the concept of a function itself. In describing the virtue and vice of the eye, Socrates asks his interlocutor, "And could eyes perform their function well if they lacked their peculiar virtue and had the vice instead?". Thrasymachus responds, "How could they, for don't you mean if they had blindness instead of sight?". Thrasymachus's response entails a dyadic view of virtue and vice, but it also suggests a specific way of understanding what the function of something is. Lacking a function is the vice, having the function is a virtue. Thus, an eye functions virtuously, that is, well, if it allows us to see, an ear functions well if it allows us to hear, and so on. To put it more simply, there is no difference between functioning and functioning well. Socrates' response is non-committal, "Whatever their virtue is, for I'm not asking about that". Thrasymachus claimed earlier that ruling entails ruling well, which supports the conflation of functioning and functioning well.

Now, in the case of a pruning-knife, one of Socrates' examples, notably absent from Aristotle's account, there is arguably no difference between it carrying out its function and it carrying out its function well. If the knife cuts, it is performing its function well. If it does not cut, it fails to perform its function at all. However, in other cases, it makes sense to distinguish mere functioning and functioning well. A harpist may play the harp, but not necessarily well. As Aristotle explains, in the case of the excellent harpist, "we add to the function the superior achievement that accords with virtue" (*EN* I 7 1098a10–11).

Therefore, when Aristotle concludes in his premiss (5) that the function of an F is the same in kind as the function of an excellent F, he intends to contradict the Thrasymachean account. On Aristotle's account of function, all human beings have the same function, but only the excellent human being carries out that function *well*.

This difference between Aristotle and Thrasymachus is significant because the Thrasymachean account of function may be thought to support the view that the point of ethical virtues is to remedy natural defects in human beings. According to Thrasymachus, blindness is the vice or defect of the eye. The vice is the lack of virtue, sight. The blind person lacks the function of seeing. It is a small step to think of ethical vices as lacks of function, and the ethical virtues as correctives. Aristotle's account of function in his *Nicomachean Ethics* is subtly different from the Thrasymachean view, and also marks an advance on his discussion in the *Eudemian Ethics*. There, he implies that the function of a human being and of an excellent human being is *to function well*, not merely to function (*EE* II 6 1106a16–25). According to the Nicomachean account, bad human beings do not lack the human function, but only the excellent human being carries out that function well. Vices are not lacks of function, nor are virtues correctives of such lacks. The Nicomachean function argument is therefore important in Aristotle's rejection of the remedial view.

6. REJECTING REMEDIAL VIEWS

There are practical as well as philosophical reasons for rejecting the remedial views. Apart from fostering the idea that humans are inherently bad,[39] remedial views support a frame of mind that finds great and expensive measures in a crisis much better than the preventive measures that would have made the intervention unnecessary in the first place. Korsgaard's medical example is instructive. In modern medicine, funding for expensive and heroic measures is preferred to preventive

---

[39] It is easy to confuse the perfection of human qualities with the correction of defects. The term "imperfection" is ambiguous between what has not yet been perfected and what is defective.

medicine.[40] The same goes for measures to help the environment or to deal with famine and drought. There is a general idea that one should intervene only when something has gone very wrong, but there is less of an obligation to create the conditions for things to go well in the first place. Remedial views also bolster the idea that if materials, in this case the emotions, can be exhibited and acted on well or badly, they must have been bad all along. Such views breed scepticism about goods.

Finally, some explanation is needed of where the remedial views come from, and why Aristotle is interpreted in these ways. Perhaps because the mention of the cardinal virtues suggests Platonic influence, commentators have imported the views of Plato's purple passages against desire and emotion.[41] Or perhaps the remedial views come from the Christian idea of original sin, according to which, after the Fall, human beings had to leave the garden of Eden, the Judaeo-Christian equivalent to the isles of the blessed, for a hostile world where they had to work for a living. Succeeding generations are inherently sinful, and the sinful tendencies need to be corrected by the ethical virtues. Yet, the Christian commentators on Aristotle do not seem to share a remedial view. Augustine, in *De Trinitate*, disagrees with Cicero and argues that the virtues can exist even in the state of bliss. Aquinas also seems to eschew a remedial view (*ST* question 67). Perhaps, then, more recent philosophers are the culprits. Hume, in his *Treatise on Human Nature*, describes the golden age of the poets as a useful fiction that shows that the human conventions regarding justice are "intended as a remedy to some inconveniences".[42] Kant, according to the traditional view, thinks that virtue often consists in overcoming one's emotions.[43] In Chapter 10, I argue that Hobbes is another culprit, showing how the non-remedial view puts Aristotle's ethic of virtue at odds with a particular kind of social contract theory. Hobbes thinks that human beings

---

[40] As, e.g., Williamson explains, in the foreword to *Gene Therapy* (Lemoine and Cooper 1996), "Although understandable in terms of the trials that are taking place, it is a pity that gene therapy has been described primarily in terms of catastrophic diseases … Genes are really about health. Using genes for health is an approach which emphasizes their essential usefulness".

[41] For example, Plato's *Phaedo* 83–4.

[42] Hume 1888, 494.

[43] See, e.g., the first paragraph of ch. IX of Kant's *DOV*.

naturally desire to better one another (the Aristotelian vice of injustice or greed), and fear and glory are overwhelming sources of motivation. In order to live in peace and security, human beings need to remedy these desires by coming to an agreement that is contrary to nature. According to Aristotle, human beings are naturally social.

Wherever the remedial views come from, Aristotle is not wittingly the source. The non-remedial view is an important thesis in Aristotle's ethic of virtue. It supports and is supported by Aristotle's doctrine of the mean. It explains a puzzling feature of the function argument. It also supports Aristotle's humanism, a point to be further elaborated in Chapter 6, and it contributes to Aristotle's account of particular virtues, as we shall see in the following chapter.

4 Listing the Virtues

In his *Nicomachean Ethics*, Aristotle lists the following dispositions as ethical virtues: bravery, temperance, generosity, magnificence, magnanimity, a virtue concerned with honour on a small scale, mildness, truthfulness, wit, and friendliness. As we have seen, the first five are named, the second five are nameless. These are followed by justice and equity.[1] The list is interesting both for what is included and for what is omitted. For example, Aristotle thinks that wit and friendliness are virtues. Kant does not. Aristotle treats pusillanimity as a vice, but it is treated as an important virtue by one modern Utilitarian.[2] Hope, not on Aristotle's list, is often considered to be an important virtue, and Aristotle is frequently chided for omitting charity and benevolence.[3] Asceticism, meekness, and self-sacrifice, Aristotelian vices, are often touted as virtues. On a more popular note, self-discipline tops William Bennett's influential list,[4] and faith is important too. These are not virtues according to Aristotle. Followers of Ayn Rand praise greed,

---

[1] It is not clear whether Aristotle's list is supposed to be exhaustive. Before discussing the ethical virtues in detail, Aristotle comments, "at the same time it will also be clear how many virtues there are" (*EN* III 5 1115a5), but he may merely be saying that it will be clear how *many* there are, as opposed to the shorter lists of his philosophical predecessors. Cf. Stewart 1892, 282 who thinks that all Aristotle means here is that the list is not limited to the four traditional cardinal virtues of wisdom, courage, temperance, and justice. (Wisdom, of course, is not an *ethical* virtue according to Aristotle.)

[2] See Driver 2001.

[3] The complaint about benevolence goes back to Bentham. See Louden 1992, 40. For a more recent complaint, see, e.g., Crisp 2000, xviii.

[4] Bennett 1993.

making and keeping money, and self-assertion.[5] Others yet again praise sympathy or compassion, and tolerance. Yet others talk of environmental virtues.[6]

Given the possible candidates for virtues, it is important to consider the basis for Aristotle's list if we are to see how he would rule out or rule in the modern suggestions about what the ethical virtues are. In Chapter 2, I argued that the existence of Aristotle's nameless virtues contradicts the influential idea that the basis for Aristotle's list is simply the views of his time, and therefore that the list is generated in a very conservative fashion. In Chapter 3, I rejected the view that the virtues are remedial and therefore that the basis for the list is that the virtues remedy defects in human nature or in the world.

In the first section of this chapter, I consider some other suggestions about how Aristotle's list of ethical virtues is generated that have been made on Aristotle's behalf. I argue that these factors need to be combined with the three aspects of the doctrine of the mean, described in Chapter 1. In the second section of the chapter, I compare Aristotle's controversial views about which dispositions count as virtues and which as vices, with some modern suggestions. The point of this section is to continue the argument of Chapters 1 and 2 that the doctrine of the mean has substantive consequences about what the ethical virtues are, and to show that it is plausible to think that Aristotle has a contribution to make to virtue ethics as opposed to contending moral theories.

1. GENERATING THE VIRTUES ON ARISTOTLE'S LIST

One suggestion is that Aristotle is generating the virtues merely by considering the sorts of dispositions that contribute to a happy life both for the agent and for others. For example, someone who has healthy self-esteem, like the human being with magnanimity, will have a happier life

[5] For some sample writings in this vein, see www.aynrand.org.

[6] On the "ethic of care" see, e.g., Gilligan 1993 and Noddings 1984. On environmental virtues, see, e.g., Jamieson 2007, although he views them from a Utilitarian point of view.

than someone who is plagued with self-doubts, like the pusillanimous person. The magnanimous person will also be able to help others more effectively if he is not worrying about himself. Similarly, the temperate person will be in good health, generally a pre-requisite for happiness.[7] Since he is temperate, he will also not take more than his fair share of goods, thus enabling others to lead happy lives as well. Truthfulness promotes trust and enables communication to take place, again enabling citizens to lead happy lives, and so on.

Although it is possible to argue for the Aristotelian ethical virtues along these lines, Aristotle himself does not explicitly provide any such arguments. The consequentialist aspects of the ethical virtues are not to the fore in any of his discussions, although, as I shall explain in Chapter 7, the virtues are to be pursued both for their own sakes and for the sake of happiness.

Nor does Aristotle present any arguments beginning from a merely subjective account of happiness, although such arguments are possible. For example, at one point Irwin argues that even a purely subjective or conative account of happiness would support courage and temperance, because temperance requires concern for one's good on the whole, as opposed to the satisfaction of this or that immediate desire, and courage requires such a concern in contrast to present fears that might paralyse one's pursuit of it. Irwin argues that the conative account is insufficient because it only allows for a minimal degree of virtue, and more needs to be said about which desires should be pursued at the expense of which others.[8] A different objection is that, on such an account, the virtues of courage and temperance would have much broader spheres than Aristotle himself allows, since present desires and fears are not restricted to physical pleasures and the battlefield. While the strategy of arguing from a conative account of happiness is attractive, since it suggests that the moralist should be able to convince almost anyone to become virtuous, it has difficulties that Aristotle wisely avoids. I consider the question of Aristotle's view of the appropriate student of ethics in Chapter 9.

---

[7] Health is one among three considerations presented for being temperate at *EN* III 12 1119a15. S. White 1992 shows how each ethical virtue can be considered in relation to a different external good.

[8] Irwin 1988, 382–4.

One might think that considerations about happiness enter in a different manner. As I explained in Chapter 3, Section 5, Aristotle argued in Book I that the well-functioning human being will be happy, and so it may seem reasonable to look for considerations from Aristotle's function argument in his discussion of particular virtues. First of all, one might consider human beings and other creatures. Aristotle nowhere argues that human beings have functions by analogy with other creatures having functions, as do Foot and Hursthouse.[9] The human function, according to Aristotle, is precisely what is distinctive of human beings, although it may include or require functions shared with other creatures but which are carried out in a distinctively human fashion. Aristotle occasionally mentions such differences in his discussion of particular ethical virtues. For example, he compares the vice of intemperance with the behaviour of non-human animals (*EN* III 10 1118b1–4), and bravery is contrasted with the behaviour of wild animals who are in pain or frightened (*EN* III 8 1116b24–1117a9). Elsewhere, Aristotle says that wild boars are not really brave, even though they are thought to be so (*EE* III 1 1229a25–6). As we saw in the discussion of the nameless virtues, according to Aristotle, human beings are the only animals capable of having a sense of humour, which helps explain the importance of the virtue of wit.

More importantly, though, human beings are the only animals with full-fledged *logos*, the power of reasoning and of using a language, since all of the ethical virtues in the *Nicomachean Ethics* require practical wisdom, which involves *logos*, it may appear promising to look at each ethical virtue with respect to reason, because each virtue requires the discriminating use of reason.[10] Such discussion will not be sufficient for generating the ethical virtues. We need to know precisely what kind of reasoning is involved, and how the reasoning relates to the emotions and appetites. In short, we will also need to have an understanding of the doctrine of the mean.

[9] Foot 2001, ch. 3, Hursthouse 1999, chs. 9 and 10.
[10] For example, Korsgaard 1986 esp. 276 argues that the virtues produce and maintain rational activity. On this view, one would still need to distinguish practical reasoning from theoretical reasoning and reasoning used in other skills.

While reason is certainly important, then, it is not sufficient to generate the particular virtues, although, as I explain below, it may be sufficient to rule out certain candidates for virtue. Nor is it sufficient to generate the particular virtues merely to explain the different spheres of each virtue. Since each ethical virtue covers a different aspect of human life, commentators have traditionally divided the virtues by their spheres.[11] While the first virtues on Aristotle's list relate to particular emotions and types of actions, the next ones relate to different types of activities in different contexts. However, merely providing a sphere is still not enough to generate a virtue. Someone might agree that there is a sphere of giving and taking, but think that the appropriate disposition involves taking as much as one can, as in the "virtues of selfishness" discussed below.

To address these problems, Aristotle lists his virtues using all the features of his doctrine of the mean. Each virtue is a disposition in relation to the emotions and is not itself an emotion, and there is a triadic structure of virtue and vices. To generate the virtues, then, Aristotle needs to use both considerations arising from general human psychology and the human way of life, *and* his doctrine of the mean. If human psychology and way of life, including the fact that humans are social animals, can give one the spheres of the virtues, only the doctrine of the mean can say what the *good* dispositions in those spheres are. That is why Aristotle takes such pains to show that each of his ethical virtues is in a mean, not merely the first five ethical virtues on his list, which are familiar named virtues, but also the second five, which are nameless.

2. CANDIDATES FOR VIRTUE, ANCIENT AND MODERN

In this section, I consider some virtues that have a controversial status on or off Aristotle's list. But first, a caveat. Given Aristotle's doctrine of the mean, it should not be possible to say what good people

[11] See, e.g., Aquinas 340, 113. Nussbaum 2000 presents a neo-Aristotelian account based on human capacities, and Irwin 1988, 366–7 also discusses the realization of capacities.

do independently of a particular context. In presenting his virtues and vices in a triadic structure, then, Aristotle must be presenting what virtuous people will do "for the most part". The vices, then, present dispositions that result in indiscriminate behaviour. The virtues are discriminating. The discussions of the virtues on Aristotle's list should provide the materials for the universal premisses of Aristotle's practical syllogisms, to be discussed in Chapter 8.

Perseverance and Endurance

We should expect Aristotle to argue that mere perseverance and endurance cannot by themselves be virtuous dispositions; we need to know that the virtuous person is persevering at the right time, for the right reasons, and so on. Persevering at a futile or vicious endeavour would hardly be a virtue,[12] just as Aristotle points out that persevering in a false belief is not good (*EN* VII 2 1146a16–18; 9 1151b4–6). Nevertheless, one might think that correct perseverance or correct endurance might be ethical virtues. Aristotle does not mention perseverance as a separate virtue, perhaps because it is a capacity that is actualized in the exercise of any virtue, and is not a virtue in itself. Although Aristotle does not mention perseverance, *karteria* (hardiness, resistance, endurance) appears on Aristotle's list of ethical virtues in his *Eudemian Ethics* (*EE* II 3 1221a9). It is a mean between luxuriousness and a nameless condition. The luxurious person endures no pain even if it is good for him, and the nameless person endures all pain alike. The virtuous person endures the right sort of pain on the right occasions, and so on.

Interestingly, *karteria* does not receive a longer treatment in Book III of the *Eudemian Ethics*, and nor does it appear on Aristotle's list of ethical virtues in the *Nicomachean Ethics* (*EN* II 7). In one of the common books, it and luxuriousness are discussed along with self-control and lack of self-control. There, *karteria* is compared unfavourably to self-control (*enkrateia*), which is also not a virtue (*EN* VII 7 1150a36–1150b1). Perhaps Aristotle has decided that *karteria* is more a matter of natural temperament than it is a virtue. In his *Eudemian Ethics*, he had already noted that some people who are very soft about some things, for

---

[12] Cf. Plato's *Laches* 192C on why endurance is not identical with bravery.

example, heat and cold, are brave, and some who are hard and enduring are also cowardly (*EE* III 1 1229b1–3). If *karteria* is a matter of physical constitution, that would explain why it is not a full virtue, and so does not conform with Aristotle's requirement of unity among the virtues, which I discuss in the following chapter.

Shame and *Nemesis*

At the end of his list of ten ethical virtues and before his discussion of justice, Aristotle lists two means "in the emotions", shame and *nemesis*, being properly indignant at the undeserved good fortune of others (*EN* II 8 1108a30–b6).[13] While Aristotle does not explicitly deny that *nemesis* is a virtue, it is reasonable to suppose that Aristotle links it with shame because he means to reject both.

The reason that these means are not virtues cannot be simply that they concern the emotions, because the other virtues concern the emotions too. In his *Eudemian Ethics*, Aristotle explains that these dispositions are not virtues because they do not involve choice (*EE* III 7 1234a24). He says that they *are* emotions, by which he presumably means that they are merely a matter of temperament. In a later discussion, Aristotle argues that shame is more like an emotion because those who feel ashamed blush, just as those who feel fear turn pale (*EN* IV 9). In the *Eudemian Ethics*, shame and proper indignation are treated as natural virtues. Shame is said to contribute to temperance, and proper indignation is said to contribute to justice (*dikaiosunē*) (*EE* III 7 1234a31–2). In his *Rhetoric*, proper indignation is treated as an emotion (*Rh.* II 9).

In the *Nicomachean Ethics*, Aristotle gives a further reason why shame is not a virtue, which has nothing to do with emotions and choice. The reason is that it would be odd to have a virtue whose exercise depends on having done something wrong. It is unclear whether the shame Aristotle is describing here is quite the same as the reaction of shyness, which seems to be described in the *Eudemian Ethics*. In any case, one can feel ashamed without having done anything wrong.

[13] Interestingly, Grant 1874, 507 links shame and *nemesis*, noting that in Protagoras's great speech in Plato's *Protagoras*, Zeus gives human beings two gifts: shame and *dikē*, the counterpart of Aristotelian *nemesis* (*Protagoras* 322C).

Faith and Piety

Although Christian faith and ancient Greek piety are very different, the one being expressed primarily in one's beliefs and the other in one's actions, it is still appropriate to consider whether Aristotle considers piety important. Piety is mentioned as one of the four ancient Greek cardinal virtues by Aeschylus and Isocrates,[14] and it warrants a whole dialogue by Plato, the *Euthyphro*, although it is no longer discussed in his *Republic*. Aristotle does not include it on his list, and only mentions it once in the whole of his *Nicomachean Ethics*, and then only to excuse his criticism of Platonist friends. Although both the truth and friends are dear, he says, it is pious to honour the truth first (*EN* I 6 1096a16–17).

It might be argued that piety makes an appearance in the final book of the *Nicomachean Ethics*, where Aristotle says that we should strive to be as near as we can to immortal (*EN* X 7 1177b31–4).[15] I have argued that we should not take these comments on the gods too seriously (Chapter 3, Section 3), and I address the matter further in Chapter 10, Section 2. True, Aristotle does allow for priests and temples in his *Politics* (*Pol.* VII 9 1329a27–30; VII 13 1331b4–18), but piety sometimes appears simply as a means of getting the citizens to do what is independently good. For example, Aristotle suggests that the legislator rule that pregnant women must make a particular sacrifice at a temple a certain distance from home, but the point of this law is to make sure that pregnant women take healthy walks (*Pol.* VII 16 1335b12–16). Piety does not play any role in Aristotle's discussion of the mean.

Hope and Sympathy

Hope is an especially important virtue in Christian virtue ethics, and sympathy is very important in Hume's influential ethical framework. It is not clear how Aristotle would categorize hope, because only confidence is discussed in Aristotle's list of emotions in *Nicomachean Ethics*

---

[14] Aeschylus *Septem ad Thebas* 610 and Isocrates *Helen* 31.

[15] See Broadie 2003 who takes seriously piety's appearance at *EN* X 1179a22–32.

and *Rhetoric.*[16] However, if Aristotle were to put hope (*elpis*) in the same category as sympathy (or compassion, *eleos*), they would both be emotions according to Aristotle, not dispositions, and so are in the wrong genus to count as virtues.[17] Since they are emotions, they can be used well or badly, at the right or wrong time, in the right or wrong way, and so on, as specified in Aristotle's doctrine of the mean. Indiscriminate hope or indiscriminate sympathy would not be good, according to Aristotle. As Aristotle explains in his discussion of states that are not to be confused with true bravery, hopefulness, exemplified by those who are "of good hope" (*euelpides*) is not a virtue, since it may be based on a misestimation of one's own abilities. Similarly, misplaced sympathy would not count as virtuous either.

A defender of hope and sympathy might counter that hope and sympathy are always appropriate, contrary to Aristotle's view. However bad things get, hope is always appropriate, and, however unworthy someone might appear, sympathy is always in order. Here, Aristotle might respond that the virtues involve both feelings and actions, and actions done in accord with one's hopes or sympathies might not always be appropriate or productive. For example, hoping that global warming will cease on its own is inappropriate and unlikely to be productive. Hope and sympathy need to be properly directed, just like the other emotions.

Alternatively, one might wonder whether there could be particular dispositions relating to hope and sympathy, just as there is a disposition relating to anger, that is, mildness. Since Aristotle thinks that bravery is concerned with confidence and fear, he would probably say that a disposition relating to hope should relate to both hope and pessimism, but such a virtue would not be the Christian virtue. If the disposition in question turns out to be some type of endurance,[18] Aristotle would

[16] *EN* II 5, *Rh.* II 5.

[17] "Pity" is the usual translation of *eleos* ("sympathy"), but, while it fits Aristotle's discussion of the voluntary well, the definition in *Rhetoric* II 8 1385b13–16 shows that it is inexact. Pity is usually given to those we think inferior to ourselves. Aristotle describes it as caused by some undeserved evil that we might expect to befall ourselves or some friend of ours, and soon.

[18] See, e.g., Foot 2001, 97.

not accept such a virtue in any case, as I argued above. Sympathy is a
trickier matter, but having the right amount of sympathy, at the right
times, and so on is no doubt subsumed under the virtue of equity, discussed below.

Charity and Benevolence

It has long been thought that Aristotle has no room for the virtues of
charity and benevolence. The complaint about benevolence goes back
to Bentham, who thinks that all the virtues should be types of benevolence.[19] True, Aristotle does not think that indiscriminate giving or
indiscriminate goodwill are appropriate, but the correct kind of giving
and the correct kind of benevolence are praised as the virtues of generosity, magnificence, and friendliness (or "kindness" as it is translated by
Engberg-Pedersen).[20]

Generosity involves giving and receiving from the right people at
the right time, and so on (*EN* IV 1). Magnificence includes a form of
philanthropy, since it may involve giving on a large scale. According to
Aristotle, the magnificent person may provide funding for large public projects, like outfitting a ship for military use, or putting on a play,
or he may act as an ambassador, entertaining dignitaries from abroad.
He may also display his virtue in large private expenses, for example,
in holding a wedding or in building a house. The virtue has an aesthetic aspect. Not only does it involve supporting the arts, but it also
involves carrying out the various public projects tastefully. While the
good person enjoys possessions that are fine but have no use, according to Aristotle (*EN* IV 3 1125a11–12), Aristotle considers functional
objects to be better if they have aesthetic value.[21]

Friendliness involves treating people one meets in the right way (*EN*
IV 7). As Aristotle is well aware, we need to treat people differently in
order to give them the same respect. According to Aristotle's nameless

---

[19] See Louden 1992, 40. For a more recent version of the same complaint, see,
e.g., Crisp 2000, xviii.

[20] Engberg-Pedersen 1983, 87–8.

[21] Compare the way that art is functional in African societies, as described by
Wingo 1998.

virtue of friendliness, we should treat friends and strangers differently. This does not mean that while one should be polite to one's friend one should be rude to a stranger, but rather that what it takes to be pleasant to each is different. For example, it is inappropriate to greet a stranger the way one would a long lost friend, and vice versa.

For practical reasons, it is likely that Aristotle restricts his virtues to those that govern transactions with people whom one happens to meet, but it is not difficult to apply these virtues to those who live beyond city boundaries. While it would be appropriate, and altruistic, to give money to an independent agency to combat hunger among children overseas, this would not be the appropriate way to deal with one's own hungry child; one should feed her oneself. Nevertheless, one's concern, though differently expressed, would apply to children overseas as well as to those at home.

Finally, Aristotelian generosity is far more radical than present charity. According to Aristotle, the generous person must also take from the right sources, since the virtue is a mean concerned with giving *and taking* (*EN* IV 1 1120b30–2). According to Aristotle, robbers and gamblers count as ungenerous, as do those who earn money from occupations exploiting other people (*EN* IV 1 1121b31–1122a13). Giving aid to others in our own community and overseas may count as charity, but, given the source of most people's incomes, present-day charity may be less generous than people like to think.

Asceticism, Meekness, and Self-sacrifice

Just as indiscriminate emotion cannot constitute virtue, so lacking any emotion cannot constitute virtue either. According to Aristotle's doctrine of the mean, the good person must have the emotions he should, at the time he should, in the manner he should, and so on. Therefore, while it might be right not to have any particular emotion on a particular occasion, it would not be right never to have any emotions at all. Aristotle explains that people are wrong to define the virtues as states of being unaffected,[22] "That is why [i.e., because people become bad by pursuing certain pleasures and pains in the wrong way, at the wrong

---

[22] He perhaps has Speusippus in mind.

time, etc.] people define the virtues as states of being unaffected or at rest, but they do so incorrectly because they speak unconditionally and fail to add 'how one ought' and 'how one ought not' and 'when' and all the rest" (*EN* II 3 1104b24–6 cf. *EE* II 4 1222a3–5).

With regard to physical pleasures, insensibility, according to Aristotle, is a vice (*EN* II 7 1107b6–8 cf. III 11 1119a5–7). Similarly, inirascibility in the sphere of anger is a vice. Both are vices of deficiency in Aristotle's triadic system. Depriving oneself of all physical pleasure and never responding to insults is to be a self-sacrificing type of human being. A Christian might respond that chastity and self-sacrifice are virtues, and that they do fit Aristotle's doctrine of the mean, being appropriate on the right occasions, for the right people, in the right way. However, Aristotle is not arguing that particular actions may or may not be appropriate on different occasions, but about whether a general disposition to do actions of a certain kind is appropriate. Even if soldiers are required to sacrifice themselves in battle in certain situations, for example, Aristotle does not consider a self-sacrificing mentality to be a good one to have. In fact, he comments that the best soldiers may not be brave ones (*EN* III 10 1117b17–19). Furthermore, if one accepts Aristotle's triadic scheme, one cannot consider self-sacrifice a virtue because it is unclear what the vice of deficiency would then be.

Self-control

According to Aristotle, self-control (*enkrateia*) is not a virtue (*EN* IV 9 1128b34). This view is a clear consequence of Aristotle's doctrine of the mean, because the virtuous person has and acts on the right emotions at the right time, and so on, whereas the self-controlled person is conflicted and acts correctly despite having the wrong appetite. One might think that since self-control is only described in the sphere of temperance, Aristotle might think that self-control is a virtue in other spheres. However, it is unclear how Aristotle can countenance the virtuous person having the wrong emotions – ones that need to be conquered – and remaining virtuous. As he says, the virtuous person should enjoy doing virtuous actions (e.g., *EN* I 8 1099a17–20; II 3 1104b2–8).

True, the brave person might prefer not to be on the battlefield, or the truthful physician might prefer not to have to break the bad news to her patient, but their preferences are not bad emotions to be overcome by self-control; rather they are preferences for the situations to be different, not preferences to behave or feel differently in these very situations. Self-control or self-discipline, the centrepiece of Kant's and Bennett's ethics, is not an Aristotelian virtue.

Social Virtues

In his *Lectures on Ethics*, speaking of Baumgarten's qualities of accessibility, affability, politeness, refinement, propriety, courtesy, and ingratiating and captivating behaviour, Kant says that the social virtues are not virtues because they "demand no self-control or sacrifice, do not conduce to the happiness of another and have no bearing on his wants, but merely upon his pleasures" (*LE*, 236–7). Earlier, Kant treats such virtues as gentleness and sociability as only "externals" (*LE*, 218). Aristotle would agree that his virtues of mildness (gentleness), friendliness, wit, and so on do not demand self-control or sacrifice, but that is because none of the Aristotelian virtues do. As we saw above, self-control is not a correct disposition in relation to the emotions. Nor are the Aristotelian virtues of wit and friendliness mere externals. As we saw in Chapter 2, Aristotelian wit is not a matter of delivery but a matter of sensitivity about which jokes are appropriate to make and to appreciate and which are not, and friendliness may be very important in diplomacy, a point that will resurface in Chapter 10.

Humility

Whether or not Aristotle includes the virtue of humility depends on what one's idea of humility is. According to some, humility concerns human beings' relationship to God, and so Aristotle's account of the magnanimous person, who has the right view of himself and little concern about others' good opinion of him, unless they are virtuous too, is perfectly compatible with a person who is humble when he compares himself with God.[23] Magnanimity concerns great honour and is the virtue between the vices of pusillanimity and vanity.

[23] Thanks to A. Gómez-Lobo and M. Byrd for helpful discussion of these issues.

By contrast, the Utilitarian philosopher, Julia Driver, has argued that humility consists in not knowing how good one is and that humility is a virtue.[24] On this view of humility, Aristotle does not accept that humility is a virtue because it is part of the vice of pusillanimity. Interestingly, Aristotle's discussion suggests a Utilitarian rationale for rejecting the disposition as a virtue. If the pusillanimous person thinks badly of himself, he will not put himself forward to receive the appropriate honours and offices, and will therefore not be helping either himself or his community in the way he should. However, it is the eminent Victorian Utilitarian, Sidgwick, who unwittingly gives an Aristotelian critique of humility as construed by Driver:

> As we saw, it is only inadvertently that Common Sense praises the tendency to underrate one's own powers: on reflection it is generally admitted that it cannot be good to be in error on this or any other point. But the desires of Superiority and Esteem are so strong in most men, that arrogance and self-assertion are both much commoner than the opposite defects, and at the same time are faults peculiarly disagreeable to others: so that humility gives us an agreeable surprise, and hence Common Sense is easily led to overlook the more latent and remote bad consequences of undue self-distrust.[25]

In other words, pusillanimity is praised because people view it as the opposite of the Aristotelian vice of vanity. They fail to apply Aristotle's doctrine of the mean and see the virtue of magnanimity, which comes between the two vices.

The Virtues of Selfishness

Briefly, the virtues propounded by the followers of Ayn Rand, consistent with her "virtue of selfishness", line up with many of the vices of excess in Aristotle's list of triads, for example, greed and strong self-assertion.[26] In arguing that these dispositions are virtues, their proponents often begin by pointing to the Aristotelian vices of deficiencies,

---

[24] For example, Driver 2001.
[25] Sidgwick 1884, 429.
[26] See www.aynrand.org.

for example, pusillanimity, looking for their opposites and applying a dyadic rather than a triadic system to reach the dispositions they consider virtuous.

Unlike Christian thinkers who may see human beings as menial creatures in comparison with God, Rand, like Nietzsche, thinks of "man as a heroic being". Therefore, a more sophisticated follower of Rand might ask why, since her heroes are geniuses, or, at least, aspire to be so, they do not deserve much more than the average person and – even if one accepts a triadic system – why the Aristotelian excesses should not be appropriate for them. There are two possible responses to this question. First, the heroes may not be correct about their super-human powers. Second, even if they are correct, having better abilities does not necessarily make one a more virtuous person, according to Aristotle. What is important is how one is disposed towards and uses the abilities one has, and being disposed in the correct way requires having dispositions in a mean.

Equity over Justice

Aristotle devotes a whole book of the *Nicomachean Ethics* to justice (*EN* V [=*EE* IV]). In the first two chapters, he distinguishes two types of justice: general justice, which includes the whole of ethical virtue "as it relates to another"; and particular justice, which is a particular ethical virtue and has its own sphere. There are also two types of particular justice: distributive justice and rectificatory justice. In addition, there is equity. While Aristotle's account of particular justice is notorious in failing to fit the doctrine of the mean in the same way as the other virtues, equity, which is justice but better, according to Aristotle, perfectly embodies the mentality of the person whose virtues are in a mean.

As Aristotle himself points out, and has been much discussed in the literature, justice is a mean in a different way than are the other ethical virtues, because it concerns an intermediate position between having too much for oneself while others have too little and having too little oneself while others have too much (*EN* V [=*EE* IV] 5 1133b30–1134a1). In other words, it is a mean because it refers to a state of affairs in the polis rather than a disposition of the individual.

Justice also fails to fit the doctrine of the mean in a second way. According to Aristotle, it is impossible to do injustice to oneself. Anything one might do to oneself deliberately cannot count as injustice. Aristotle even explains suicide, which he takes to be unjust, as a crime against the polis. Therefore, the vice of deficiency does not exist, and we are left with a dyad, rather than a triad, of different possible dispositions. While it would be nice to think that a rationale for Aristotle's view is to uphold the thesis that anything anyone does to another unjustly also cannot be willingly suffered, there is no evidence that Aristotle held such an enlightened position. Justice remains *sui generis* in Aristotle's account; there is only one way to be unjust and that is by giving oneself more than one's due.[27] Even the partial judge is greedy for a penalty, claims Aristotle, an apt description of the jurors in Aristophanes's famous play, *The Wasps*, and of many modern judges whose performances are rated by the number of their convictions.

In the second case, it is noteworthy that Aristotle's view here is inconsistent with his general rejection of the Socratic view that self-destructive behaviour cannot be voluntary. In the first case, we must look to the special relationship between justice and the laws. Although what is just is so independently of human thought, distributive justice (the fair distribution of goods and offices) and rectificatory justice (compensating victims for ill treatment) depend on the law and a political system. This explains why the otherwise irrelevant taxonomy of political systems appears in the middle of Aristotle's book on justice. The best laws and political system will best promote the other ethical virtues, according to Aristotle, as we shall see in Chapter 10, so there is a sense in which the particular types of justice are logically posterior to the other ethical virtues. If that is so, we should not expect them to fit individuals in the same way as do the other ethical virtues, but this does not mean that the individuals best suited to set up the laws and political system, and to administer them, should not be prime examples

---

[27] Perhaps this is why Aristotle attributes to the unjust person the motive of *pleonexia* (greed, or desire to overreach and gain more for oneself at the expense of others). For an influential argument to the effect that there is no particular motive that the unjust person necessarily has, see Williams 1980.

of human beings with a mean disposition, and that is why Aristotle emphasizes the virtue of equity (*EN* V [=*EE* IV] 10).[28]

Justice, according to Aristotle, is embodied in the correct laws, and Aristotle is acutely aware of the limitations of laws, even correct ones, in embodying justice. It is precisely because the laws have limitations due to their completely universal nature that equity is needed. The person who has equity has something superior to justice, according to Aristotle. The equitable person follows the spirit rather than the letter of the law, when a situation arises that makes this appropriate. The equitable person's mentality *involves* reason and is not merely *in accordance with reason*, as this distinction was explained in Chapter 5. She does not mechanically apply the laws as given but looks to the particularities of the situation and applies sympathetic judgment. Here, then, applying one aspect of the doctrine of the mean trumps the literal application of the law, even where the law as it stands is the best any legislator might do to legislate justly. (Aristotle notes that the law is no less correct for being universal.) The best sort of just person is the equitable person, and such a person must have her character in a mean.

3. EXTENDING THE VIRTUES

One might wonder whether Aristotle's list can be extended to include other virtues. While it is not the aim of my book to go beyond Aristotle's own theory, I offer the following reflections on green virtues and tolerance as examples of how an Aristotelian ethic of virtue could be extended. The simplest way to introduce green Aristotelian virtues would be as expansions of, or analogues to, existing Aristotelian ethical virtues. For example, as the Aristotelian virtue of generosity involves giving and taking the right amount, for the right reason, from the correct source, and so on, and not erring on the prodigal or stingy side, so a parallel virtue would involve taking resources from the environment and giving them back in the right way, for example, by recycling, sustainable agricultural practices, and so on, avoiding being prodigal with

[28] For an excellent account of equity, see Sherman 1989, 13–22.

scarce resources or miserly when they are needed. Just as temperance is in a mean between insensibility and intemperance, so a temperate green virtue would be in a mean between indifference to the environment and non-human animals and abuse of them.

Tolerance is a particularly good candidate for an Aristotelian mean. Intolerant people often call tolerant people intolerant for failing to tolerate the intolerant. The confusion can be dispelled if we treat tolerance as an Aristotelian virtue, in a mean between intolerance and apathy. Tolerant people tolerate the right people at the right time, and so on. Those who do not tolerate anyone different from themselves are intolerant. Those who tolerate everyone and everything have the vice of apathy. While "intolerance" correctly describes the disposition of those who cannot abide those different from themselves, "tolerance" suggests that the virtuous person merely puts up with, rather than respects, other people. The term "tolerance", like the term "mildness" for the nameless virtue concerning anger, does not quite have the right connotations to capture the virtue. Tolerance, I think, is therefore another important nameless virtue.

4. MORE NAMELESS VIRTUES AND THE DOCTRINE OF THE MEAN

In this chapter, I have completed the argument of Chapter 2 that the doctrine of the mean has substantive consequences about what the ethical virtues are. I have argued that the doctrine of the mean is a more important factor in generating the virtues on Aristotle's list than has previously been thought. In particular, along with the more generally accepted factors, the following considerations turned out to be necessary: (a) whether the disposition in question is a disposition in a mean or merely an emotion or just a matter of temperament; (b) how it is in equilibrium, allowing its possessor to have the right emotions and do the right actions at the right time, in the right way, and so on; and (c) how it belongs to an Aristotelian triad. Justice is the exception, but it is trumped by a superior type of justice that is compatible with the doctrine of the mean, that is, equity.

I have also argued, by comparison with other views, that Aristotle's list of virtues is far from uncontroversial. It differs significantly from Kant's list, and it also treats as vices self-sacrifice and self-aggrandizement. Aristotle's doctrine of the mean, then, turns out to be more informative than its detractors suggest, and perhaps there are more nameless virtues waiting to be discovered.

5 Uniting the Virtues

A central and controversial thesis of Aristotle's ethics[1] is that it is impossible to have one ethical virtue fully without having all the rest.[2] Given that Aristotle thinks that there are many different virtues, as we have already seen in previous chapters, the problem is not how there can be many different virtues given the fact that they are united in some way, but why, if the ethical virtues are distinct from one another, it is impossible to have one fully without having all the rest.[3]

Aristotle has already provided one possible answer. As we saw in Chapter 1, the doctrine of the mean is first and foremost a doctrine of equilibrium, not moderation. If we imagine the different ethical virtues as the central points of different spokes on a wheel that is balanced on a central pivot, then just as the wheel will not balance if it is out of kilter in any direction, so one cannot have any one virtue fully – be properly balanced – unless one has all the rest.[4] Only if one's dispositions are in equilibrium will one have the correct emotions and act accordingly on the right occasions. Aristotle's direct argument for his thesis is consistent with

---

[1] Aristotle is often said to subscribe to the "reciprocation of the virtues" instead of to the "unity of the virtues" to distinguish his view from Socrates' account. But Socrates' account is itself controversial, as explained below.

[2] McDowell 1979 is similar in aim, but he approaches the topic from a different angle and subsumes the good person's mentality and motivation under perception.

[3] For an opposing view of the central problem, see Deslauriers 2002.

[4] Ackrill also connects the ideas of balance, the doctrine of the mean, and the unity of the virtues, although from a slightly different point of view (Ackrill 1973, 23).

this picture, but ultimately relies on a deeper insight about the connection between ethical virtue and thought, captured by a new distinction introduced by Aristotle himself, which will be revisited in later chapters.

Aristotle introduces his thesis and his new distinction in the context of Socrates' view (*EN* VI [*EE* V] 13 1144b32–1145a2).[5] He distinguishes his own view from that of Socrates by treating the ethical virtues as states of the non-rational part of the soul (*psuchē*). In dividing the soul so that it has both a rational and a non-rational part, and in conceding that each virtue is typically exercised in its own particular sphere (e.g., *EN* II 1 1103b14–21) and may be typically associated with one or more different emotions (for example, mildness is associated with anger, bravery with fear and confidence), Aristotle appears to be making the thesis hard to defend. If the ethical virtues can be distinguished so clearly, it is hard to see why one cannot have one without another. Two objections spring to mind. First, since the ethical virtues are associated with the emotions, might not one be temperamentally suited to one virtue but not to another?[6] Second, given that the virtues are typically exercised in different circumstances, might not one have the knowledge or reasoning suited to one ethical virtue but not to another?[7]

[5] Socrates himself does not distinguish intellectual from ethical virtue nor practical from theoretical intellectual virtues. In the following, I shall only address the question of the unification of ethical virtues with one another and with practical wisdom (*phronēsis*). I shall leave the thorny issue of the place of theoretical wisdom (*sophia*) in Aristotle's scheme to Ch. 10.

[6] For example, the more Plato departs from the Socratic picture and incorporates temperament into his account of the virtues (and other good qualities he wants rulers to have), the more concerned he seems about how the virtues go together. In the *Republic* he is concerned about how the future ruler must combine various good qualities (*Republic* II 375C–E, VI 503C cf. *Theaetetus* 144B) and in the *Statesman*, the stranger considers the "heretical" suggestion that the virtues of *sōphrosunē* and *andreia* are not only different but mutually exclusive, so that it may be impossible for the same person to have both (*Statesman* 306B–308B). Aristotle himself (although here probably reporting a contemporary trope) suggests that the virtues may only be combined in men in their prime (*Rh.* II 14).

[7] A third objection, that there may be circumstances in which the claims of one virtue conflict with the claims of another, is addressed briefly by the author of the *Magna Moralia* (*MM* II 3 1199b36–1200a11). I discuss the question of whether Aristotle can countenance modern moral dilemmas in Ch. 6.

The answer to these questions rests on Aristotle's distinction between acting "in accordance with the correct reason" (*kata ton orthon logon*) and having a disposition "involving the correct reason" (*meta tou orthou logou*), introduced specifically to support his main thesis. This distinction, of which I provide an original interpretation, shows how, despite the division of the soul, the properly virtuous person is literally someone of perfect integrity.[8]

I. SOCRATES, ARISTOTLE, AND THE DIVISION OF THE SOUL

Socrates' own position is highly controversial. A crucial issue in Socratic scholarship concerns whether Socrates thinks (1) that all the different virtue-names stand for the same thing – the knowledge of goods and bads (which Aristotle refers to as "practical wisdom") – so that there is really only one virtue, or whether he thinks (2) that there are different virtues that are parts of a whole, either as species of practical wisdom, or as varieties of practical wisdom.[9]

[8] Someone considering the *Magna Moralia*'s two-tiered account of moral development (*MM* II 7 1206b20–6) might think that, according to Aristotle, the bad person's soul is in harmony too, but this idea is at odds with Aristotle's description of the bad person at *EN* IX 4 1166b1–29. I discuss the two-tiered view in Ch. 9.

[9] Those accepting the first interpretation, which stems at least from Menedemus of Eretria (Plutarch *On Moral Virtue* 440E–441D quoted in Long and Sedley 1987, section 61B), include Penner 1973 and 1992, Irwin 1977, 86–90, and Taylor 1976, especially 103–8. Vlastos 1972 is the chief modern proponent of the second interpretation. Ferejohn 1982 and 1984 and Woodruff 1976 hold that there is a closer connection between the different virtues than that they are species of the same genus. Since I do not think that the notion of contingent identity is coherent, I represent their view as being that the different virtues are *varieties* of one and the same species. The view of Kraut 1984, 260–4, although *sui generis*, is nearer to this view than to Vlastos's. (Here, I am grateful to Richard Kraut for helpful responses to questions on his views on the Socratic thesis.) There is also some dispute about whether there is a consistent doctrine in the early Platonic dialogues. See, e.g., Devereux 1992.

Each interpretation of Socrates has its own drawbacks from the point of view of uniting the virtues. The second, which allows that there is more than one virtue and more than one part or species or variety of practical wisdom, needs supplementing to explain why one needs all of these to have any one of them. The first interpretation shifts the problem to an earlier stage. If the *metaphysics* is correct, we can see why if one has one virtue one has them all – there is only one virtue, an intellectual one, to be had! However, we still need to be convinced that there *is* only one virtue and one *intellectual virtue* to be had. Ordinarily, we talk about brave actions as distinct from temperate actions as distinct from just actions. Aristotle himself points out that if justice and courage were identical, "justly" must be identical with "courageously" (*Top.* VII 1 151b32–4). But it seems odd to say that someone who pays their taxes justly, for example, is also behaving courageously.

There are two possible ways to lessen the impact of this oddity. First, a Socratic might broaden the scope of the "virtues" so that it no longer seems odd to say that a just action is also a temperate and courageous one.[10] Second, he might argue that the virtues are to be individuated, not by the "types" of behaviour that result from "them" in different situations, for example, acting correctly in situations of danger (for courage) or acting correctly in one's dealings with others (for justice), but by the state that is at the root of all those types of behaviour, practical wisdom.[11] Strictly speaking, on this account, there is only one type of behaviour involved, virtuous behaviour. To act courageously is simply to act with practical wisdom. To act justly or temperately is to act with practical wisdom as well. Virtue is to be identified with an intellectual state.

Although Aristotle presents his own position as a refinement of Socrates', it is not completely clear what Aristotle takes Socrates' own position to be (*EN* VI 13).[12] What is clear is that Aristotle's own

[10] Irwin 1977, 87 and Penner 1992, 2, argue that this is precisely what Socrates does.

[11] See Penner 1992, 6, 1973, 166–8 and Irwin 1977, 134–5.

[12] Since Aristotle says that Socrates thought that the virtues are *phronēseis*, using the plural, he is often thought to endorse the second interpretation of Socrates, according to which Socrates thinks that each virtue is a different species of *phronēsis*. Aristotle is praised and blamed accordingly (Vlastos 1972, 233 and fn 28, and Penner 1992, 21 fn 35). However, he might equally well be

position combines elements from each interpretation of Socrates: he thinks that there are several ethical virtues (as in interpretation (2)) but that they involve just one intellectual virtue, practical wisdom (as in interpretation (1)). Aristotle claims that practical wisdom is a single state and that once one has it, one will have all the ethical virtues.[13] But Aristotle cannot argue that there is only one intellectual virtue involved in the same way as can Socrates on the first interpretation of his position. First, Aristotle thinks that there are several ethical virtues; second, Aristotle gives these virtues quite narrow scope;[14] and third, Aristotle does not think that only an intellectual state is involved in good conduct. Temperate actions really are different from courageous actions according to Aristotle, and they differ because they stem from different non-intellectual states, the Aristotelian ethical virtues.

expressing the view that, according to Socrates, each virtue is a *variety* of one single species, or, indeed, (although inconsistently) that it is an instance of the same thing. (Irwin translates Aristotle's comment by "[instances of] intelligence" (Irwin 1985, 170), compatible with the first interpretation of Socrates' view. Presumably, the idea is that merely being exercised in different types of circumstances – if that is what accounts for the use of different virtue-names on different occasions – does not show that a different state is being exercised; there is just a different instantiation of the very same state. On this account, though, Aristotle is inconsistent. Aristotle too should think that there are *phronēseis* [plural], if these are instantiations of the very same state, but he never expresses his own view in these terms.) The medieval commentator, Eustratius, even thinks that the Socrates of Plato's *Republic* is meant here (*CAG* 20, 400), but he has no modern followers.

[13] The Greek word *mia* (one) is clear in the disputed text (*EN* VI 13 1145a1–2). Aquinas notes that the unity of *phronēsis* provides an important underpinning for Aristotle's thesis about the unity of the virtues (*CANE ad. loc.*). The Medievals in general made much of *phronēsis* as the unifying factor connecting the virtues. Hence, their worries about whether there is more than one *phronēsis* and, if there is, whether there is a unifying general *phronēsis*. For a discussion of these issues, see Lottin 1955, 343–64.

[14] However, there is an interesting discrepancy between the Eudemian and Nicomachean accounts of the scope of courage. In the *Nicomachean Ethics*, the primary sphere of courage is the battlefield (*EN* III 7 1115a32–5). In the *Eudemian Ethics*, there is no such explicit restriction (*EE* III 1).

Unlike Socrates, Aristotle divides the human soul into three parts: a nutritive part concerned with growth, digestion, and reproduction; an appetitive part concerned with sense-perception, appetites, and the emotions;[15] and a rational part, itself divided into two parts, one devoted to practical thinking, the other to theoretical thinking such as mathematics and astronomy, which according to Aristotle concern necessary truths (*EN* I 13, VI 1 and 3). According to Aristotle, each part of the human soul has its own virtues except for the nutritive part (*EN* VI 12 1144a9–10). Ethical virtues are dispositions of the appetitive part of the soul (*EE* II 1 1220a10 cf. *EN* I 13 1103a3–10). Practical wisdom is a virtue of that part of the rational part of the soul that is concerned with practical reasoning (*EN* VI 5 1140b25–8). Aristotle defines practical wisdom as a disposition involving reason (*meta logou*) concerning what is good and bad for human beings (*EN* VI 5 1140b4–6 cf. 1140b20–1).

While the author of the *Magna Moralia* says starkly that Socrates "did away with the non-rational part of the soul" (*MM* I 1182a20), Aristotle's comments on Socrates' position in *EN* VI are less extreme. Aristotle describes Socrates' own position not in a Socratic framework, but within an Aristotelian framework according to which there is a distinct non-rational part to the soul. Aristotle objects that Socrates fails to accommodate the non-rational part of the soul in the correct way; he places all the virtues in only one part of the soul. According to Aristotle, in so doing, Socrates mistakes the relationship of the intellectual state involved in ethical virtue with the states of the non-rational part of the soul (he thinks that the virtues are identical with *phronēseis* [the plural of practical wisdom] and that they are instances of reason [*logous*] rather than involving reason [*meta logou*] [*EN* VI 13 1144b19–21, 1144b29–30]), and that is because he mistakes the very nature of the intellectual state involved itself. According to Aristotle, thinking that the virtues are instances of reason is equivalent to thinking that the virtues are branches of knowledge (*epistēmas*) (*EN* VI 13 1144b28–30), and branches of knowledge, on Aristotle's account, are

---

[15] In his *Nicomachean Ethics*, Aristotle includes appetite (*epithumia*) among the emotions (*pathē*) (*EN* II 5 1105b21–3). For a discussion of this issue, see Leighton 1982, section 3.

not related to the condition of the non-rational part of the soul (e.g., *EN* VI 3 1140b13–16).[16]

I wish to suggest that Aristotle's criticisms of Socrates, rather than preventing him from being able to unify the virtues, actually provide a way of solving the problems. First, Aristotle complains that Socrates was wrong to say that the virtues *are phronēseis* ("practical wisdom" in the plural), even though he was right to say that they are *not without practical wisdom* (*EN* VI 13 1144b19–21). Second, Aristotle notes that "Socrates thought that the virtues are lines of reason because he thought that they were branches of knowledge (*epistēmas*), while we say that they are involving reason (*EN* VI 13 1144b28–30)". In the intervening passage, what involves reason has been given a special meaning. Aristotle says that philosophers of his day are wrong to say that ethical virtue is in accordance with the correct reason, where the correct reason is what is in accordance with practical wisdom. According to Aristotle, ethical virtue is a disposition that is not only in accordance with correct reason but also involves the correct reason and the correct reason is practical wisdom. I wish to suggest that the obscure distinction between merely being in accordance with the correct reason and involving the correct reason, when properly understood, can explain how Aristotle can unify the virtues even though he differs from Socrates in dividing the soul.

I shall argue that the ethical virtues involve the correct reason when the soul of the good person is fully integrated. My argument will proceed as follows. First, I shall explain the distinction between merely being in accordance with the correct reason and involving the correct reason (Section 2). Next, I shall explain the claim that ethical virtue involves the correct reason (Section 3), and therefore why Aristotle thinks that the ethical virtues are united (Section 4). I shall also explain why the large-scale ethical virtues on Aristotle's list do not undermine his thesis (Section 4), and finally, I shall use the distinction between merely being in accordance with the correct reason and involving the

---

[16] I take it that Aristotle is using terminology from his own account of human psychology to characterize and to amend Socrates' position, consistently with his general procedure, defended in relation to Plato by Fine 1992, especially 13–15.

correct reason to show how Aristotle can respond to the objections to his view raised at the beginning of this chapter (Section 5).

2. THE DISTINCTION BETWEEN "INVOLVING THE CORRECT REASON" AND BEING MERELY "IN ACCORDANCE WITH THE CORRECT REASON"[17]

One traditional and influential way of understanding the distinction between being merely in accordance with the correct reason and involving the correct reason is as the distinction between acting merely on external prompting and being in a state in which one has internalized the principles on which one acts.[18] There are two advantages to such an interpretation. First, since Aristotle defines technical skill (*technē*) too as involving true reason (*EN* VI 4 1140a20–1), what Aristotle says about ethical virtue is strictly analogous to what Aristotle says about learning a skill like house-building or writing or medicine.[19] As Aristotle explains, someone learning how to write may first follow what the teacher says. When he is proficient, he will act *in accordance with the grammatical skill in himself* (*EN* II 4 1105a23–6). Hence, with skills too, there is a distinction between acting on external prompting and, when an expert, acting on principles one has internalized oneself. Second, the distinction appears to solve one of the puzzles about practical wisdom that Aristotle raises (*EN* VI 12 1143b28–33). The exact worry is not clearly spelled out, but Aristotle seems to be asking why one cannot become (I supply the next two words) ethically virtuous

---

[17] Some of the issues raised in this section intersect with those addressed by Burnyeat 1980 and elaborated by Sherman 1989, especially section 5.

[18] See Heliodorus, *CAG* 19, 133; Stewart 1892, vol. 2, 111; and Gauthier and Jolif 1958, vol. 2, pars II, 557.

[19] Aristotle often uses the doctor's reasoning as an analogy for practical reasoning (*EN* VI and VII), even though he thinks that there is a sharp difference between *technē* and *phronēsis*, which I address in Ch. 8. Medicine seems different from other technical skills. Indeed, there was dispute in ancient times about whether it should be classified as a *technē* at all. (See "Hippocrates", *On Ancient Medicine*, a defence of medicine as a *technē*, perhaps written by a pupil of Protagoras.) For more on medical analogies, see Chs. 8 and 9.

simply by following the advice of someone else, when one *can* become healthy just by following the advice of a doctor, but without learning medicine oneself. If ethical virtue involves the correct reason in the sense just described, this would explain why one cannot have it simply by consulting one's local guru.[20]

Despite the advantages of such an interpretation of the distinction between what is in accordance with the correct reason and involving the correct reason, there is one "fatal objection", to use the expression of J. A. Smith.[21] Surely Socrates too would have allowed that ethical virtue involves the correct reason if involving the correct reason simply means that one is not merely acting on external prompting, but on principles that one has internalized oneself. Smith's alternative, now accepted by Hardie, Irwin, and Broadie and Rowe,[22] is that Aristotle's "involving the correct reason" is not stronger but weaker than being "in accordance with the correct reason", and is equivalent to not without reason (*ouk aneu logou*). According to Smith, Aristotle thinks that being in accordance with the correct reason does not mean merely in conformity with reason but marks a stronger connection. Ethical virtue spans both a disposition that is *caused by reason* (previously translated as "in accordance with the correct reason") and a disposition (previously translated as "involving the correct reason") that need only be *accompanied by reason*. It is in accordance with the correct reason when the agent has practical wisdom.

In my view, Smith is right that Aristotle's complaint against Socrates is mystifying on the traditional interpretation of the distinction between involving the correct reason and being in accordance with the correct reason, but he is wrong in his diagnosis of the trouble.

---

[20] This raises a problem, for the puzzle can now be reformulated as follows: Why isn't having a state short of virtue good enough (e.g., for the ruled)? A full answer would have to bring in the happiness and autonomy of the agent, but this would appear to alter the terms of the original puzzle. Health would then be parallel to happiness as opposed to ethical virtue. The following passage in the text suggests that Aristotle may indeed make this slide.

[21] Smith 1920, 20.

[22] Hardie 1980, 236–9, Irwin 1985, 349; 1999, 254, and Broadie and Rowe 2002, 188. Ross and Crisp's translations are consistent with my view. See Crisp 2000, 117–18.

The problem arises, not because involving the correct reason is weaker than being in accordance with the correct reason (which would leave the puzzle about why one needs practical wisdom to be a good person unsolved), but because the analogy with skill on which the interpretation rests breaks down. I shall first explain why, and then I shall explain what "involving the correct reason" must mean in the case of ethical virtue.

In the very passage in which he draws the analogy between acquiring a skill and acquiring ethical virtue (*EN* II 4), Aristotle himself notes the limits of the analogy, pointing out that the person who has learnt to be good must not only know what he is doing himself, but must also (a) have the correct rational choice (*prohairesis*) and (b) act from a stable and reliable disposition. The claim that rational choice is needed for ethical virtue accords with the suggestion of the author of the *Magna Moralia* that what is wrong with considering the ethical virtues to be merely in accordance with the correct reason is that then someone might act justly without any rational choice, nor recognition of fine things, but by some non-rational impulse that just happens to accord with what the correct reason would prescribe (*MM* I 34 1198a16–21). To be ethically virtuous, then, it is not enough to have some impulse that merely happens to line up with the demands of reason.

Correct motives are all important. Presumably, the idea is that one can have and exercise a skill such as house-building, for example, whatever one's motives, whether these be to help out a friend or to make money or to spoil the environment, whereas one can only have and exercise ethical virtue if one's motives are correct. Learning a skill, then, does not require getting one's motives correct, whereas becoming ethically virtuous does.[23] For example, as Aristotle comments elsewhere, the person who thinks that the virtues should be possessed for the sake of external goods "does fine things only incidentally" (*EE* VIII 3 1249a15–16). I discuss this type of "civic virtue" in more detail in Chapter 7. The fine-and-good person, by contrast, thinks the virtues should be possessed for their own sakes, and nobility (*kalokagathia*), complete virtue, Aristotle claims, is the result of all the individual

---

[23] For more on ethical virtue and skill, see Ch. 8.

virtues.[24] Here, Aristotle appears to consider it not just an intellectual mistake, but a moral one too, to treat ethical virtue as a skill.

Aristotle here seems to underestimate the effect of motives on whether one is merely competent at a skill or has it in an exemplary fashion.[25] Be that as it may, although Aristotle defines skill as a state "involving reason" (*EN* VI 4 1140a20–1), he clearly does not think that it involves reason in the same way as does ethical virtue. Hence, it is a mistake to understand the ethical and technical distinctions between involving the correct reason and being in accordance with the correct reason as strictly analogous. However, it is also a mistake to conclude that involving the correct reason is weaker than being in accordance with the correct reason. Rather, it takes more for ethical virtue to involve the correct reason than it does for a skill.[26] For ethical virtue to involve the correct reason, one's reason and motivation must be fully integrated. I now turn to the question of how this is to be accomplished.

[24] Woods suggests that the passage on *kalokagathia* has been misplaced in the present version of *Eudemian Ethics* and was originally placed after the chapter identical with *EN* VI 13, where Aristotle raises the issue of the unity of the virtues (Woods 1992, 172). Kenny suggests that the merely good person's motivation should be understood as a second-order and not a first-order motivation for external goods (Kenny 1992, 14 draws an analogy with Rule-Utilitarianism). But the fact that Aristotle mentions the fine-and-good person and not the merely good person as having the particular virtues suggests that Aristotle might not agree that the merely good person *can* have all the virtues. Indeed, having a second-order aim for external goods undermines one's first-order aims in a way in which a second-order aim for virtue will not. See Ch. 7 and Gottlieb 1996.

[25] Aristotle seems to concede elsewhere that vice may affect not just the *exercise* of a *technē* one already has, when he allows that intemperance can change the arts of medicine or writing (*EE* VIII 1 1246b28), but the text is corrupt, and the word "not" may have dropped out. See too *EN* VI 5 1140b13–16 on pleasure and pain altering judgments but not those about the triangle.

[26] I do not mean to suggest that the paradigm of Aristotelian moral education is first to learn the right principles from others and later to assimilate them in the correct way. There is no reason why the good person should not arrive at a reasoned understanding of the virtuous life from his own experience. The term "internalization", insofar as it suggests the first option alone, is misleading and I shall not use it from now on.

3. ETHICAL VIRTUE "INVOLVES THE CORRECT REASON"

The integration of reason and motivation is tricky to describe. Aristotle says that in order for one's ethical virtue to involve the correct reason, one's rational choice (*prohairesis*) must be correct, but he also says that it is ethical virtue that makes one's rational choice correct (*EN* VI 12 1144a20). Aristotle never clearly explains where rational choice belongs in the soul. In *Nicomachean Ethics*, he explains that rational choice is the result of deliberation from a wish for what one thinks to be good (*EN* III 3 1113a10–12).[27] There, its motivational force would appear to come from the rational part of the soul. In *EN* VI, rational choice is described as a combination of thought and motivation, and it is said to be the efficient cause of action, and even identified with the human being (*EN* VI 2 1139b4–5). Here, rational choice seems to be thought of as what combines the thought of the rational part of the soul with the motivation of the rest of the soul. At any rate, the motivation of the rest of the soul would seem to have to mesh with the motivation of the rational part of the soul for rational choice to be effective.

Indeed, this proves to be the case, for according to Aristotle, both the akratic and enkratic person have the correct reason and the correct rational choice, but neither of these is virtuous, nor do they have practical wisdom.[28] It is clear why the akratic person lacks virtue; he acts on a recalcitrant desire. However, the enkratic person manages to overcome his recalcitrant desire and so to act as his reason prescribes. Yet, even he is not deemed to have virtue. Having practical wisdom, then, would appear to require more integration of the soul than I have so far described. To be in a state that involves the correct reason requires not just mastering the impulses of the non-rational part of the soul so that one's rational desire wins out, but being in a state that causes one to have those non-rational impulses in such a way that they do not conflict with what reason prescribes (cf. *EE* II 2 1220b18–20). According to

[27] Here, I am reading *"kata tēn boulēsin"* at *EN* III 3 1113a12.

[28] On the akratic having the right *prohairesis*, see *EN* VII 10 1152a17, but Aristotle may not be completely consistent on this point. I revisit the akratic and enkratic in Ch. 8.

Aristotle, in the temperate person the appetitive part of the soul must harmonize with reason, and both the appetitive and rational parts of the soul must have the same target, the fine (*EN* III 12 1119b16).[29] The temperate person has an appetite for the things he should, in the way he should, and when he should, just as reason directs.

As Aristotle points out elsewhere, "The excellent person is in harmony with himself and strives for the same things with the whole of his soul" (*EN* IX 4 1166a13–14).[30] It appears, then, that ethical virtue will not involve the correct reason until reason is fully integrated with the emotions. Again, Aristotle's account of the integration is sketchy and can only be gleaned from odd remarks in other works. According to Aristotle, having an emotion typically involves three things: (1) an impression (*phantasia*, the way things strike one that falls short of a full-blown belief)[31] of something as good, bad, pleasant or painful, either present or imminent (*Rh.* II 1–11); (2) a physiological reaction or disturbance (*de An.* III 9 432b26–433a1; *MA* 703b5–20), or some pleasure or pain connected with the impression (*Rh.* II 1–11); and (3) some impulse to avoid or pursue the object of the emotion (*de An.* III 9 432b26–433a1 cf. *MA* 703b5–20). The relationship between the three is not completely clear. Aristotle says that the relationship between physiological reaction and impulse is that of matter to form (*de An.* I 1 403a30–b2). Sometimes he suggests that the impression will cause the physiological disturbance (*Top.* VI 13 151a16); elsewhere he allows that being in a disturbed state may cause the impression (*Insomn.* 2 460b1–10). My main concern is where reason enters the picture. Although it has been argued that the impulse involved in an emotion is "at the mind's command" (*de An.* III 9 432b26–433a1 cf. *MA* 703b5–20),[32] commentators have ignored a passage where Aristotle

---

[29] Hence, the analogy at *EN* III 12 1119b13–14 is misleading: "Just as the child's life must follow the instructions of his guide, so too the appetitive part must follow reason".

[30] Cf. Plato's *Republic* 518, alluded to by Aristotle at *EN* VI 12.

[31] Cf. Cooper 1996 who translates *phantasia* as an "immediate impression", 91. *Phantasia* is in a different part of the soul from opinion (*doxa*) (*EE* VII 2 1235b28–9).

[32] Both passages are quoted in full by Furley, who argues that the mind does not command the physiological reaction associated with an emotion, but it

explains that an impression also may be *"caused by thought* or by sense-perception" (*MA* 702a17–21, my emphasis).

In his ethical works, Aristotle also seems to assume that reason can, although it does not necessarily, affect all three parts of an emotion, since it tells one when and how one should feel an emotion as well as what its objects should be. If practical wisdom is an intellectual state that concerns what is good or bad for a human being and how things strike one reflects this state, it seems reasonable to suppose that ethical virtue involves the correct reason when reason enters not just at the stage of desire but affects the content of the impression as well.[33] In short, ethical virtue involves the correct reason when the reason of practical wisdom is fully integrated with, and not just running parallel to, the workings of the non-rational part of the soul. This, according to Aristotle, is what Socrates' account failed to show.

For ethical virtue to involve the correct reason, then, the functions of both parts of the soul must be intimately connected. Aristotle says that it does not matter whether one thinks of the soul as having parts or whether the parts are related as the convex to the concave (*EN* I 13 1102a28–32; *EE* II 1 1219b32–4). The second analogy may be intended to stave off Socratic objections to "parts" of the soul. Although the second analogy perhaps does not apply very well to the soul of the non-virtuous person, when applied to the soul of the virtuous person it is suggestive; the ethically virtuous person has practical wisdom, the intellectual side to virtue, and ethical virtue, necessary for the emotional and motivational side. One cannot have either side properly without the other, just as one cannot have the convex without the concave. Aristotle gives an excellent summary of the integration of the soul in *EN* X: "Practical wisdom is yoked to virtue of character, and it to practical wisdom, since the starting points of practical wisdom are in accordance with ethical virtues and the correctness of ethics is

does command the "secondary reaction" that leads to action (Furley 1967, 57). Belfiore follows Furley's interpretation and treats the desire involved in the emotion as what is commanded by the mind (Belfiore 1985, 349–61). Sherman suggests that, according to Aristotle, a physiological reaction by itself is no emotion (Sherman 1994).

[33] This explains Aristotle's claim that someone cannot have *phronēsis* and be akratic at the same time (*EN* VII 10 1152a6–9).

in accordance with practical wisdom. Being fitted together with the emotions too, the ethical virtues must belong to our composite nature" (*EN* X 9 1178a16–20).

4. INTEGRATING THE SOUL

At this stage, one might wonder why one should think that Aristotle has shown how the different virtues are united by showing how the *soul* of the good person is to be properly integrated. Indeed, it may seem puzzling why, in his discussion of the Socratic thesis, Aristotle does not clearly explain how the particular Aristotelian ethical virtues go together, instead of drawing the obscure distinction that he does. I wish to suggest that to explain how ethical virtue must involve the correct reason just is to show that the different ethical virtues must be united.

The fact that ethical virtue involves the correct reason is the key to Aristotle's thesis about the unity of the virtues. Since ethical virtues are dispositions of the non-rational part of the soul, and since one does not have them until one has fully incorporated the correct intellectual disposition, in order for the good person to have any ethical virtue, he requires the intellectual disposition that will allow him to have the appropriate emotions, directed at the correct objects at the correct time, and hence to act accordingly. But he will not have that intellectual disposition unless he has those ethical virtues that embody it, because an inappropriate emotion or motive in any sphere will undermine that intellectual state; indeed, a vice in any one area may undermine virtuous activity in any other area. As Aristotle says, "vice perverts us and causes us to be deceived about the origins of actions" (*EN* VI 12 1144a34–6), and, as he explains, the origin in action is what one ought to do. Furthermore, an incorrect intellectual judgment in one area may undermine a correct judgment in another area. Someone who has merely learnt a list of rules to follow may act in accordance with the correct reason but will not reliably do the right thing.

I shall give two examples: one in which an incorrect emotion in one sphere may lead to an intellectual mistake in another area, and one in which an intellectual mistake in one area may lead to an incorrect emotion in another sphere. First, according to Aristotle, the generous person is someone who not only gives to the right people at the right time for the right reasons, but is someone who *receives* from the right sources as well (*EN* IV 1 1120a31–1120b4). Someone who is unjust, then, and who steals from people out of greed, cannot, on this account, make the right judgments when it comes to the sphere of the virtue of generosity.[34]

Second, someone who has too high an opinion of himself and unwarranted self-esteem, giving him the vices of vanity and boastfulness, will presumably also lack the virtue of mildness, since he will think that others are belittling him when they are not, a thought that will affect the impression associated with anger, and so will become angry on inappropriate occasions.

It is precisely because the rational and non-rational parts of the soul are connected in the way that they are that a vice in any one area may undermine an Aristotelian virtue in any other.[35] That is why, in order to have any particular virtue fully, one must be free of all the other vices, and hence one must possess all the other virtues.[36]

5. RESPONDING TO THE OBJECTIONS

At the beginning of the chapter, I raised two objections to Aristotle's claim that one cannot have one ethical virtue without having all the rest. First, since the ethical virtues are associated with the emotions, might not one be temperamentally suited to one virtue but not to another? Second, given that the virtues are typically exercised in

[34] Sharples suggests that this point could be used to support Bernard Williams's doubts about the existence of the Aristotelian particular vice of injustice, which is characterized by the motive of greed (Williams 1980). However, Williams's arguments that any inappropriate emotion may subvert justice support my claims about the unity of the Aristotelian ethical virtues.

[35] This may not necessarily happen (see the end of Section 5), but one would have to be very lucky if it did not. On courage, probably the hardest virtue to accommodate on my account, see Heinaman 1993.

[36] On the supposed problem of accommodating the "large-scale" virtues, see the Appendix.

different circumstances, might not one have the knowledge or reasoning suited to one ethical virtue but not to another?

After contrasting his own view with that of Socrates, Aristotle concedes that one can have one *natural virtue* without having another, although one cannot have one virtue proper without having all the rest. As Aristotle elsewhere explains, each virtue has a natural and a proper form (*EE* III 7 1234a28–30). The natural form is without practical wisdom and intellect (*nous*) (*EE* III 7 1234a24–30 cf. *EN* III 8 1117a4–5). It is a matter of sheer temperament.[37] Aristotle explains what natural virtue is by saying that it is to virtue proper (almost!) as cleverness (*deinotēs*) is to practical wisdom (*EN* VI 13 1144b2–4). The analogy is obscure.[38] To explain it, I shall first give an account of what Aristotle thinks cleverness is.

Aristotle describes cleverness as "the capacity to do the actions which promote whatever target is assumed and to hit upon them".[39] If its target is fine, cleverness is included in practical wisdom, when used for ill it is unscrupulousness. It cannot be a purely executive capacity, because Aristotle says that there is nothing to prevent the clever person from being akratic (*EN* VII 10 1152a10), and he describes the akratic as like a city that passes all the right laws but does not put them into practice (*EN* VII 10 1152a20–1). I therefore suggest that it is a capacity for instrumental reasoning that enables one to act; the akratic may have this as an *intellectual* capacity, but without the appropriate emotional basis it will not always be effective or correct. Hence, there are three kinds of people who may be *deinos*: the good person, the bad person, and the person who is not quite good (the akratic or enkratic).

If we take cleverness as it applies to all three persons as the appropriate term in Aristotle's analogy between natural virtue and virtue proper and cleverness and practical wisdom, the analogy is quite inapt.

---

[37] See too *HA* VIII 588a18f and, for the way in which people can and should adjust for different natural tendencies, *EN* II 9 1109b1–7.

[38] In the actual text, the analogy is the wrong way round; Aristotle says that *phronēsis* is to cleverness as natural virtue is to virtue proper.

[39] The Greek manuscripts have "them" instead of "it" at *EN* VI 12 1144a26, cf. "them" in the description of what is probably the same capacity at *EE* II 11 1227b39–1228a1. I therefore think, with Stewart 1892, that "them" is better, since someone with cleverness alone may not necessarily hit the mean, as I explain below.

The person with natural virtue is predisposed to have full ethical virtue, whereas the person with cleverness is not necessarily predisposed to have practical wisdom. The relationships between natural virtue and cleverness and that between cleverness and practical wisdom are therefore quite different.

If, instead, we take the cleverness of the person who is not quite good as the term in Aristotle's analogy, the parallel that Aristotle wants to draw becomes much clearer: both natural virtue and cleverness are employed in accordance with the correct reason, but in different ways. (Hence, Aristotle's comment that natural virtue is to virtue proper *almost* as cleverness is to practical wisdom is still appropriate.) Natural virtue is in accordance with the correct reason in comparison with virtue proper because it is the sort of temperament that makes a person do the things that a virtuous person would do (presumably within a suitably narrow range of human experience) but without being in the appropriate intellectual disposition. Cleverness, in comparison with practical wisdom, is in accordance with the correct reason when its deliverances are separate pieces of information, and it is not properly grounded in the correct emotional life. For example, the clever person, like one of the mock brave people I shall be discussing in Chapter 7, may "know" the piece of information that he should stand his ground and how to do it, and act accordingly, but without the emotional life of the magnanimous person, will only do so when he is being watched. Without the correct emotional backing, cleverness is a much attenuated intellectual skill.

Aristotle can happily concede, then, that one may be temperamentally suited to one virtue but not to another, and that one may have the attenuated intellectual ability to match the virtuous person's behaviour in some cases but not in others, but he thinks that neither natural virtue nor cleverness are sufficient for virtue proper. Each enables one to act in accordance with the correct reason, but neither are states involving the correct reason. Hence, both are unreliable. The person who is temperamentally suited to one virtue may harm himself when faced with more difficult circumstances, or may express the wrong reaction when the situation calls for an emotional response outside the usual sphere (cf. *EN* VI 13 1144b8–9). (Someone naturally mild, for example, may act correctly because all the situations he has faced merely call for a quiet response and not for an angry response.) The person with the intellectual wherewithal ungrounded in the correct emotions will go astray in cases where his emotions are awry.[40]

According to Aristotle, virtue is a stable and reliable disposition (*EN* II 4 1105a34). The person who has the wrong emotions but matches the virtuous person's behaviour nonetheless and the person who has the right emotions but matches the virtuous person's behaviour without the correct intellectual state are both simply lucky.[41] Virtue proper, then, involves the correct reason.

6. INTEGRITY

Although Aristotle divides the soul, he argues that in the ethically virtuous person the soul's parts have the same fine aims and function not just together but in an integrated fashion. When a person's soul has reached this state, he has ethical virtue that involves the correct reason. Although there are people who may appear to have one ethical virtue without having the others, on closer inspection they turn out to be acting merely in accordance with the correct reason and not from an ethical disposition that involves the correct reason.

Aristotle's view that the virtues are united, then, provides a philosophical foundation for the common-sense view that the properly virtuous person is someone of perfect integrity. It is also consistent with the analogies used to support the first aspect of the doctrine of the mean because, if the good person is always in equilibrium, such a person needs to have all of the ethical virtues in order to confront all eventualities in life without falling out of kilter. In order to remain balanced, such a person will need to have their emotions and reason going hand in hand, having the correct emotions at the correct time, for the correct reasons, and so on.

---

[40] Hence, the good person must have transcended his temperament. Aristotle suggests that a person with a melancholic temperament may suffer from *akrasia* (*EN* VII 10 1152a18–19, 27–30).

[41] Here, I am extrapolating from the obscure *EE* VIII 2 1248b3–7. (A modern analogy to this distinction would concern the difference between having true belief and having knowledge.)

In the second part of this book, I explain in more detail the type of ethical thought engaged in by the good human being, and why and how it is connected with ethical virtue. In Chapter 7, I return to the theme of the good person's motivation and I also show why Aristotle thinks that the person of integrity makes the best friend. In Chapter 8, on the controversial practical syllogism, I show how Aristotle expands his idea that practical wisdom requires ethical virtue and conversely. I begin with the question of whether Aristotle can deal with ethical dilemmas, a question naturally arising in the light of his views about the unity of the virtues and the integrity of the good human being.

Chart of Aristotle's particular ethical virtues: *Nicomachean Ethics* II 7 1107a28–1108b10

Vice of Deficiency	Virtue	Vice of Excess	Sphere
Cowardice	Courage	Rashness	Fear and confidence
Insensibility*	Temperance	Intemperance	(Physical) pleasures and pains
Stinginess	Generosity	Wastefulness	Giving and taking
Niggardliness	Magnificence	Ostentation and vulgarity	Giving on a large scale
Pusillanimity	Magnanimity	A sort of vanity	Honour and dishonour
Indifference to honour*	Virtue concerned with honour on a small scale*	Honour-loving	Honour and dishonour on a small scale
Inirascibility*	Mildness*	Irascibility*	Anger
			Association in words and actions:
Self-deprecation	Truthfulness*	Boastfulness	Truth
Boorishness	Wit*	Buffoonery	What is pleasant in amusement
Quarrelsomeness	Friendliness*	Obsequiousness	The rest of what is pleasant in life
[Suffering injustice]	Particular Justice Equity	Injustice (caused by greed)	See *EN* V

*These are nameless according to Aristotle.

PART II

ETHICAL REASONING

6   Moral Dilemmas

In the previous chapter, I argued that Aristotle thinks that it is impossible to have one ethical virtue fully without having the rest, because ethical virtue involves reason (it is *meta logou*) and so the reason and feelings of the good person are completely integrated. One might therefore expect the good human being to be free of inner conflict and regret, and that is exactly how Aristotle describes him (*EN* IX 4 1166a27–29). Indeed, according to Aristotle, the good person will feel neither shame nor disgrace because he will never voluntarily perform base actions (*EN* IV 9 1128b20–33).[1] One might also expect it to be impossible for the demands of one virtue to conflict with the demands of another, and indeed, consistently with that view, the author of the *Magna Moralia* writes that the demands of bravery cannot conflict with those of justice, even in particular circumstances (*MM* II 3 1199b35–1200a).[2] It is reasonable to assume that the ethical virtues are meant to be internally consistent as well.

All of these further claims make Aristotle's view about the unity of the ethical virtues even more controversial from both an ancient and modern point of view. It is often thought that the Greek tragedians show how life contains situations where even the good human being is faced with a tragic dilemma and must do something that is not virtuous

[1] This point is challenged by Curzer 2005 on different grounds from those discussed below, but his and Drefcinski's 1996 arguments are refuted by Roche, unpublished.

[2] True, Aristotle does say at one point that the truth should trump piety, but piety is not listed as a particular ethical virtue (*EN* I 6). I discussed Aristotle's view of piety in Ch. 4.

and that will shatter her fragile goodness.[3] It is also argued that there are situations where the good person is faced with conflicting demands and where, even if he makes the right choice, he will have done something shameful and will be left with "dirty hands" and a special sort of regret.

For those who think that dilemmas are an essential part of moral life, and hence an important part of any ethic of virtue, Aristotle will no doubt stand accused of being simplistic and his theory naive, if he has nothing to say about them. Nevertheless, in his discussion of voluntary action, Aristotle describes a case in which a tyrant asks a person to do something disgraceful in order to save his family from being put to death. For the person in question, this would seem to be a paradigm moral dilemma. Michael Stocker has made an important case that the resulting act is a case of dirty hands, so it is reasonable to ask whether Aristotle does countenance such dilemmas after all.

I begin with the example of the tyrant, and then consider what Aristotle would say about tragic situations. I argue that Aristotle does not, after all, subscribe to the modern analysis of moral dilemmas, which I present in Section 2, but that, in fact, his account is more, rather than less, sophisticated than the modern analysis of such situations, and that this conclusion depends on one aspect of his doctrine of the mean.

1. THE EXAMPLE OF THE TYRANT

In his discussion of voluntary action in *Nicomachean Ethics* III, Aristotle mentions some problem cases where it is hard to say whether an action is voluntary or not. His most familiar example is the case of a ship's captain throwing cargo overboard in a storm. Aristotle wonders whether the captain's action is voluntary or not. The captain *does* decide to throw the cargo overboard, but, on the other hand, he does not seem to have much choice. A less familiar example is the case of the tyrant. If a tyrant threatens to kill your family unless you do something shameful, and you do it, is that a voluntary action? The example of the tyrant is

---

[3] The phrase "the fragility of goodness" is Martha Nussbaum's (Nussbaum 1986).

intriguing, and Stocker has argued that it is an example of a particular sort of moral dilemma, a case of dirty hands.

Now, the issue here is not whether Aristotle thinks that there *are* situations like ones in which a tyrant asks you to do something terrible or face the consequences, but what the philosophical analysis of such situations should be. A person who believes in moral dilemmas will think that Aristotle is committed to a particular analysis of such situations, so I begin by giving the sort of analysis to which such a person thinks Aristotle is committed and will then consider whether such an analysis is right. Although most people are familiar with moral dilemmas in everyday life, giving a characterization of such dilemmas without begging any philosophical questions is extremely difficult. In the following, I am particularly indebted to the characterizations of Hursthouse and Stocker.[4] In the first part of this chapter, I assume that Stocker is right that Aristotle thinks that the agent should do what the tyrant says, but, in Section 5.3, I question that assumption as well.

2. TWO TYPES OF DILEMMAS: A PRELIMINARY DISCUSSION

The two types of dilemmas I wish to consider are cases of dirty hands (or resolvable dilemmas) and tragic (or irresolvable) dilemmas. Cases of dirty hands have the following features:

(1) The agent wants a and also wants b and cannot have both.
(2) The agent has to choose between x and y, when x and y are both bad but not equally bad.

---

[4] Stocker and Hursthouse draw on a vast range of existing philosophical literature, and both have considered the problem in the light of Aristotle and virtue ethics. Stocker explicitly connects Aristotle's account of voluntary action with cases of dirty hands (Stocker 1990, ch. 3). Hursthouse discusses moral dilemmas in her book on virtue ethics (Hursthouse 1999), and she has a separate discussion of Aristotle's account (Hursthouse 1984). There, she argues that Aristotle's account is not so much about legal responsibility but that "the emphasis of Aristotle's discussion is on the virtuous character, on, for instance, how it can be that an agent could do an action which is what-is-called unjust without this counting as inconsistent with his virtue" (Hursthouse 1984, 253).

(3) Choosing x over y is the right decision.

(4) The action is nonetheless somehow wrong, shameful, and the like,[5] and

(5) There is a "remainder", and the agent has a special type of regret.

According to the first feature, the agent has inconsistent desires, but these may only be inconsistent in the situation. For example, if I want to avoid hurting others and I want to save lives, these are generally compatible desires that may only become inconsistent in a particular situation. As it stands, the first feature may turn trivial choices into cases of dirty hands, so often the first feature is expressed not as a conflict between mere desires but as a conflict between moral principles, for example, the principle not to break one's promises and the principle to save lives. Conflicts may also arise from applying just one principle, for example, that one should keep one's promises. If a person makes two promises, and it turns out that in honouring the one he is unable to honour the other, this would be a moral conflict as described in feature (1).

Since any analysis involving conflicting *principles* would appear to beg the question against an Aristotelian view right off the bat, since, according to Aristotle, ethical claims are "for the most part", in what follows, I shall argue that Aristotle does not accept the other features of the analysis, irrespective of feature (1).

The second feature needs to be spelled out in more detail, because, in many of the examples given of cases of dirty hands, the choice in question is between doing x and letting y happen, for example, allowing someone else to do y. For example, the choice may be between doing something bad oneself or allowing someone else to do something worse. Considering the outcomes, then, choosing to do something bad oneself as opposed to allowing someone else to do something worse is the right decision. However, when it comes to assessing the action, it is assumed that: (a) the badness of one of the options is not simply cancelled out by the rightness of the decision; and (b) doing something

---

[5] Cf. Stocker's characterization: "An act is one of dirty hands if (1) it is right, even obligatory, (2) but is none the less somehow wrong, shameful, and the like" (Stocker 1990, 51–2).

oneself is in an important way worse than merely letting someone else do something. Thus it is assumed that actions are worse than omissions, even if, from a different viewpoint, the agent makes the right choice. These points, I think, are what account for what philosophers have dubbed "the remainder", something left over that the agent feels squeamish about. In a case of dirty hands, the agent does something "somehow" bad herself. This stains her character and for this a special type of regret is in order.

Tragic dilemmas have the following features:

(1) The agent does not want to do x or y (with the provisos of the discussion above).

(2) The agent has to choose between doing x and doing y where both are equally wrong.

(3) Whatever decision she makes is wrong.

(4) Regret, and even guilt and remorse, are not strong enough to describe the remainder. Instead, "A virtuous person's life will be marred or even ruined, haunted by sorrow that she had done x".[6] Tragic dilemmas are tragic because the agent, through no fault of her own, is put in a situation where she has to make a choice, and whatever she chooses will mar the rest of her life.[7] This last point is often understood to mean that the virtuous person's character is not only stained but destroyed. I consider the stronger understanding of this feature below.[8]

---

[6] The quotation is from Hursthouse 1999, 77.

[7] According to Hursthouse 1999, a tragic dilemma is a particular kind of irresolvable moral dilemma and "An irresolvable moral dilemma is usually specified as a situation where doing x and doing y are equally wrong, but one has to do either x or y, or one in which two moral requirements conflict but neither overrides the other (roughly)" (44). An irresolvable dilemma, she explains, is "a situation in which the agent's moral choice lies between x and y and there are no moral grounds for favouring doing x over doing y" (63). A tragic dilemma is a situation "in which even a virtuous agent cannot emerge with her life unmarred" (75). Hursthouse ends up revising the aspect of the dilemma that says that whatever one does is equally wrong, so that the virtuous person makes the right decision, even if the action is "too terrible to be called 'right' or 'good'" (79).

[8] Hursthouse 1999 does not favour the stronger version.

3. ARISTOTLE'S ACCOUNT OF VOLUNTARY ACTION: IS THERE A SPECIAL TYPE OF REGRET?

Aristotle is interested in the topic of the voluntary and its contrary, the involuntary,[9] because virtue concerns feelings and actions, and praise and blame are awarded for voluntary ones, and pardon, and sometimes pity, for involuntary ones (*EN* III 1 1109b30–2). Presumably, Aristotle has in mind involuntary *bad* actions in the case of pardon and pity. Aristotle does not say what is suitable for involuntary good actions.[10] Nor does he discuss voluntary and involuntary feelings in the following account.

An action is voluntary, according to Aristotle, if (a) the origin of the action is in the agent (this includes any motivating desire or emotion), and (b) if the agent knows all the particulars of the situation – who he is, what he is doing, about what or to what he is doing it, what he is doing it with (if applicable) and for what result, and in what way. Not knowing what is appropriate to do does not make the action involuntary. In addition, if someone does something wrong failing to know some salient particular but later has no regret, his action is not involuntary but falls under the separate category of "not voluntary".

It is tempting to interpret this separate category along act Utilitarian lines, supposing that the agent finds out about an undesirable consequence of his action after he has acted and should therefore regret the action with hindsight. However, this is not Aristotle's view. He is referring to something that the agent could have known at the time of the action, not something that happens subsequently and can only be known later on. In general, consequences of actions do not reflect on the goodness or badness of actions in the same way in Aristotle's and in act Utilitarian theory. For example, whether soldiers in a war ultimately win victory is irrelevant to whether they acted well on the battlefield on Aristotle's account, but not on the act Utilitarian's.

---

[9] For an account of why these customary translations of *hekōn* and *akōn* are apt, especially because they enable the reader to see where Aristotle departs from ordinary Greek usage, see Meyer 1993, 9–14. For a defence of the neologism "counter-voluntary" for "involuntary", see Broadie and Rowe 2002, 38.

[10] Aquinas comments that one should not be praised for these (*CANE* 383, 128). Thanks to Jeff Christ for his helpful question here.

Be that as it may, the new category of the "not voluntary", in addition to the involuntary, has struck many as peculiar, but if the appropriateness of praise and blame, pity and pardon is a major consideration for Aristotle, Aristotle's category would seem to be apt, since pity and pardon would hardly be appropriate for an agent who has no regrets for the action himself.[11]

Nevertheless, Aristotle's separate category raises a puzzle. According to Aristotle's general account, a good person should be free from regret, unlike the bad person, but here Aristotle suggests that a good person who unwittingly does something wrong should have both pain and regret. Modern philosophers distinguish agent-regret – regret that I was causally responsible for this action, that I could have done otherwise – from general sorrow, such as can be shared with a spectator.[12] Aristotle says that the agent has regret *for the action*. He does not say whether the agent is thinking about the action from a first-person or third-person point of view. Certainly, the agent knows that she, and nobody else, performed the action; the origin was in her. On the other hand, according to the case under consideration, she was not responsible for her ignorance, so the regret does not seem to involve blame, as it would do if she had done the action in full knowledge of all the particulars, or if she had been responsible for lacking the knowledge at issue.

When Aristotle says that the agent has regret for the action, I take it that the agent has regret for the action involuntarily done, but I do not think that the good agent will blame herself for doing it, so a certain type of agent-regret will be absent. Repentance, in particular, would be out of place.[13] For present purposes, however, all that matters is that whatever regret the agent here has, it is not the same as that of the bad person who regrets voluntarily doing something bad. Although Aristotle's good person may have regrets, then, these will

---

[11] For this and alternative accounts, see, e.g., Bostock 2000, 109–10, although he is dismissive of them all.

[12] For example, Williams 1981b, 28. The phrase "could have done otherwise" is never found in Aristotle's writings. I have changed Williams's locution from regret felt by a spectator to general sorrow because I doubt that there is any such thing as *regret*, as opposed to sorrow, felt by a spectator, even if the spectator can use such locutions as "That was regrettable".

[13] So would forgiveness, *pace* Sachs 2001, 36.

not be the same type of regret as the bad person whose conflicted character Aristotle describes elsewhere (*EN* IX 4). Nevertheless, the good person will experience a real psychological "remainder", and it reflects her good character. To adapt J. L. Austin's famous example, if I am delighted that I shot my neighbour's donkey, even though by mistake, something is amiss with my character.[14] The regret experienced, then, is very different than the regret supposedly experienced in cases of dirty hands. The latter regret reflects a stain on the agent's character, not anything good about it.

Therefore, there are two important differences between the regret Aristotle describes here and the special type of regret required for cases of dirty hands. First, the regret is "for the action", and so the agent has no need to blame herself. Second, the regret reflects something good about the agent's character, not anything bad.

4. THE PROBLEM OF MIXED ACTIONS

In the midst of his discussion of voluntary and involuntary actions, Aristotle imagines the case of a tyrant who tells you to do something shameful (*aischron*) or else your parents and children will die. Aristotle likens the case to being in charge of a merchant ship in a storm. If you accede to the tyrant or throw the cargo overboard, is your action voluntary or involuntary?

There is a case to be made for each. On the one hand, throwing cargo overboard in a storm looks involuntary because the agent does not seem to have a real choice. The ship's captain will either lose the cargo or he will lose the crew and the cargo. His predicament is the same as that of someone accosted by a highwayman with the words "Your money or your life". Here, either you give up your money or you give up your life and your money.[15] Similarly, if the case of the tyrant is supposed to be parallel, we must suppose that if you do not help the tyrant in order to save your family, the tyrant will kill your family and find someone more susceptible to his threats to do his dirty work. Whatever you decide,

---

[14] Austin 1956–7, 48–9.
[15] Stampe (unpublished), 12–14.

the shameful thing will be done, so there is no real choice. On the other hand, since we would praise the captain in a storm for sensibly throwing the cargo overboard and would blame him for doing otherwise, and praise and blame are awarded to what is voluntary, we must think that the action is voluntary. Again, if we would blame the agent for leaving his family to their deaths, we must think that the action of helping the tyrant is voluntary.

Aristotle does not present arguments for and against in these terms. He does not consider the possibility that the actions in question are involuntary at the time, although he does say that sometimes people are praised when they endure something shameful or painful as the price of what is great and fine, and blamed when they endure something shameful for no particularly fine result (*EN* III 1 1110a19–23). Although he calls the actions "mixed", he says that they are more like voluntary actions (*EN* III 1 1110a11–12 cf. 1110b6). The reason for this is that whether they are choiceworthy depends on the time when they are performed. Aristotle points out that, in the case of mixed actions, it is up to you whether you do the action or not – the origin is in you – and that actions should be assessed with reference to the particular occasion when they are performed. Therefore the "mixed" actions are voluntary, but what accounts for them being "mixed" is that they are involuntary without qualification (*haplōs*). For example, throwing cargo overboard is voluntary on the particular occasion when there is a storm and in order to save the crew, but without qualification, that is to say without the qualifications "in a storm and to save the crew", throwing cargo overboard is not something that anyone would want to do.

Aristotle's comments about the "involuntary without qualification" are obscure. Some have suggested that they are partly voluntary and partly not, or voluntary under one description and not under another.[16] I think that these comments make best sense when considered by analogy with what Aristotle says about certain things that are goods without qualification.[17]

All unqualified goods are ones that are good for and in the hands of the good person, but some are not always good because they may be

---

[16] For more on these options, see also the following section.
[17] See Gottlieb 1991, 35–8.

bad for someone who is not good. For example, health is good without qualification, but it is not always good because it would be bad for a bad person, allowing him to do more bad things. If Aristotle were to say that health is bad for a bad person but good without qualification, he would not mean that health is bad for the bad person and also partly or in some weird sense good for him in his present situation. Similarly, then, when Aristotle says that an action is voluntary, but involuntary without qualification, he need not mean that one and the same action is voluntary and partly or in some weird sense involuntary for the agent on the same occasion. His point is that a rational person would voluntarily throw the cargo overboard, for example, in the present situation when that is what is necessary to save the crew, even if she would not voluntarily throw the cargo overboard if the situation were different.[18]

According to Aristotle, what happens in the particular situation is what counts. He says, "For at the time they are done they are choice-worthy, and the goal of an action accords with the specific occasion; hence we should also call the action voluntary or involuntary on the occasion when he does it. Now in fact he does it willingly" (*EN* III 1 1110a12–15). Therefore, the action up for assessment should be described in as much detail as possible, including the goal.[19] In this way, Aristotle can rule out rigging the assessment as involuntary by picking out the description one likes.[20]

However, Aristotle does point out that it is difficult to know what to endure for the sake of what, and that we pardon those who do things they ought not to do in situations that go beyond human endurance.

---

[18] One might wonder how Aristotle can say that the same action x is voluntary in this particular situation but involuntary without qualification. The answer is that this is not exactly right, but if one distinguishes the matter and form of an action, the form being given by the goal, one can argue on Aristotle's behalf that the matter of the two actions is what is the same on both occasions. The form is different and therefore so are the actions as a whole. See also the following footnote.

[19] See Charles 1984, esp. ch. 2, for the teleological elements in Aristotle's philosophy of action.

[20] Modern philosophers are often tempted to talk about actions performed "under a description", e.g., Kenny 1979 and, most recently, Broadie in Broadie and Rowe 2002, 312. For arguments against, see Stampe (unpublished).

If pardon is appropriate for involuntary acts, acts in situations that go beyond human endurance must be involuntary.[21] Some things, however, should not be allowed to happen, even if they mean one's own death, Aristotle says, a claim consistent with his contention elsewhere that the magnanimous person will not think life worth living at all costs (*EN* IV 3 1124b9). The evaluation of action, then, depends very much on the particular circumstances and the particular stakes involved, consistently with the second aspect of Aristotle's doctrine of the mean.

5. MIXED ACTIONS AND MORAL DILEMMAS

5.1. Regret

As we have seen, cases of dirty hands are ones in which the agent comes to the right decision, but the act is somehow wrong or shameful and so there is a remainder, reflected in the agent's regret. If we suppose that the case of the cargo and the case of the tyrant are parallel in respect of what the agent should do as well as whether the agent acts voluntarily (although this is dubious because, as I argue later, the details of the case of the tyrant are left out),[22] the options in these scenarios are not equally bad, and the agent comes to the right decision in throwing cargo overboard or in helping the tyrant. The question then is whether the act is "somehow wrong or shameful" and whether there is a remainder, on Aristotle's account.

According to Aristotle, the agent in the case of the tyrant is asked to do something shameful, but "through fear of greater evils or on account of something fine". The agent here acts in order to stave off something worse, or on account of something fine, presumably saving the life of his family. The act is a mixed one. If one just takes these introductory remarks of Aristotle into account, a natural way to interpret Aristotle is

---

[21] The connection is made more explicit in *EE* II 8 1225a20–30.

[22] Stocker argues that the hostage case, the jettisoning, and Alcmaeon's matricide form an explanatory series showing that the man in the hostage case can act, not only voluntarily, but also rightly in complying with the tyrant's threat (Stocker 1990, 57).

to say that there really is an involuntary as well as a voluntary element in the agent's mixed action. He voluntarily acts to achieve the good goal, but he involuntarily takes the repugnant means, helping the tyrant. Now the agent can be praised for the good part of the action and can be pitied or pardoned for the bad part. Although Aristotle never explicitly says whether the agent who throws the cargo overboard or who helps the tyrant does or should experience regret, Aristotle does say that pain and regret are appropriate reactions to bad actions one has done involuntarily, as we saw above.[23] Presumably, then, the agent can regret the involuntary part of the action, just as she regrets doing something bad unwittingly, but be pleased about the good part. On this account, the action is "somehow wrong" and there is a remainder, regret at involuntarily doing the bad part.

Leaving aside the question of whether it is coherent to suppose that actions have parts in this way, a more pressing problem with this interpretation is that it would seem to make too many actions mixed ones. In fact, it would seem to make any action mixed that had a necessary means that one would rather not take, for example, not just throwing cargo overboard but paying the crew. It may appear arbitrary where we should draw the line.[24]

Aristotle's next remarks, however, show that "mixed" actions are to be understood rather differently and in a way in which defuses the worry about drawing a line between them and other voluntary actions. A mixed action is voluntary at the time, according to Aristotle, even though it is involuntary without qualification, as explained above. If this is correct, then Aristotle should say that the act is also bad without qualification. Without the qualification that one's family is in the power of the tyrant, it would not be an act that any good person would want to do. However, with this qualification, it is the right thing to do. If the agent does feel regret, then, this must somehow reflect the fact that

[23] See also Meyer on the Eudemian argument connecting the requirement of pain or regret with what is forced or contrary to one's voluntary impulse (Meyer 1993, 82–4).

[24] Paying the crew is an example of Stocker 1990, 60. He thinks that the puzzle can be solved by specifying the way in which acts contribute to an agent's happiness. Irwin also notes the puzzle, and thinks that it can be solved by specifying further features of Aristotle's examples (Irwin 1999, 202).

the actions in question are without qualification bad and involuntary. For an action to be without qualification bad and involuntary is not for it to be bad in all circumstances. If this is so, what the agent must be regretting is being in a situation where a qualified action is the best one can do. But of course, this particular action in this particular situation is neither bad nor involuntary, so the agent has no need to blame him or herself for what transpired at the time.[25]

On either interpretation, Aristotle has the resources to explain a "remainder" in terms of the agent's regret, although he does not explicitly do so anywhere in the text. However, in neither case will the agent's regret be directed at himself as blameworthy. The agent either regrets being in a situation where the best option was one he would not otherwise choose, or he regrets part of an action he only involuntarily did. Such regrets are fundamentally different from the bad person's regrets, which are directed at bad actions voluntarily performed. There is nothing in Aristotle that suggests that in complying with the tyrant's demands in the case described, the agent's character has been stained and that he has dirty hands. Thus, although Aristotle can explain various aspects of the situation, including the agent's reluctance to act and subsequent regret, for Aristotle these features would have to be evidence that the agent is a good person rather than evidence that the agent has lost some of his integrity.

But in fact, Aristotle does not mention any regret on the part of the agent, probably because he holds the stronger view that the agent has nothing to regret here at all, if he does the right thing. Perhaps this is because mixed actions are fundamentally different from those involuntary actions where one lacks the appropriate information to act correctly. Presumably, in the latter cases, the regret also shows that the agent would have acted differently had she had the appropriate information. In the case of mixed actions, the agent would not have acted differently for any reason.

---

[25] Cf. Hursthouse who describes two Aristotelian mixed actions as follows: "The virtuous cargo owner jettisons his cargo without hesitation or regret. Naturally he regrets the circumstances that make this necessary, but the cargo is, after all, worthless in comparison with the lives on board...In a time of famine the virtuous person undermines his own health sharing the little food he has with his friends and family; he regrets the circumstances that make this necessary, but does it gladly all the same" (1984, 264).

5.2. The Structure of Aristotelian Decision-making

Up to now, I have been considering features (4) and (5) of cases of dirty hands, concerning remainders and regret. I now wish to turn to the first three features of such cases. According to these features, the structure of the dilemma is that one must choose between two options, x and y. In the case of the tyrant, the options consist in letting the tyrant kill one's family or doing the shameful thing. Both choices are bad, but one is worse than the other. According to this analysis, the content of the choice is what explains the subsequent remainder and regret. One regrets that one has to do something rather than merely let something happen, and one regrets the option one chose, "doing the shameful thing".

However, this interpretation of the situation is light years away from Aristotle's understanding. He does not see the problem as being what to choose *instead of* what, but what to choose *at the price of* what. As he says, "it is nevertheless hard to determine what should be chosen at what cost and what should be endured for what gain" (*EN* III 1 1110a29–30, tr. Crisp). This point is hammered home by Joachim, although he sees it as a purely grammatical issue.[26]

According to Aristotle, when the agent finally decides to "help the tyrant to save his family's lives", he hasn't decided to "do something shameful period". In addition, Aristotle here does not seem to draw a big distinction between letting something happen and doing something oneself, since he thinks that "if no is up to us, so is yes" (*EN* III 5 1113b8). Some might think that what a tyrant does is not up to oneself the way that doing what is shameful is. It may be especially relevant that the tyrant is also a moral agent. (Consider, for example, a situation in which hostages are taken. If you refuse to accede to the hostage-takers' demands, are you clearly responsible for the deaths of the hostages?) That Aristotle is not interested in issues like this is shown by the fact that he thinks that the case of the tyrant and the case of the cargo are the same in matters of voluntariness, even though a tyrant is a moral agent and a storm is not. The way in which Aristotle describes decision-making, then, is antithetical to modern descriptions of moral dilemmas and conflict.

[26] Joachim 1951, 98.

5.3. Factors in the Decision about the Tyrant

So far, I have been assuming, with Stocker and for the sake of argument, that the case of the cargo and the case of the tyrant are parallel not just in respect of whether the agent acts voluntarily, but also in respect of what the agent should do as well. Once this was done, I have argued that, on Aristotle's account, there is no special regret based on some special remainder, as fits the analysis at the beginning of this chapter, and therefore nothing shameful left dangling (except the fact that what the agent does would be shameful in other situations). What is more, Aristotle does not analyse the dilemma as consisting of two competing options – do one shameful thing (leave your family to die) or do another shameful thing (whatever the tyrant wants).

At this point, however, I should like to point out that, *contra* Stocker, it is not at all clear what Aristotle intends us to conclude is the correct action in the case of helping the tyrant. Suppose we provide some more details. The agent is Socrates, and if Socrates fails to help the tyrant, not only he but his family will be killed. But we are still missing a lot more. What exactly is the tyrant asking Socrates to do? Is there another way of helping his family escape? Is whatever the tyrant wants Socrates to do really in the tyrant's interest? If not, could not Socrates persuade him of that? The idea that the options are to do the shameful thing the tyrant wants or let one's family be killed is exactly the either/or analysis of moral dilemmas that I have been arguing that Aristotle rejects. Aristotelian practical reasoning is more complicated than the version of simple competing options given by those who propose the modern analysis of modern dilemmas. The agent has to sort out the particular factors in the situation, deciding which are most important and what the options really are. Here, the second aspect of Aristotle's doctrine of the mean is very much in play.

But suppose there is a situation where one should help the tyrant. Doesn't this mean that one has done something shameful that prevents one from exercising one's virtue and therefore being happy? The agent, *ex hypothesi*, has done the best she could in the circumstances. True, her happiness may be at stake, but not because she has done something shameful and hasn't exercised her virtue, but because the external goods needed for a happy life are severely lacking. This is the type of situation I describe in the following section.

6. A TRAGIC DILEMMA

Even though Aristotle does not discuss any tragic dilemmas, it is worth asking whether there could be any on his account. Consider Sophie's choice. Described as a tragic dilemma, her two options, giving up either of her children to certain death, are equally bad, but she has to make a choice. Any decision will be wrong, and there seems to be no good goal in sight. If Sophie acts, her life is marred for ever. Aristotle would no doubt describe the situation differently. Sophie has to give up one child, or both will be taken. According to Aristotle, if she is a good person, she will do the finest actions she can, just as a good general will make the best use of his forces in war, and a good shoemaker will produce the finest shoe from whatever materials he has been given (*EN* I 11 1100b35–1101a5). Therefore, she will make the best of a terrible situation and retain her integrity. Of course, she may regret having been in such a dreadful situation, she may even have nightmares about it for the rest of her life, but these will not be the same kind of regrets that accompany an irresolvable dilemma as analysed above.

The question remains whether Sophie's life will be "marred and ruined". Sophie will not have become a bad person, so in that respect, according to Aristotle, she will not be "wretched", but, like Priam, she may not be happy either (*EN* I 11 1101a6–8).[27] This should not be surprising, since in Aristotle's view, virtue is not sufficient for happiness and, very plausibly, the good person cannot be happy on the rack (*EN* I 5 1095b34–1096a1).

7. ARISTOTLE'S HUMANE VIEW AND THE DOCTRINE OF THE MEAN

Although Aristotle can perhaps account for certain psychological costs of facing harrowing choices, he does not allow (a) that the good person

---

[27] I take it that Aristotle uses the terms "blessed" and "happy" interchangeably here, otherwise his discussion is inconsistent with the rest of Book I. Hursthouse describes Aristotle's account in the same way (Hursthouse 1999, 75). My conclusion is the same as Nussbaum's view about what Aristotle would say about the tragic heroine, Hecuba (Nussbaum 1986, 418 para 2 and 419).

will ever voluntarily do a bad action in a bad situation (he will either do the finest thing he can in the situation – a choiceworthy action – or he will rather die), and hence he does not allow (b) that a good person's regret regarding an action done in a bad situation should be directed at the agent's own character. By contrast, those who believe in dirty hands and tragic dilemmas often think that the agent has done something voluntarily that fundamentally compromises his character,[28] and that therefore the regret felt is and ought to be deep and abiding.

Such a position may appear particularly compelling, especially when those who are faced with life-or-death decisions often hold themselves responsible in a deep way, even when they know that they could not have done any better in the situation and that having to make the choice was not up to them. Their regret is not just for what they did not want to do, but, and this is what makes the situation tragic, what they *did* want to do at the time. That is what shows that they have lost the good characters they used to have. On this account, for example, the shamefulness of what the tyrant asks one to do does not simply disappear when viewed in the context of the correct action in the circumstances, but it remains to haunt the agent and to cast a stain on his character.

According to Aristotle, if the good Aristotelian human being does the right thing in obeying the tyrant (and, as I have argued, whether it is in fact the right thing depends on many factors), his action is praiseworthy, there is no stain on his character, and therefore the type of regret that amounts to self-reproach is out of place. The shamefulness perhaps does not completely disappear, since it explains why the agent would not help the tyrant if there were no special circumstances, and it also explains his reluctance to do so. But what takes precedence for Aristotle is the actual situation in all its myriad details, and this is consistent with a central tenet of Aristotle's philosophy as expressed in Aristotle's doctrine of the mean and elsewhere, that what is right or wrong depends on the particular circumstances. In saying that the shamefulness should attach to the action and hence to the agent's character, Aristotle's opponents are not making allowance for the very specific context.

Those who believe in tragic dilemmas and the like are often also struck by the fact that human life is saturated with luck. We are lucky

---

[28] Hursthouse 1999 is excluded from this group.

where we are born, our gender, who our parents are, the society and country we live in, our personalities, the people we meet, what characters we develop, what plans we have, whether our plans come to fruition, and so on. Tragic dilemmas are supposed to show that what characters we *have* is just a matter of luck too. But, in order for the tragic dilemma to be tragic, the agent has to think of herself not as the plaything of luck, for then she should forgive herself her involuntary action, but as someone with a deep and abiding centre. She must take complete responsibility for her action in the circumstances, and her feelings must reflect this responsibility. But, of course, neither her actions nor her feelings nor her circumstances are ultimately up to her. While we pity the protagonist her fate, she is unable to pardon herself, and we pity her for being unable to do so.[29]

For Aristotle, by contrast, the world and our view of it are coherent. The views of agent and spectators will not be incompatible, although their feelings will be different. Both are justified in taking the same view. The agent can be distressed at being in the bad situation but be pleased she acted rightly. The spectators can pity the agent for being in such a bad situation but praise her for doing the right thing in the situation.

One might argue that where others see the glass as half empty, Aristotle sees it as half full. Where others see a world of luck in which people vainly suppose they have some control, Aristotle sees a world of opportunities in which, however circumscribed they are and barring situations where one should give up one's life, it is up to us to do the finest acts we can. Aristotle's account is fundamentally humane. Praise is due to those who do the finest acts they can in their particular circumstances. If these circumstances may include their own position, resources, (non-ethical) abilities, and so on, as I argued in Chapter 1, the best that a slave can do in a particular situation will be very different than the best a freeman can do in the same situation.[30] As mixed actions show, what is bad without qualification may be justifiably praiseworthy when the details and goal are fully spelled out.

---

[29] See, e.g., Nagel 1976, Nussbaum 1986. This is not Hursthouse's 1999 view.
[30] For a modern nuanced account of the mixed actions of the oppressed, see Card 1999.

When Stocker says that Aristotle's discussion of voluntary action contains "some of his more penetrating ethical thoughts",[31] he is right. What is penetrating about Aristotle's discussion is that he shows how tragic dilemmas can be resolved in a way that is compassionate to those who find themselves in them and without denying that such dilemmas are difficult, and he also shows that resolvable dilemmas are more difficult than proponents of the modern analysis suggest; there are more factors to be taken into account than two black-and-white alternatives.

Aristotle's rejection of the modern analysis has both practical implications and an important implication for his relationship to modern ethical theorists, as we have seen. The idea that Kant's ethical theory entails that there are situations in which an agent, however good, has to do something wrong in response to a moral dilemma, is at least as old as Sartre's famous paper, "Existentialism is a Humanism", although recent Kantian commentators have interpreted Kant's principles of action in a more flexible way.[32] Aristotle's view is far from Sartre's Kant. It buttresses his thesis about the unity internal to and between the different virtues, and it also interlocks with one important aspect of the doctrine of the mean.

[31] Stocker 1990, 51.
[32] For example, Herman's "principles of presumptive deliberation" (Herman 1993) and Sherman 1997, ch. 7.

7 Fine Motivation

The point of this chapter is to present an account of the good human being's motivation, including the way in which the good human being is motivated to care for her friends, that is conducive to Aristotle's ethic of virtue and is consistent with Aristotle's claim, discussed in Chapter 5, that ethical virtue involves and is not merely in accordance with reason.[1] According to Aristotle, the virtuous person is distinguished by the fact that he acts *for the sake of the fine.* Any account of Aristotle's ethics as an ethic of virtue will therefore have to explain what this means, because the locution is obscure. Modern commentators often connect it with Aristotle's view that the good person does the right thing, for example, the generous action or the brave deed, *for its own sake,* but the locution "for its own sake" has proved just as puzzling, since, according to Aristotle, something can be chosen both for its own sake and for the sake of something else.

I first show how Aristotle's view is plausible by comparing it with Plato's views. Next, I discuss and raise difficulties for Kantian and Utilitarian interpretations of Aristotle's view. This is important if Aristotle's views are to belong to the genre of virtue ethics that is distinct from Kant or Utilitarianism. I conclude that choosing x for its own sake and for the sake of y makes sense taken at face value, provided that y does not undermine one's choosing x in the first place. I then turn to cases of mock bravery, where choosing x for the sake of y does undermine the initial choice, and I explain how Aristotle's account of

[1] For an alternative approach to the topic, see, e.g., Richardson Lear 2004, 123–46.

cases of mock bravery elucidates the incorrect, and therefore, the correct motivation on the part of the good person.

Here, I also compare "civic bravery" with the civic disposition that Aristotle attributes to the warmongering Spartans, whom I discuss further in Chapter 10. I argue against a Kantian interpretation of Aristotle's account of civic virtue in *Eudemian Ethics* VIII 3. Value is objective and is not conferred by the good person's motivation. Again, this highlights a distinctive feature of Aristotelian virtue ethics.

Finally, I consider how the good person is motivated to care for his friend for the friend's own sake. Commentators have taken Aristotle to mean that if x and y are friends of good character, x cares for y simply because y has a good character, where good character is a repeatable general property. I argue that Aristotle does not think that one cares for a friend merely derivatively from the friend's general character, and that he is right not to do so. I also explain how Aristotle's example of mother and child is telling. Most important, I show how a good friend needs to be someone of stable character and integrity, as explained in Aristotle's doctrine of the mean and his thesis about the unity of the virtues, in order to be cared for for himself.

1. ARISTOTLE AND PLATO

Aristotle claims that there are three types of ends: those that are chosen only for the sake of something else; those that are chosen for their own sake and for the sake of something else; and those that are chosen only for their own sake (*EN* I 7 1097a25–34). Only one good fits the final category, happiness. Examples of goods in the first category are musical instruments, tools, and riches. Examples of goods in the second category are honour, pleasure, virtue, and understanding (*nous*), which are chosen both for their own sake, according to Aristotle, and for the sake of happiness.

The Greek word for "chosen" (*haireton*) can also mean "able to be chosen" or "ought to be chosen". Although Aristotle begins the passage by talking about what "we choose", it is reasonable to assume that Aristotle is considering goods that both are and ought to be chosen by a good rational agent.[2] Riches, of course, could be chosen for their own sake and not for the sake of anything else, but in Aristotle's view, this would not show that riches belong in the second category. Aristotle is describing how the good person will and ought to make his choices.

At first sight, Aristotle's threefold distinction appears to match Plato's classification of goods in *Republic* II 357B–D. The three categories are as follows:

(1) Goods loved for their own sake and not for their consequences, e.g., joy and harmless pleasures.
(2) Goods we love for their own sake and for their consequences, e.g., thinking, seeing, and being healthy.
(3) Things that are onerous in themselves but good for their consequences, e.g., physical training, medical treatment when sick, medicine itself, and other ways of making money.

Glaucon here challenges Socrates to show that justice, which most people put in category (3) because it is burdensome in itself but to be practised for its rewards (*Republic* II 358), really belongs in the best category (2). Like Aristotle, Glaucon must be discussing goods that *ought to be loved* in certain ways, otherwise it makes no sense to challenge Socrates to show that a good that most people in fact do love only for its consequences, justice, belongs in a different category from the third.

The differences between Aristotle and Plato are instructive. First, Aristotle thinks that Plato's category (1) is the best category.[3] Second, Aristotle's equivalent to category (1) contains only one good, happiness, which is not merely good for its own sake, but the ultimate goal of everything else. Third, the use of the items in Aristotle's equivalent to category (3) is not necessarily painful or onerous.[4]

---

[2] Cf. Williams's remark that "his [Aristotle's] discussion, for instance, of things which can be pursued for their own sake is confined to things which a sane and rational man would pursue for their own sake" (Williams 1962, 291).

[3] One might wonder why we should value something most if it is not used for anything else, rather than if it is. Aristotle shows awareness of this problem in *Fr.* 12 (*Protrepticus* 52.16–54.5).

[4] Aristotle does call the life of money-making "in a way forced" (*EN* I 5 1096a6), but I agree with Stewart 1892, 68–9, who argues that this means not that

In the midst of his criticisms of Plato's Form of the good (*EN* I 6), Aristotle objects on the Platonists' behalf that there may be two types of goods only one of which partakes in the single Form. He notes that there are some things that are pursued and loved for their own sake (*kath'hauta*) and others that produce these things or preserve them or prevent their opposites (*EN* I 6 1096b10–14). Aristotle gives as examples of the former, thinking (*phronein*), seeing, certain pleasures, and honours. He says that even if we pursue these for something else, one would still put them among the first group (*EN* I 6 1096b18–19). Aristotle's examples are significant in that they cut across Plato's first two categories in the *Republic*, but they fit Aristotle's own examples of things chosen for their own sake and for the sake of something else in *EN* I 7. Again, the things that according to Aristotle produce the things that are pursued for their own sake or preserve them or prevent their opposites are not necessarily onerous.

Plato sees no difficulty in something being chosen and choiceworthy both for its own sake and for the sake of something else. As Glaucon says to Socrates, "You agree that justice is one of the greatest goods, the ones that are worth getting for the sake of what comes from them, but much more so for their own sake, such as seeing, hearing, knowing, being healthy, and all other goods that are fruitful by their own nature and not simply because of reputation. Therefore, praise justice as a good of that kind, explaining how – because of its very self – it benefits its possessors and how injustice harms them. Leave wages and reputations for others to praise" (*Republic* 367C–D, tr. Grube/Reeve). The discussion might suggest that the consequences of such goods are merely artificial or a matter of what people think, but that cannot be right. The consequences of health do not depend on people's opinions, nor do the consequences of true justice. Being healthy is choiceworthy both for its own sake and for the sake of all the things one is able to do when one is healthy. Similarly justice, which turns out to be a state of

violent means are used to make money (Eustratius's view), nor that the life of money-making is compulsory (Grant 1874 and Aquinas *CANE* 71, 22), but that the money-getting life, when and because it goes beyond people's needs and has no end or limit, is "contrary to nature". In his *Politics*, Aristotle argues at length that acquiring wealth is only necessary up to a point. Beyond that point, it is an unnatural pursuit (*Pol.* I 8–9).

the psyche analogous to health, is choiceworthy for its own sake and, for example, for the good effects it has on others. These effects do not depend on opinion.

2. KANTIAN AND UTILITARIAN READINGS

Although the above interpretation of Plato's category (2) suggests a similarly straightforward way of understanding Aristotle's goods that are choiceworthy both for their own sake and for the sake of something else, commentators have been puzzled by Aristotle's category (2). For example, Prichard, a Kantian, says that Aristotle is simply being inconsistent in saying that something can be pursued for its own sake and for the sake of something else. Prichard treats the two as mutually exclusive. If x is desired for its own sake, x is an ultimate aim, and so the desire for x is an independent desire. On the other hand, if x is desired for the sake of something else, x is not an ultimate aim, and so the desire for x depends on the desire for something else.[5] (Presumably, choiceworthiness too, according to Prichard, is also conferred in only one of these ways.) Others have argued that what Aristotle means by the claim that virtue, for example, is chosen both for its own sake and for the sake of happiness, is that it is desired on some occasions merely for happiness and on other occasions merely for its own sake.[6] This interpretation concedes to the Kantian the incoherence of something being chosen for its own sake and for the sake of something else at one and the same time.

An alternative interpretation draws on the ideas of the Utilitarian, J. S. Mill. Mill argues that happiness is the only thing desirable as an end, and everything else is only desirable as a means to that end. (Like Aristotle, Mill conflates what is desired, what is able to be desired, and what ought to be desired, though with less justification, since on Mill's official view, happiness is purely subjective and yet the general happiness ought to be desired.) To those who object that virtue is also an end, Mill claims that virtue, besides being a means, can be desired in itself

---

[5] Prichard 1967, 250–1.
[6] Kraut 1976 and 1989 cf. Kenny 1965–6, 28.

and can become part of the end. Mill concludes more generally, "there is in reality nothing desired except happiness. Whatever is desired otherwise than as a means to some end beyond itself, and ultimately to happiness, is desired as itself part of happiness, and is not desired for itself until it has become so".[7]

The idea of "parts" of happiness is not alien to Aristotle's thinking. For example, in the *Eudemian Ethics*, Aristotle warns that disputes arise because people tend to confuse the indispensable conditions for happiness with the parts of happiness (*EE* I 2 1214b26–7). According to Aristotle, the two should be distinguished just as one should distinguish the indispensable conditions for being healthy from being healthy (*EE* I 2 1214b14–16). Again, Aristotle explicitly refers to "parts" of happiness in his *Rhetoric* (*Rh.* I 5), although the list goes beyond what is listed in *EN* I 7. According to Ackrill, although Aristotle no longer uses the terminology of parts and whole in the *Nicomachean Ethics* because he now realizes that it is too crude to capture his view, nevertheless "when Aristotle says that A is for the sake of B, he need not mean that A is a means to a subsequent B but may mean that A contributes as a constituent to B" and "that this is what he does mean when he says that good actions are for the sake of *eudaimonia*".[8]

Although Ackrill himself does not explicitly draw this inference, one might suppose that it makes sense to say, following Mill, that A is chosen *for its own sake and for the sake of B* if A is chosen *as a part of B*. Leaving aside difficulties concerning the metaphysics of parts and wholes,[9] there are other problems with this view. First, wealth, a part of happiness in the account in the *Rhetoric*, is not considered to be choiceworthy both for its own sake and for the sake of something else in the *Nicomachean Ethics*. True, Aristotle may have changed his mind here, but even if he has, this example raises an awkward problem. Are there parts that are choiceworthy solely because of their contribution to some whole, and if so, what sense does it make to say that these are choiceworthy also for their own sake? Why are they not merely instrumentally

---

[7] Mill's *Utilitarianism* "Of what sort of Proof the Principle of Utility is susceptible", ch. 4, 37.

[8] Ackrill 1974, 29–30 cf. 19.

[9] Ackrill 1974, 22 and Kraut 1989, 210–27.

valuable? By analogy, a blade is a part of a lawn-mower, but it does not follow that the blade is choiceworthy apart from its contribution to the lawn-mower, and if it is not so choiceworthy, what makes it choiceworthy for its own sake? Perhaps its being choiceworthy for its own sake is simply its being choiceworthy for the sake of the lawn-mower, but then it would appear to be no different from those things that belong to the category of things choiceworthy merely for the sake of something else. The mere distinction between parts and wholes, then, does not seem to distinguish things that are choiceworthy merely for the sake of something else and those choiceworthy both for their own sake and for the sake of something else. Another account is needed.

3. TAKING ARISTOTLE'S DISTINCTIONS AT FACE VALUE

In view of the difficulties above, and the intelligibility of Plato's second category of goods, I propose to take Aristotle's distinctions at face value. Aristotle himself explains that we choose virtue, honour, and the rest for their own sake because we would still choose them even if they had no further result, but we also choose them for the sake of happiness because we believe that through them we shall be happy. An analogy may be helpful. Just as an athlete chooses to run a race just to participate but also in the hope of winning first prize, but would still choose to run even if there were no prizes (a sane athlete would certainly not want to win a prize for a race without running), so the good person will desire virtue both for its own sake and for the sake of the happiness it will bring, even if it turns out, by some misfortune, not to bring happiness. She will not want happiness by any other means. Both running a race and virtue have something to be said for them in their own right, but that does not mean that at the same time they cannot be chosen for other reasons too.

Choosing x for its own sake and for the sake of y is perfectly coherent provided that choosing x for the sake of y does not undermine one's choosing x in the first place.[10] For example, it is coherent to choose to

---

[10] See too Gottlieb 1996, 10–11.

run a race for its own sake and for the sake of winning, provided that the wish to win does not make one not want to run the race at all. An athlete who perversely wished to win by doing away with all his opponents would not qualify as wanting to run the race *for its own sake* as well as for the sake of winning. An athlete who wishes to win by running the race wishes to run the race for its own sake as well as for the sake of winning, even when winning cannot be guaranteed. Similarly, it makes perfect sense to choose virtue for the sake of happiness, provided that one's desire for happiness does not undermine one's choosing virtue in the first place.

Whether or not the proviso is fulfilled depends on what happiness is, according to Aristotle. If happiness were identical with reputation or pleasure or power, wishing for it might very well undermine one's choice of virtue, since one can achieve all three without virtue. On Aristotle's account, though, happiness is identical with none of these things. Nor is it identical with an aggregate of goods, so that getting one more of the goods in the aggregate would be worth abandoning one's choice of virtue. Happiness, in Aristotle's view, is not the sort of thing that can be maximized, so a desire for happiness on the part of someone who has the correct view of what true happiness is will never undermine a desire for virtue.

Here, it might be objected that one's choice of honour, one of the goods Aristotle says is chosen for its own sake and for the sake of happiness, can be undermined by one's wish for happiness. Here, it is certainly true that one's wish for Aristotelian happiness will undermine a choice for indiscriminate honour (or recognition). Only honour from the right sources would be choiceworthy. However, one's choice of honour from the right sources would not be undermined by one's wish for Aristotelian happiness. Although the right kind of honour cannot guarantee happiness, wishing for happiness will not undermine one's choice of the right kind of honour.

Finally, one might object that on this interpretation there is no room for Aristotle's third category, for it will turn out that there is nothing that is and ought to be chosen *merely* for the sake of something else and not also for its own sake. Take Aristotle's example of a musical instrument. A violinist does not choose this particular violin *merely* in order to play music; she chooses this violin rather than that one because there is something to be said for it independently. Perhaps it has a special tone or feels more comfortable. All that may be true, but what would not be true is that the violinist, in so far as she is a violinist, would choose the instrument even if it did not result in playing music at all. But, one might retort, nor would one choose virtue if it did not result in activity in accordance with virtue. Perhaps, but according to Aristotle, one would and should choose it regardless of whether it led to all the trappings of a happy life.

4. THE FINE AND THE BRAVE

An explication of choosing x and doing x *for its own sake*, where that is fully compatible with acting for the sake of happiness as well, does not fully explain what it means to act "for the sake of the fine" (*kalou heneka*), because other things besides virtue come in the category of goods wanted for their own sake and for the sake of happiness, according to Aristotle. I wish to suggest that the nearest Aristotle gets to an explication of acting for the sake of the fine is in his discussion of bravery.

Bravery is the first individual virtue to be described by Aristotle and the only one to be contrasted not just with the corresponding vices but with a set of similar but different states (*EN* III 8). Before introducing the states in question, Aristotle repeats the point that courage is a mean, and that the brave person stands firm *because that is fine* (*hoti kalon*). My suggestion is that the states contrasted with bravery show the mentalities and motives to be contrasted with the correct mentality and motive of the brave, and hence of the generally virtuous, person. We discover what it means to act for the sake of the fine by seeing what the alternatives are. The method is a familiar one. Aristotle often explains what x is by examining and distinguishing things that fail to be x. For example, in his account of the voluntary (*to hekousion*), Aristotle explains what count as voluntary actions by examining behaviour that is not voluntary. He uses the same method in his accounts of rational choice (*prohairesis*) (*EN* III 2) and practical wisdom (*EN* VI).

All of those who have the five mock states that Aristotle describes stand firm in battle, at least up to a point, and so resemble the brave person on a superficial level. It is not that they sometimes act for the sake of the fine and sometimes do not, rather it is that they lack the mentality and general motivation of the brave person. There are five states: civic bravery, experience and expertise, spirit (*thumos*), hopefulness, and ignorance. If one counts the two forms of citizen bravery, there are six.

According to Aristotle, civic bravery is the closest to true bravery. Presumably, this is because the citizens do stand their ground whereas the others flee when things get difficult. There are two kinds of civically brave citizens: those who stand firm to avoid reproach and legal penalties and to win honours; and those compelled by their superiors, for example, by commanders striking their troops. The former are better, according to Aristotle, because they are motivated by shame and a desire for honour, whereas the latter are simply motivated by fear and by the avoidance of pain. Aristotle concludes that one must not be brave because of force but because it is fine (*EN* III 8 1116b2–3). Here, then, Aristotle is showing that action for the sake of the fine must be voluntary. The good person must not be acting under coercion. Nor must the good person be acting merely in order to gain rewards or to avoid penalties, since if there were no such reward or penalties, he would have no reason to act well.

Next, Aristotle discusses experience and expertise. Here, Aristotle complains that Socrates thought of bravery as an expertise (*epistēmē*), but, according to Aristotle, experienced soldiers only appear brave because they know that certain alarms are groundless. When the alarms are not groundless, they run. Although they are expert at using their weapons and are stronger and fitter than the others, they are not brave.[11] They are more afraid of being killed than of disgrace, and so are worse off than those who have citizen bravery. It is doubtless unfair of Aristotle to imply that Socratic bravery is of this type. Nevertheless, it shows that acting for the sake of the fine is not the same as having a simple skill or technique, a point that foreshadows Aristotle's distinction between practical wisdom and skill in *EN* VI, to be discussed in Chapter 8.

---

[11] Cf. "Bravery is not what makes men more daring fighters, otherwise strength and wealth would be bravery" (*EE* 1230 a11–12).

Aristotle discusses three more states not to be confused with real courage. First, spirit (or emotion or anger) (*thumos*). According to Aristotle, acting merely because of one's emotion does not make one brave. As Aristotle says, "Now brave people act because of what is fine (*dia to kalon*), and their emotion cooperates with them. But beasts act because of pain" (*EN* III 8 1116b30–2). Otherwise, according to Aristotle, hungry asses and adulterers would be brave. Bravery caused by emotion is natural virtue and is true bravery once rational choice and the goal are added, but spirit, in the form of anger, where this involves desiring the pleasure of revenge, is never the correct motive. Here, Aristotle is saying that merely acting on emotion is not to act for the sake of the fine, but having emotion is not incompatible with so acting.

Second, hopefulness. Those who have hopefulness are confident, according to Aristotle, because they think they are invincible. When things turn out differently from how they expect, they run. What they have is similar to liquid courage, the apparent bravery people exhibit when drunk. Such people, then, do not have the correct view of their own abilities. Finally, ignorance. Ignorant people, according to Aristotle, seem like hopeful people but are inferior. They stay a while, but when they realize their mistakes, for example, the identity of their adversary, they run.

Acting for the sake of the fine, then, is different from acting in all of these ways. None of the reasons these characters have for standing their ground have overriding weight for the truly brave person. He does not stand his ground merely to avoid reproaches or to gain honour (although he thinks that true honour is important), nor merely because he has the skill to fight, nor just because he is angry or hopeful or unaware of the true nature of the situation. If the brave person is angry, fearful, or confident, this is because he is aware of the true nature of his abilities and of the situation and has the appropriate emotions in the circumstances. In such a case, he will not desert his post if he thinks that no honour is forthcoming, or no pleasure (of revenge). His fine motivation is not undermined by desires for glory and pleasure.

Characterized in these terms, the Aristotelian truly brave person appears to be an admirable character, the sort of person whose general priorities would make him or her admirable in peacetime as well as in war, whereas the characters who exhibit the other states have general priorities that would make them less than admirable both in war-time and in peace. Therefore, Aristotle's discussion about civic mock bravery can be generalized, and is generalized by Aristotle himself in a passage at the end of his *Eudemian Ethics*, to which I now turn.

5. THE FINE AND THE GOOD

In his *Eudemian Ethics*, Aristotle distinguishes the disposition of the fine-and-good person and a "civic disposition", much like civic brav-ery, which he attributes to the Spartans (*EE* VIII 3). According to Aristotle, the Spartans wish to possess virtue for the sake of natural goods, for example, wealth and power, and so the natural goods are not both good and fine for them as they are for the person who is fine and good. Aristotle seems to be assuming here that Spartan society is ideally arranged so that the only way to attain the desired natural goods is by doing what one should. Otherwise, the Spartans' desire for these goods will undermine their grounds for acting virtuously and hence their choice of virtue. This will happen whether the Spartans' desire for the natural goods is a first-order or second-order desire.[12] The case is similar to Aristotle's description of civic bravery. The civic brave stand their ground to avoid penalties and to gain rewards, and, luckily for them, the penalties and rewards are so arranged that they have no grounds to act differently. However, it is still true that if the penalties and rewards were altered, the grounds for remaining at their posts would be gone, and so would they.

This preceding passage from the *Eudemian Ethics* has been taken to support a Kantian reading of Aristotelian motivation, because the fine-and-good person's actions and goods appear to become fine simply because of the fine-and-good person's fine motivation.[13] There are two points against such a reading. First, everything Aristotle says here is still compatible with acting for the sake of the fine and for happiness

---

[12] Kenny 1992, 14 draws an analogy with Rule-Utilitarianism and suggests that the motivation in question should be understood as a second-order desire for external goods.

[13] Whiting 1996.

at the same time, which would be unacceptable to a Kantian. Second, the discussion in the *Eudemian Ethics* explains why the good person, who acts for the sake of the fine, can also desire goods without such a desire undermining her choice of virtuous actions. The answer is that her desire for goods is conditioned by being motivated for the sake of the fine, so that any goods attained by other than virtuous means would be unwanted. Goods do not become fine simply because of a person's motivation, rather, goods obtained by virtuous means and used for virtuous ends are the ones worth wanting by the fine-and-good person. According to Aristotle, "a person is fine-and-good because, among goods, those that are fine for themselves [sc. the virtues] are fine for him, and because he is a practiser of fine things, and for their own sake. Fine things are the virtues and the deeds resulting from virtue" (*EE* VIII 3 1248b34–7, tr. Woods). Since the person of civic disposition is only motivated by the desire for natural goods and "does fine things only incidentally" (*EE* VIII 3 1249a15–16), civic virtue cannot be true virtue. Therefore, the discussion in the *Eudemian Ethics* does not show that value is conferred by the good person's motivation.[14]

In conclusion, it is, *pace* Prichard, perfectly intelligible to choose something for its own sake and for the sake of something else, and without using a Millian interpretation. Acting for the sake of the fine is best explicated by Aristotle's account of different types of mock bravery. To use the terminology of Chapter 5, the truly brave person's disposition involves reason and is not merely in accordance with it. Although civic virtue comes closest to acting for the sake of the fine, as Aristotle shows, it still falls short, even when things are arranged so that outwardly one cannot tell the difference between the fine-and-good person and the person of merely civic disposition. However, the difference is not one that supports a Kantian interpretation of Aristotle's text.

6. CARING FOR A FRIEND FOR THE FRIEND'S SAKE

Aristotle says that a friend is the greatest external good, and he accordingly devotes two whole books of his *Nicomachean Ethics* (VIII and IX),

[14] Whiting 1996.

as well as another whole book of his *Eudemian Ethics* (VII), to the topic of friendship. Aristotle's discussion ranges from friendship between individuals to the bonds between fellow citizens. According to Aristotle, a human being can only be self-sufficient if he has friends. Friends, including family, are necessary not only for living a happy life but also to help one develop the good character to be able to enjoy a happy life in the first place.[15] We learn about ourselves by interacting with our friends, and we also enjoy activities far more when they are shared.[16] A friend is "another self", someone one can identify with, and whom one notices reciprocating one's own good wishes. It is not surprising, then, that Aristotle thinks that the best, the most reliable, and the most pleasant friend a person can have is someone of good character. There are two other types of friendship, based on utility and pleasure respectively, but these are not as good and are more easily dissolved.

A central problem in Aristotle's account of friendship is how Aristotle can say that a good friend cares for his friend for the friend's sake, when Aristotle also says that the good human being is motivated by his own happiness. As we have seen, there is a perfectly clear way in which the good human being can care about particular things both for their own sakes and for the sake of his own happiness, and so this problem drops away. There does remain another problem that has given rise to new Kantian interpretations of the text, and that is what Aristotle has in mind when he says that only good people can be friends with each other because of the other person himself. For example, Vlastos and Whiting take Aristotle to mean that if x and y are friends of good character, x cares for y simply because y has a good character, where good character is a repeatable general property, and they chide and praise Aristotle for this suggestion respectively.[17]

I shall argue that it would be right to chide Aristotle if he held this view, but that what Aristotle says does not support this reading of the text, and that his discussion is more complicated, allowing good friends

---

[15] On the importance of including family among friends and considering other family members as other selves, not just in Aristotle's account of ethics, but also in his analysis of tragedy, see Schollmeier 1998.

[16] Cooper 1980, 320–30 and Sherman 1997, 187–216.

[17] Vlastos 1973 and Whiting 1991. Whiting's article includes a debate with Brink 1990.

to care for one another in a way that is not simply derivative from caring for good character itself.

Aristotle says, "It is clear that only the good [can be friends with each other] because of themselves" (*EN* VIII 4 1157a18–19). Aristotle is here contrasting friendships of character with friendships of utility and friendships due to pleasure. In the second type of friendship, the friends only care for each other because they are useful; in the third, they care for each other because they are pleasant. These points suggest that in the first type of friendship, the friends care for each other because they are good. Hence, both Vlastos and Whiting attribute to Aristotle the view that the good person cares for a friend only in virtue of the friend's good character and so is not concerned for her "in the uniqueness and integrity of his or her individuality".[18] Vlastos considers this a "fatal flaw" in both Plato and Aristotle's views. Nagel makes a related point when distinguishing sexual attraction to a particular individual from the case of liking an omelette. In the case of an omelette, any omelette with the requisite characteristics would do as well, but that is not true in the case of a particular person.[19] In other words, a friend is not replaceable in the way that an omelette is. One can give up a friend and gain another, but the second will be a new friend, not a replacement for the first. Against Vlastos, Whiting argues that there is no fatal flaw in Aristotle's account, because disinterested affection, as constituted by appreciation of a person's excellences, has much to be said for it, and the view that we care for *this* person has the unwelcome implications that I care for x because x is unique or because x arises from this sperm and this egg.[20] Whiting elaborates the view, arguing that the good person cares about good character in itself, and so values that character not only in herself but also in others, caring derivatively about this or that person for solely pragmatic reasons.

When contrasted with selfishness and possessiveness, disinterested affection does indeed seem a promising feature of a good friendship. As I explained in Chapter 1, the triadic nature of the doctrine of the mean is supported by the idea that there are three mentalities, and the one exemplifying correct self-love, and not selfishness, is the one that

[18] Vlastos 1973. Whiting 1991 quotes the salient passages from Vlastos, 12–13.
[19] Nagel 1969, 43.
[20] Whiting 1991, 13.

characterizes the good human being who is suited for the primary kind of friendship. Such a person will not relate to anyone in a selfish and possessive way, but it does not follow that such a person must relate to a friend only derivatively, unless the alternative is somehow incoherent.

Whether caring for *this* human being is incoherent depends on how the idea is understood. Caring for x because x is unique is not the same as caring for *this* person, because being unique is a general property that many share. As for caring for x because he comes from this sperm and this egg, it is important not to confuse the origin of the object of concern with the grounds for caring for it. When Aristotle discusses the different features of friendship, his favourite example is that of the relationship between mother and child (*EN* IX 4 1166a5–6 cf. *EN* VIII 8 1159a28–33). The example is telling, because a mother cares not for good character in itself and then derivatively for her child, but she loves her child, this very being, and therefore wants him or her to have a good character, not for the sake of good character in itself but for the sake of the child. Of course, in the example of mother and child, the child cannot reciprocate the mother's good wishes in the same way, and so this is not an example of the primary type of friendship. However, even in the case of loving someone who has a good character, one will want that person to retain her good character not merely derivatively but for her own sake because it is good *for her*. As Aristotle says, those who wish goods for their friends for the sake of their friends are friends most of all (*EN* VIII 3 1156b9–10). If the good person were primarily interested in good character, she would do better to spend her time reforming bad people rather than hobnobbing with the good.

If Aristotle does not think that caring for a friend for the friend's own sake is merely derivative from caring for good character, the question remains why he thinks that it is only possible between friends of good character. The answer is to be found in the passage where Aristotle lists parallel features in the way the good human being relates to a friend and the way in which he relates to himself (*EN* IX 4). According to Aristotle, the good human being wishes goods for his friend as he wishes good for himself. He wishes his friend to exist for the friend's sake as he wishes himself to survive. He likes to spend time with his friend, just as he does by himself. He makes the same choices as his friend, just as he is of one mind with himself. He shares his friend's pleasure and pain, just as he finds the same things pleasant and painful when he is by himself.

The main point about the good human being is the fact that he is a stable individual with the same character over time, and this point is nailed home by Aristotle in the very next passage where Aristotle describes the disintegrated nature of the person who is not virtuous. Such a person is conflicted, never pleased or pained by the same things, and thoroughly miserable. According to Aristotle, the moral is that we should try to be good so as to be disposed in a friendly way to ourselves and become a friend for someone else. The point of this conclusion is not simply that a human being cannot have the right attitude towards someone else if he is not good, but that he cannot be the proper object of friendship for anyone else if he is not good. Only a good person has the integrity of character that allows a friend to relate to him himself. One can only relate properly to a friend *as a stable individual* if that friend has a good character. Otherwise, one is relating to a conglomeration of conflicting desires that changes from day to day.[21]

According to Aristotle, then, the good person does not care primarily for a repeatable general property that just happens to be instantiated in this or that human being, but he will be attracted to other good human beings precisely because they have stable good characters that enable the friend to have a continuing, reliable, and trustworthy relationship with a stable individual himself.

It is therefore possible to explain what Aristotle means by acting "for the sake of the fine" and doing things "for a friend's own sake" without resorting to any Kantian interpretations. In the first case, Aristotle's comments about choosing x for its own sake and for the sake of y should be taken at face value, and his discussion of mock bravery should be re-evaluated. In the second, Aristotle's comments on familial friendships should be given the weight they deserve. From the perspective of virtue ethics, Aristotle's account of the motivation of the good person is understandable in its own terms. In the following chapter, I show how the account is developed under the aegis of Aristotle's arguments about the practical syllogism.

[21] Cf. *EE* VII 6 1240b15–18.

8 The Practical Syllogism

The argument of this chapter is that Aristotle's practical syllogism, despite the qualms of modern commentators,[1] is at the heart of Aristotle's ethic of virtue. This chapter connects the different strands of Aristotle's thought on ethical virtue, motivation, and practical wisdom, and it completes the argument of Chapter 5 that ethical virtue and practical wisdom go hand in hand.

I begin by raising a long-lived puzzle about how to distinguish Aristotelian practical wisdom (*phronēsis*) from a technical skill (*technē*), and arguing that the solution comes, not from Aristotle's metaphysics, but from his account of the virtues, especially the nameless virtue of truthfulness. I then raise the further problem whether Aristotle is begging the question when he says that the difference between practical wisdom and a technical skill is that the former requires ethical virtue whereas the latter does not. In Chapter 5, I discussed Aristotle's controversial claim that it is impossible to have all the ethical virtues fully without having practical wisdom, and that it is impossible to have practical wisdom without having all of the Aristotelian ethical virtues fully (*EN* VI 13 1144b30–1145a1). I now turn to Aristotle's practical syllogism, which, on my interpretation, makes the connection between ethical virtue and practical wisdom even clearer.

In the sphere of formal logic, Aristotle is famous for discovering the syllogism (a piece of reasoning consisting in two premisses and a conclusion), and for categorizing all the valid forms of syllogisms with

---

[1] Natali, alluding to such scepticism, entitles a chapter on the practical syllogism "Perhaps it doesn't exist. No-one knows what it is about" (Natali 2001, 63).

premisses containing subject and predicate terms. One of these valid forms, according to Aristotle and as I explain below, is the basis for the appropriate form for setting out reasoning in the theoretical sciences, but it is controversial whether there is any such analogous form for practical reasoning.[2] I argue that there is indeed such a thing as a syllogism that is practical and of specific ethical import,[3] that it is analogous to the correct theoretical syllogism in an important way, and that the explanation for its practical and ethical nature is to be found in the much-neglected part of the minor premiss that reveals the agent to have the virtue salient to the situation at hand.

Formulating a correct ethical practical syllogism presents various difficulties. First, Aristotelian "practical" wisdom is not broadly practical. Aristotle draws a sharp distinction between practical wisdom and productive reasoning or skill (*technē*), and yet almost all of the examples in the *Nicomachean Ethics* and elsewhere relate to skills. As we have already seen in Chapter 1, Aristotle's favourite skill is medicine, but, while it is analogous to practical wisdom, according to Aristotle, it is not the same. In his *Nicomachean Ethics*, instead of presenting a complete and detailed example of a valid ethical practical syllogism, as opposed to an example of the argument form, Aristotle supplies snippets of medical reasoning, albeit applied to the agent and not to a separate patient, and parts of reasoning that have gone awry in the sphere of temperance.

A second difficulty is that it is not immediately clear whether the practical syllogism is supposed to represent the actual reasoning processes of the good person or an *ex post facto* explanation of action or the person's motivation or the justification for their action or some combination of the above.

Therefore, in order to formulate a correct ethical practical syllogism, I first consider the parallels between it and the theoretical syllogism, and examine some pieces of analogous reasoning, including technical reasoning, from *de Anima* and *de Motu Animalium*. I concentrate on

---

[2] See, e.g., the doubts of Annas 1993, 92. Broadie 1991, esp. 229 and Reeve 1992 think there is an analogy, but Broadie draws a different parallel from mine, which I discuss below, and Reeve concentrates on the status of the major ("universal") premiss.

[3] Kenny also distinguishes an ethical syllogism from the technical ones, but does not focus on the first part of the minor premiss (Kenny 1979, esp. 112–24).

how the practical syllogism explains virtuous action, but I also briefly
address the role of the syllogism from a first-person point of view.

I argue that the minor premiss of the ethical practical syllogism is
very important. I also argue that the ethical practical syllogism will
only be used by the good human being, consistently with the idea that
ethical virtue "involves reason", as explained in Chapter 5 and elaborated in Chapter 7. The practical syllogism is an ethical topic.

1. THE PROBLEM OF DISTINGUISHING PRACTICAL WISDOM AND TECHNICAL SKILL

In *Nicomachean Ethics* VI, Aristotle explains what practical wisdom is by
contrasting it with other mentalities or ways of thought. He first distinguishes practical wisdom from theoretical wisdom (*sophia*). According
to Aristotle, theoretical and practical wisdom belong to different parts
of the rational part of the soul, have different types of objects, and
involve different procedures. Theoretical wisdom has necessary truths
as its axioms; practical wisdom is concerned with what could be otherwise, contingent truths. Theoretical reasoning involves demonstration
or deductive reasoning while practical reasoning involves deliberation.
Aristotle's next and central distinction, between practical wisdom and
technical skill, is harder to draw. Unlike practical wisdom and theoretical wisdom, practical wisdom and technical skill both belong to the
same part of the rational soul, they both have the same objects, things
that admit of being otherwise, and they both may involve deliberation.
Technical skills involve deliberation to varying degrees, according to
Aristotle. Spelling involves no deliberation, whereas skills like naviga-
tion and medicine involve quite a lot. Deliberation relies on principles
that hold only "for the most part" and so experience, judgment, and
perception are important.

In addition, Aristotle often uses examples of technical skills as analogies for ethical virtue and practical reasoning. Aristotle explains his
doctrine of the mean by likening hitting the mean to an archer hitting
the target. He also points out that, in praising a product, we say that
nothing can be added or taken away, just as the doctrine of the mean
says that we should avoid excess and deficiency. In the argument from

function, Aristotle compares the function of a human being with the function of artisans and musicians. Finally, as we will see in the later part of this chapter, Aristotle explains ethical practical reasoning with snippets of reasoning from medicine and dietetics. All these similarities between practical wisdom and technical skill show that there is a special challenge to Aristotle to explain how practical wisdom and technical skill differ, if indeed they do.

There is a further difficulty. Technical skills do not form a homogeneous class. It might be thought that the skill involved in shoemaking differs from that involved in playing the harp as much as it does from ethical reasoning. True, the three differ, but why think that they differ *in kind*? Socrates, as Aristotle is well aware, classified them all together.

I shall begin by listing the differences that Aristotle notes between practical wisdom and technical skill that are at the root of the problem. First, practical wisdom aims at an unqualified goal, whereas technical skill aims at a qualified goal, a goal that is needed to attain some further goal (*EN* VI 2 1139b1–2). Practical wisdom is concerned with action, whereas technical skill is concerned with production (*EN* VI 4 1140a2–5). Practical wisdom relates to the whole of life, whereas technical skill relates to a restricted area (*EN* VI 5 1140a28–31). The goal of practical wisdom is doing well, whereas the goal of technical skill is something other than itself (*EN* VI 5 1140b6–7). Practical wisdom requires ethical virtue (*EN* VI 13 1144b30–2), whereas technical skill does not. Practical wisdom, unlike technical skill, is a virtue. It cannot be intentionally misused (*EN* VI 5 1140b20–4), nor can it be forgotten (*EN* VI 5 1140b28–30). A further point of difference can be gleaned from an earlier book. According to Aristotle, the products of a technical skill can be evaluated without considering the state of the agent. The actions produced by ethical virtue and practical wisdom cannot (*EN* II 4 1105a26–34).

Aristotle's distinctions have invited a slew of objections. The first objection relies on the heterogeneous nature of technical skills. While shoemaking may aim at a goal beyond the exercise of shoemaking, that is, shoes, in the absence of records and compact discs, playing the harp aims simply at playing the harp. Also, there is no reason why a shoemaker might not aim at just the shoemaking. Perhaps, like other artists, he likes the process but has no interest in the final product. Second, there is great difficulty in distinguishing action and production.[4] Consider a generous action. Aristotle says that generosity involves money, but he then expands this to include anything measurable by money. If we include time and help, it is reasonable to suppose that if mending my neighbour's fence is the generous thing to do, action and production are one and the same. Similarly, if doing the brave action produces victory, action and production would also appear to be one and the same. Third, it might be thought that technical skill does require ethical virtue, just as much as does practical wisdom. For example, the best golfers have endurance, patience, and so on. Fourth, Aristotle may appear to be begging the question in claiming that practical wisdom is a virtue, whereas technical skill is not. Socrates would accept the peculiar features of practical wisdom but argue that it is still a technical skill. Finally, it may be disputed whether, even in the case of technical skill, the products can be evaluated apart from the maker. It may make a big difference whether an object is manufactured or home-made, for example. Even in Aristotle's time, one might evaluate a child's effort differently from a skilled artisan.

When Aristotle says that practical wisdom has to do with living in an unqualified way (*haplōs*) as opposed to technical skills that apply to restricted areas, he is harking back to the beginning of Book I, where he explains how different skills fit together in a hierarchy. For example, bridle-making is subordinate to horsemanship, and horsemanship to generalship. The horseman uses the bridles made by the bridle-makers, and the generals make use of the cavalry's skills when going to war. Just as the higher skill makes use of the lower, so practical wisdom can make use of any other skill for its own end of doing virtuously in action. It is therefore beside the point to object that harpists aim at playing the harp and shoemakers may like making shoes for its own sake. Aristotle's point is that playing the harp and shoemaking are subordinate skills, and can be used well or badly in promoting the happy life. Practical wisdom, by contrast, cannot be used well or badly. It uses the other skills, and its exercise is not subordinate to any other faculty. Practical wisdom is not identical with any particular technical skill, nor does it

4 See, e.g., Ackrill 1978 and Charles 1984.

require any particular technical skill. Aristotle puts this point by saying
that action is not identical with production. However, this does not
mean that practical wisdom cannot make use of the skills a person has
in performing virtuous actions. Aristotle describes practical wisdom as
"capable of giving orders" (*epitaktikē*) for this very reason.

2. A SOLUTION INVOLVING TRUTHFULNESS AND THE DOCTRINE OF THE MEAN, AND A NEW PUZZLE

If practical wisdom can make use of and direct other skills, Aristotle's
discussion may now appear to fall prey to the other group of objections
relating to products. What sense does it make to say that technical
skills need products, whereas practical wisdom does not? In *Nicomachean
Ethics* II 4, Aristotle says that the products of technical skills literally
"have the well in themselves" (*EN* II 4 1105a27–8), that is, they can be
judged good or bad just by looking at the products themselves, whereas
this is not so in the case of ethical actions. In their case, the agent has to
be disposed a particular way. I take this passage to mean that products
figure into the assessment of the person's good or bad actions in a very
different way than they would in the assessment of a technical skill. For
example, if the general does not achieve victory, this reflects on his skill
as a general. But if a particular soldier's death does not result in victory,
this does not mean that he was not brave. Similarly, if a present, say a
shirt, turned out to be the wrong size for its recipient, this would not
necessarily tell against the generosity of the action. In addition, in the
case of good action, any product, even the agent's resulting happiness
over a lifetime, is irrelevant to the assessment. If the agent meets ill
luck later on, it does not mean that his present actions were any the less
virtuous.

One might object that if I offer to mend my neighbour's fence
and then botch the job, I have not done anything generous at all, so
the final product does affect our evaluation of the action after all. In
response, I agree that I have not done anything generous in this case,
but the reason is not so much the product – bad luck would not affect
the evaluation – as that I have the wrong view of my abilities and
therefore lack the Aristotelian virtue of truthfulness. I should have

offered to do something else, or if I knew I would do it badly, I should have enlisted the help of someone else (cf. *EN* IX 9 1169a32–4). A nameless virtue therefore makes an important contribution to practical wisdom.

Next, there is Aristotle's claim that practical wisdom requires the ethical virtues, whereas technical skills do not. Certainly, truthfulness is required to exercise the technical skills judiciously, but it is not required to have those skills. The best golfers may indeed have endurance, patience, and so on. However, as I have already argued in Chapter 4, making use of different aspects of the doctrine of the mean, these are not ethical virtues according to Aristotle.

Finally, there is the objection that Aristotle is begging the question when he says that the difference between practical wisdom and technical skill is that the first requires the ethical virtues, whereas the second does not, when we have no independent account of how reasoning involves ethical virtue. As we saw in Chapter 5, it is impossible to have the ethical virtues fully without having practical wisdom, and it is impossible to have practical wisdom without having the ethical virtues fully. This raises a new puzzle about how exactly practical wisdom requires ethical virtue. In the following, I formulate the type of reasoning, represented by the practical syllogism, that explains how this is the case, and I show that there can indeed be pieces of reason that are *practical*.

3. THE ANALOGY BETWEEN THE THEORETICAL AND PRACTICAL SYLLOGISM, AND THE IMPORTANCE OF THE MIDDLE TERM

At *de Motu Animalium* 7, Aristotle raises the following question: "But how is it that thought sometimes results in action and sometimes does not, sometimes in movement, sometimes not?" (*MA* 701a7–8). He answers by pointing out a parallel between theoretical and practical reasoning: "What happens seems parallel to the case of thinking and inferring (*dianooumenois kai sullogizomenois*) about immovable objects. There the end is speculation (for, when one thinks the two premises, one thinks and puts together the conclusion), but here the conclusion drawn from the two premisses becomes the action".[5] In drawing an analogy between theoretical and practical reasoning, Aristotle uses the terminology of a syllogism, mentioning premisses and conclusion. The analogy is confirmed in the *Nicomachean Ethics* where Aristotle says that in ordinary reasoning the soul affirms the conclusion, but in the productive case it immediately acts (*EN* VII 1147a26–8). To examine the analogy in more detail, my discussion begins with the theoretical syllogism and its application to Aristotelian science.

Aristotle's main discussion of the theoretical (sometimes referred to as "demonstrative") syllogism appears in the *Posterior Analytics*. The details of the theoretical syllogism are the subject of nearly as much controversy as Aristotle's practical syllogism. In addition, Aristotle's own examples of syllogisms often do not live up to his own stringent requirements.[6] The medievals helpfully formulated the following example to fit Aristotle's specifications. It consists of a major premiss, a minor premiss and conclusion thus:

Major Premiss: Rational animals are grammatical.
Minor Premiss: Human beings are rational animals.
Conclusion: Human beings are grammatical.

Here is the Aristotelian schema:

$$\quad C \qquad\qquad\qquad\qquad\qquad\qquad\qquad B$$
(1) Being grammatical belongs necessarily to rationality.
$$\quad B \qquad\qquad\qquad\qquad\qquad\qquad\qquad\qquad\qquad\quad A$$
(2) Rationality belongs necessarily (because essentially) to human beings.
$$\qquad\qquad\quad C \qquad\qquad\qquad\qquad\qquad\qquad A$$
So (3) being grammatical belongs necessarily to human beings.

B is the middle term. It is the cause or explanation why the conclusion holds true. Human beings are grammatical, that is, capable of learning a language, *because* they are rational. Their rationality explains

---

[5] I explain this comment in the following section.
[6] See Lloyd 1996, 13, who goes on to argue that there are more stringent and laxer versions of demonstration.

why they are capable of learning a language. According to Aristotle, the premisses are true, necessary, primary, immediate (they themselves do not have any further middle terms), and both prior to and explanatory of the conclusion.

This type of syllogism is not intended to mirror the research or inquiry of the working scientist. The scientist does not start with definitions and work out the science *a priori*. Nor does putting terms in the order of a syllogism alone guarantee success. The scientist must make sure that the middle term really is explanatory. In other words, she must make sure that what appear in the premisses are not mere correlations but are etiologically grounded (*A Post.* I 2–6, II 8–10, *A Pr.* II 23).[7] Furthermore, Aristotle gives examples to show that the middle term must not be too remote (*A Post.* I 13 78b22–8). Aristotle compares his examples to Anarchasis' riddle, "Why are there no female flute-players in Scythia?" and its answer "because there are no vines there" (*A Post.* I 13 78b28–31). Presumably, the answer is short for the following train of reasoning, "Where there is no drunkenness there are no female flute-players, where there is no wine there is no drunkenness, where there are no vines there is no wine. In Scythia there are no vines. Therefore, in Scythia there are no female flute-players". As Ross points out, the problem is that there might be drunkenness and yet no female flute-players, wine and yet no drunkenness, or vines and yet no wine. The point is that if the middle term gives an explanation that is too remote, it may also turn out not to be the correct explanation for the conclusion of the syllogism at all.[8]

Jonathan Barnes notes that Aristotle thought that the final results of a science would be written up in syllogistic format, and he accordingly considered Aristotle's biological works unfinished since they contain no complete syllogisms.[9] However, he also thinks that Aristotle's works would point the way to a more complete science. The pioneering work of Gotthelf and Lennox supports this idea. For example, Gotthelf has shown that proto-syllogistic reasoning does in fact abound; many

---

[7] I do not mean to suggest that Aristotle does not also discuss inductive reasoning and "demonstrations of the fact", but I take these to be earlier stages in an Aristotelian science.

[8] Ross 1949, 553–54.

[9] Barnes 1975 cf. Barnes 1994, esp. p. xii.

explanations of facts about animals are given in terms of features of the animal, which are explained by the nature of the animal or its parts.[10]

One might expect any of Aristotle's four causes to play the role of middle term, but in the biological works, not surprisingly, it is the final cause, the explanation in terms of point or function, that usually takes pride of place.

Gotthelf and Lennox's conclusions are controversial because of the laxer type of reasoning involved in the biological works.[11] However, if it be allowed that what appears in the biological works is in an important sense syllogistic, then it becomes less of a leap to suppose that the practical syllogism counts as a syllogism too, even if it contains particular terms. That is not to say that the practical syllogism is a type of theoretical syllogism; rather it is analogous to one. Aristotle carefully distinguishes practical and theoretical reasoning in *Nicomachean Ethics* VI.

3.1. Formulating the Practical Syllogism and the Analogous Middle Term

The clearest general example of the premisses of a practical syllogism appears in Aristotle's *de Anima*.[12] Aristotle says, "Since the one supposition and proposition is universal and the other is particular (the one saying that such and such a human being[13] ought to do such and such a thing, while the other says that this now[14] is such and such a thing, and I am such and such a human being, then either it is the latter opinion,

---

[10] Gotthelf 1987, esp. 167–70, Lennox 1987.

[11] See Lloyd 1996, 7–37, addressed by Lennox in his introduction to Lennox 2001. On the complexities of Aristotelian demonstration, definition, and explanation, see also Charles 2000, Part II.

[12] Hicks 1907, 572 says that the following sentence "introduces the practical syllogism".

[13] The Greek says "such and such". Hicks gives, "for while such and such a person", (Hicks 1907, 157). Similarly, Ackrill, "such a kind of man". (Ackrill 1973, 225) and Rodier "celui qui a telle qualité" (Rodier 1900, 213). Aquinas *CANE* 482 gives as an example "Children ought to honour their parents. I am a son and I ought here and now to honour my parents" but no one else is that specific.

[14] Reading "now" (*to nun*) with most of the manuscripts, as opposed to "therefore" (*toinun*) with Torstrik 1862 after Simplicius.

not the universal one, which produces movement, or it is both, but the first is more static while the other is not" (*de An.* III 11 434a16–434a2, tr. Hamlyn). In the *de Motu Animalium*, Aristotle says that the conclusion drawn from the two premisses *becomes* the action (*MA* 7). This comment is cryptic. Aristotle seems to imagine that the agent will act immediately. He says, "For example, when one thinks that every human ought to walk, and that one is a human being oneself, immediately one walks", but he elsewhere points out that the agent will act if not physically prevented (*EN* VII 1147a31–2). Presumably, then, the conclusion of the syllogism is the action itself. The default conclusion is a specification of the action to be performed.

In *de Motu Animalium* 7, Aristotle considers the productive reasoning resulting in making a coat. Aristotle renders the conclusion as "a coat must be made", or, in more idiomatic English, and applying the major premiss to oneself, "I should make a coat". (Negative conclusions, such as that I should avoid doing something now, are also possible as we shall see below.) In the following, I shall give the idiomatic rendering of the (default) conclusion, with the caveat that, in Aristotle's view, it is not possible to reach that very conclusion except by way of the major and minor premisses.

Putting these two passages together provides the following schema:

Universal Premiss: Such and such a human being ought to do such and such a thing.[15]

Particular Premiss: I'm such and such a human being. This is such and such a thing.[16]

Conclusion: I should do this [now etc.].

---

[15] One might wonder why the universal premiss does not say that such and such a human being does do such and such a thing. However, if "such and such" refers to a positive attribute, what such and such a human being *does* do will be the very same as what such and such a human being *ought* to do.

[16] It has been suggested that my particular premiss is in fact two premisses and that there are two syllogisms involved, not just one. Briefly, against this suggestion I would argue that Aristotle himself claims to be describing only two premisses and one conclusion, that my account makes more perspicuous the connection between being a good person and having a correct appreciation of the circumstances, and that Aristotle's account of *akrasia* (lack of self-control) can also be formulated with only one syllogism.

In the passage in *de Motu Animalium*, Aristotle uses the phrase, "I'm a human being" as opposed to "I'm such and such a human being". The reason for this, I suggest, is that here Aristotle is contrasting human behaviour with that of other animals, so "human" is the salient term. The appropriate kind of behaviour is related to the kind of creature one is. However, a more plausible reconstruction of the syllogism in question might refer to the health of the agent as follows:

Universal Premiss: Healthy human beings ought to take constitutionals [at the right times etc.].
Particular Premiss: I'm a healthy human being. [This is the right time for a walk etc.]
Conclusion: I should go for a walk [now].[17]

A few paragraphs further on, Aristotle mentions that walking is good for human beings. Presumably, it is good for their health.[18] He also notes, plausibly, that, when acting, people do not dwell on the premiss "I'm a human being". I shall return to this point later.[19]

I now turn to the snippets of syllogizing in the *Nicomachean Ethics*. In explaining why the person with practical wisdom must be concerned with particulars as well as universals, Aristotle says, "For someone who knows that light meats are digestible and healthy, but not which sorts

---

[17] A separate account is required for the actions of the person who is sick and merely wishes to do what is healthy. Compare Section 8.

[18] Cf. Barnes 1975, 218.

[19] The passage in the *de Motu Animalium* also introduces two types of premisses in productive reasoning; some describe what is good for human beings, others describe what is possible for them. For example, if a tailor needs a coat (something that would be good), she will work out what she needs to do first in order to make it, that is, what is possible. Controversy surrounds whether these are two types of major premiss or whether the good premisses are major, while the possible are minor (Allan vs. Wiggins in Wiggins 1975–6). My solution is that the two types of premiss alternate as follows:
Major Premiss: Healthy human beings should wear coats when they go out.
Minor Premiss: I'm a healthy human being. I need a coat.
Possible Premiss: To make a coat, I need material etc.
So (new major premiss): Healthy human beings should find the right material.
Minor Premiss: I'm a healthy human being. This is the right material etc.

of meats are light, will not produce health; the one who knows that bird meats are healthy will be better at producing health" (*EN* VI 7 1141b18–21, tr. Irwin). He also comments, "Moreover ... deliberation may be in error about either the universal or the particular. For [we may wrongly suppose] either that all sorts of heavy water are bad or that this water is heavy" (*EN* VI 8 1142a20–2, tr. Irwin).[20]

The above examples suggest that the more specific information one has, the better able one is to act. However, Aristotle seems to define the particulars in relation to the universal. If "light meats are digestible and healthy" is a universal claim, "bird meats are light" counts as a particular claim. None of this detracts from the view of *de Anima* that the very final minor premiss contains indexicals: "I am ... and this is ...". The doctor in the first example who knows that bird meats are healthy would still have to know that *this* is bird meat.

This point emerges more clearly in *EN* VII 3 1147a1–10. Here, Aristotle notes that there are two types of premiss, the universal and the particular,[21] and he presents a syllogism that has two particular premisses. He says, "Perhaps, e.g., someone knows that dry things benefit every human being, and that he himself is a human being, or that this sort of thing is dry; but he either does not have or does not activate the knowledge that this particular thing is of this sort". In other words, it is no good knowing that dry foods benefit you and that, say, bread is dry if you do not know that this is bread.[22]

The correct syllogism, then, would run as follows:

Major Premiss: Dry things benefit human beings.
Minor Premiss: I'm a human being. Bread is dry.
Final Minor Premiss: I'm a human being. This piece of bread is dry.
Conclusion: I should eat this now.

---

[20] Although this may look like decisive evidence against Cooper's view that deliberation ceases at the major premiss (Cooper 1975, 46), there is a problem involving scope in this sentence. It may also mean that there is an error about the universal in the deliberation, or [an error] about the particular.

[21] The particular here is *tēi kata meros* cf. *A Post.* I 24.

[22] *Contra* Cooper 1975, e.g., 184, and with Dahl 1984, esp. 29 and footnote 12.

Although the final minor premiss is not arbitrary, how many pre-misses there are between major and final minor premiss seems to me to be arbitrary. If one thinks of the syllogism by analogy with an accor-dion, one can insert as many premisses as one likes between major pre-miss and final minor premiss.

In the same passage in Book VII, Aristotle also distinguishes two types of universal, one relating to the agent, the other to the thing (*to men eph'heautou to d'epi tou pragmatos estin* 1147a4–5). The distinction is puzzling if one takes Aristotle to be referring to two universal pre-misses, because the distinction between what refers to the agent and what refers to the thing seems only to appear in the minor premiss. Irwin's translation refers to two universal terms. But this is equally puzzling, for how can the part of the premiss that refers to the agent be a universal term?

The solution is to consider the agent in the light of some universal attribute that she possesses, just as, in the passage in *de Anima*, the agent in the first part of the minor premiss appears as "such-and-such a human being".[23] Putting all the information together, we get the fol-lowing good medical syllogisms:

(1) Universal Premiss: Healthy human beings ought to eat light foods.
     Minor Premiss: I'm a healthy human being. This is chicken.
     Conclusion: I should eat this now.
(2) Universal Premiss: Healthy human beings ought to eat dry food.
     Minor Premiss: I'm a healthy human being. This is dry food.
     Conclusion: I should eat this now.
(3) Universal Premiss: Healthy human beings ought not to drink pol-luted water.
     Minor Premiss: I'm a healthy human being. This is polluted.
     Conclusion: I should avoid this now.

So far, I have been discussing syllogisms that are analogous to the ethical ones that are our concern. In the case of an ethical syllogism, according to Aristotle, the final universal premiss represents the result

[23] Cf. Kenny 1973, 28–50.

of deliberation. The content of the final minor premiss is given by perception. Presumably, what licenses the conclusion is the fact that the agent is the sort of person she is. If she is not that sort of person, then the universal and second part of the minor premiss will have no effect on her whatsoever. This is different from the scientific syllogism, where the inference from premisses to conclusion holds whatever kind of character one has. However, there is one extremely important point of similarity. The explanatory role of the middle term in the practical syllogism is played by the part of the minor premiss that refers to the agent. Indeed, its explanatory nature may explain why Aristotle calls it a "universal term".[24] The part of the minor premiss that refers to the agent not only licenses the move from premisses to conclusion, but it also explains why the agent acts the way she does.

What Aristotle says about the akratic dieter is consistent with the above schema. There are two beliefs: one universal and the other about particulars (*EN* VII 3 1147a25–6). The universal belief hinders the akratic from tasting (*EN* VII 1147a33), and he also has the belief that this is sweet.

On my account, the full *correct* ethical practical syllogism would be as follows:

Universal Premiss: Temperate human beings should avoid sweets (on the appropriate occasions, in the right way etc.).
Final Minor Premiss: I'm a temperate human being and this is a sweet (and this is the right occasion to avoid a sweet etc.).
Conclusion: I should avoid this now.

Here again, the first term in the final minor premiss plays an important explanatory role. It is the agent's temperance that licenses the inference from premisses to conclusion, and it is because the agent is temperate that she avoids the sweet.

3.2. The Middle Term and the Ethical Agent

It might be objected that in the *Nicomachean Ethics*, despite drawing the distinction between what refers to the agent and what refers to the

---

[24] See *A Post.* I 24 for the connection between the universal and the explanatory.

thing, Aristotle routinely omits the part of the syllogism that refers to the agent, and when he mentions it, he often does so in the form "I'm a human being" as opposed to "I'm such and such a human being".

My explanation for the omission goes back to the discussion in *de Motu Animalium* where Aristotle says that the agent does not dwell on the part of the premiss that says "I'm a human being". This makes perfect sense as long as one thinks of the parts of the syllogism simply from a first-person point of view, for it is most implausible that the agent thinks to herself "I'm a human being".[25] All that the good person will have in mind when he or she acts will be the other parts of the minor premiss. None of this shows that the first part of the minor premiss of the syllogism does not play an important explanatory role from a third-person point of view. To explain why the person acted as she did, one needs to invoke her character.

If the part of the minor premiss that refers to the agent himself is truly explanatory, why does Aristotle sometimes represent this as "I am a human being" rather than "I am such and such a human being"? I wish to suggest that here too he is referring to what a human being ought to be, namely, a good human being. As we saw in the theoretical syllogism of the *Posterior Analytics*, the explanatory term must not be too remote. "I am a human being", taken *tout court*, is too remote to play a suitable role in the syllogism. Just because I am a human being does not explain why, for example, I do the generous action (many human beings do not), unless I am a *generous* human being. But if that is the case, then "human being" in the minor premiss must be short for "such and such a human being" after all.

3.3. The Middle Term, Ethical Virtue, and Deliberation

So far, I have argued that the first part of the minor premiss of the practical syllogism plays the same explanatory role as does the middle term of the scientific syllogism. I have not argued, and I do not mean to argue, that the first part of the minor premiss *is* the middle term of the practical syllogism, but it may be worth considering a passage about

---

[25] This point also applies to the bad person. Such a person does not think to himself "I'm intemperate", for example.

deliberation in *Nicomachean Ethics* VI 9, where Aristotle does explicitly refer to a "middle term". I wish to argue that one way of understanding this passage is clearly at odds with my reconstruction, but another and preferable way of understanding the passage is congenial to my project.

In this passage, Aristotle is trying to explain what good deliberation is by contrasting it with other types of thought. In the midst of his discussion, he makes the following comment: "However we can reach a good by a false inference (*pseudēi sullogismōi*), as well [as by correct deliberation], so that we reach what we should do, but by the wrong steps, when the middle term is false. Hence, this type of deliberation, leading us by the wrong steps to what we should do, is not enough for good deliberation either" (*EN* VI 9 1142b22–6). The implication is that in good deliberation, the middle term is true. But what is the middle term?

Aquinas, in his lectures commenting on Aristotle's ethics, suggests that what has gone wrong in the false syllogism is that the agent has arrived at what he ought to do but by the wrong means. The correct middle term would then be the correct means. Along similar lines, Sarah Broadie too suggests that the parallel to the "why" in the scientific syllogism is the "how" of the practical syllogism.[26] Aquinas's example is of someone who rightly concludes that he ought to help the poor but by the wrong means, stealing (*CANE* VI, lecture VIII, section 1230).

The example is puzzling. According to Aquinas, the line of reasoning must be as follows:

(1) My aim is to help the poor.
(2) Stealing is the correct way to help the poor.
(3) I should steal this. (Or I should help the poor by stealing this.)

According to Aristotle, the correct action would be to help the poor at the right time, in the right way, from the right sources, and so on, and so the false syllogism would *not* have the right conclusion, since it is never the right time to help the poor from the wrong sources. We need to find an alternative interpretation where the middle term is incorrect but the conclusion is still true.

---

[26] Broadie 1991, 225–32.

Interestingly, Aquinas's own comments suggest an alternative. He says, "Although the end in the order of intention is like the principle and the middle term, nevertheless ...". If the aim is to be generous and to help the poor, what the agent gets wrong is what that consists in.[27] According to Aristotle, it does not consist in helping people at the wrong times from the wrong sources, and so on. Being a generous person enables one to discern what the appropriate circumstances for generosity are. Hence, the middle term, correctly understood, is the universal attribute under which the good person falls – being generous. Such an account is well within the spirit of my proposed general interpretation. In the following syllogism, what the reasoner gets wrong are the italicized passages. However, the conclusion is still true:

(1) Generous people ought to help the poor (at the right times, from the right sources etc.).
(2) *I'm a generous person.* This is a poor person in need of help. *This is the right source* etc.
(3) I should help this person (now etc.).

The reasoner is right that the poor person needs help, but he is not a generous person and so lacks the appreciation to see what the correct source for the help should be. He thinks that there is nothing wrong with stealing. In short, he is wrong about what generosity consists in and that is because he is not a generous person.[28]

4. FROM A FIRST-PERSON POINT OF VIEW

As we saw in Chapter 7, Aristotle's good person is described as acting "for the sake of the fine". While it is possible to act for the sake of the fine and for the sake of one's happiness, for example, acting for the sake of the fine is to be distinguished from acting merely for the sake of

---

[27] See too *A Post.* II 11 where Aristotle seems to be envisaging the final cause as a middle term, although the passage is obscure.

[28] An alternative suggestion is that the reasoner is wrong about a matter of fact, but this has the awkward consequence that the resulting action will not then be voluntary.

external goods such as honour or wealth, or from emotions unimbued with reason. The source of the good person's motivation is the good person's good character. It follows, then, that someone with the good person's motivation will be motivated by the considerations in the practical syllogism as I have presented it.

Rosalind Hursthouse reasonably suggests that the good person is motivated by what she calls X-reasons.[29] On my account, these include those that constitute the other part of the minor premiss, what the good person perceives in the situation that makes him act. For example, a generous person might see that this person is in need.[30] If you ask him why he helped the person in question, he will say simply, "because he was in need". The second part of the minor premiss, then, provides him with a reason to help. It is important to note that it does so only in the context of the rest of the syllogism. A mean person might equally clearly perceive that someone is in need, but take this to be an opportunity and reason for some malicious action. Acting for the sake of the fine, then, must include not just having the reason presented in the second half of the minor premiss, but as having it as a reason embedded in the larger structure that refers to the ethical virtue in question, even if the good person does not have the larger structure to the forefront of his mind when he acts. As G. E. M. Anscombe points out, "If Aristotle's account were supposed to describe actual mental processes it would in general be quite absurd".[31] Having the virtue motivates the right action and provides the justificatory reason in the second half of the minor premiss with its justificatory force. If a person is generous, generosity motivates his generous actions, and also justifies his acting when seeing someone in trouble.

5. THE ENKRATIC, THE AKRATIC, AND THE LEARNER

It has been objected that if, on my interpretation of Aristotle, a good character explains good action, it will be impossible to explain the good

---

[29] Hursthouse 1999, 127–36.

[30] Of course, this is an oversimplification. The agent has to see that it is the right time, the right person, and so on.

[31] Anscombe 1957, section 42, 79.

action of the Aristotelian enkratic agent. While the akratic person, according to Aristotle, has the correct view of what she should do, but fails to do it because of a recalcitrant desire,[32] the enkratic person apparently manages to "do the right thing" despite her recalcitrant desire to do something else. How can the enkratic person do this if she is not a good person? The answer again turns on what it is to do the right thing. On Aristotle's account, having the right motivation is part and parcel of doing the right thing. "Doing the right thing although I would rather be doing something else" means that one is not doing the right thing *tout court*, but one is doing something that only looks as if it is the right thing. In other words, there is a difference between what is *meta logou* and what is *kata logon*, as originally explained in Chapter 5.

In the case of justice, Aristotle draws a distinction between those acts that are unjust – done from unjust motivation – and those that result in injustice even though they may not have been unjustly motivated (*EN* V 8, esp. 1135b20–5). Aristotle's distinction between bravery and mock states that resemble bravery also presupposes a distinction between virtuous action and merely virtuous-looking behaviour (*EN* III 6–9), as I explained in Chapter 7. Most important, in *EN* VI 12, Aristotle raises a number of puzzles about why we need practical wisdom if we are already good, and why the advice of others wouldn't be just as helpful, as it is with health. As Aristotle puts it, "We wish to be healthy, but still do not learn medicine" (*EN* VI 12 1143b32–3). "We must begin a little further back, starting with this principle. Just as we say that some people who do just things are not yet just, for example, those doing what's prescribed by the laws either unwillingly or through ignorance or for some other reason and not for the sake of the acts themselves (and yet they do what they should and the things which it's necessary for an excellent person to do), so too, so it seems, in order to be good, one must be disposed in a certain way to do each thing, I mean in accordance with rational choice and for the sake of the things done themselves" (*EN* VI 12 1144a12–20). Rational choice cannot be correct without practical wisdom and without ethical virtue (*EN* VI 12 1145a4–5).

---

[32] He also lacks part of the correct syllogism, but a full account of how this works is beyond the scope of this chapter.

On these grounds, then, the actions of an enkratic person would surely not have the same status as those of the good person. What explains the actions of the enkratic person is her *enkrateia*, not her virtue, and it is her *enkrateia* that leads to enkratic, rather than virtuous, action. At the very least she lacks the first part of the minor premiss of the correct syllogism.

A similar objection can be made regarding the people who are learning to be good or who aspire to improve their character. Again, the explanation for any of their behaviour cannot be their ethical virtue as they do not already have it. They may aspire to be virtuous and to use the practical syllogism, but will not actually be using it until they have improved their characters. In the following chapter, I shall give a more detailed account of the Aristotelian learner.

6. ADVANTAGES OF ARISTOTLE'S ACCOUNT

In formulating Aristotle's practical syllogism, I have emphasized the first part of the minor premiss, contrary to previous commentators. There are several advantages in taking the first part of the minor premiss seriously. First, if, as I have argued, the agent's virtue plays an important explanatory and justificatory role in practical reasoning, Aristotelian virtue cannot be peeled away from his account without missing a vital component.

Second, the fact that the agent must be a certain kind of person and apply the general knowledge that comes with being such a person to herself shows how the practical syllogism can be practical. In order to act, the agent must be a certain kind of person and apply her know-how to herself, here and now. A practical syllogism with all general terms could not be practical, and it is no small achievement on Aristotle's part to grasp this point.[33]

Finally, the minor premiss of Aristotle's practical syllogism shows how and why one cannot have practical wisdom without ethical virtue

---

[33] In the twentieth century, much work has been done on the related, though slightly different, problem of the indexical "I" in action. See, e.g., Perry 1979.

and vice versa (*EN* X 1178a16–17 cf. *EN* VI 13 1144b30–1145a2), completing and complementing the argument of Chapter 5. Anscombe was therefore wrong to say that "the practical syllogism as such is not an ethical topic" but right to claim that "'[p]ractical reasoning' or 'practical syllogism', which means the same thing, was one of Aristotle's best discoveries".[34] The practical syllogism is an essential part of Aristotle's ethic of virtue.

[34] Anscombe 1957, 78, 57–8.

9 What the Good Person Has to Know

As part of the longer argument towards the conclusion that ethical virtue is central in Aristotle's *Nicomachean Ethics*, in the previous chapter
and in Chapter 5, I argued that ethical virtue requires practical wisdom
and conversely in two different ways. In Chapter 5, I explained how
ethical virtue involves reason (practical wisdom) as opposed to being
merely in accordance with reason, and in Chapter 8, I explained how the
practical syllogism that the person with practical wisdom gets right,
involves the virtues of character. However, the aspects of practical wisdom I have discussed so far have been fairly minimal, so one might
think that the person with practical wisdom needs to know a lot more
than what I have so far discussed. Therefore, in this chapter, I raise
some puzzles about what, or how much, the Aristotelian good person
has to know, and what the good student needs to know in order to
study ethics.[1] The answers have far-reaching consequences for the way
in which we should read Aristotle's own *Nicomachean Ethics*, as well as
for the appropriate way to address the immoralist.

It is uncontroversial that Aristotle thinks that knowledge is
insufficient for ethical virtue (e.g., *EN* II 1105b1–5, 12–18 cf. X 9
1179b4–10). Reading a book is no substitute for engaging in virtuous
action. However, it is unclear what knowledge, if any, is necessary for
being a good person, according to Aristotle. On the one hand, there
are philosophers, like David Wiggins, who think that the good person can grasp the situation at hand and do the right thing without

---

[1] I am using the word "knowledge" in its colloquial sense, not in Aristotle's
technical sense according to which one can only know necessary truths.

any knowledge of general principles or of other disciplines.[2] On the other hand, there are those, like Ross, who think that knowledge of general principles is required. In addition, there is a major controversy about whether or not Aristotle's ethics is based on his metaphysics and biology. If it is, must the good person know these disciplines as well?

Aristotle himself exacerbates the problem about what the good person is supposed to know by comparing the good person both to the healthy person and to the physician, because the two analogies suggest conflicting answers to the question of what the good person is supposed to know. The analogy of the good person to the healthy person suggests that the good person does not need to know very much, since one can certainly be in a healthy state without knowing much about health or what kinds of things are healthy. The analogy with the physician suggests the opposite, since one might suppose that it is not possible to be a physician without a good deal of knowledge about health. One might even think that the physician needs to know biology and other scientific disciplines as well. In that case, by analogy, one might suppose that the good person's knowledge is not restricted to the field of ethics. Perhaps he needs to know psychology, biology, and metaphysics too. In this chapter, I aim to disentangle the different respects in which the analogies hold and to explain exactly what they show about what the good person does and does not have to know.

1. THE GOOD PERSON AND THE HEALTHY PERSON

I begin with the analogy between the good person and the healthy person. This analogy appears in two places. In *Nicomachean Ethics* III, the good person is said to be the measure of goods, the true objects of wish, just as the healthy person is the measure of what is healthy, bitter, sweet, hot, heavy, and so on (*EN* III 4 1113a25–33). In Book X, the good person is said to be the measure of what is really pleasurable, just as the healthy and vigorous person is the measure of what is sweet, hot, and the

---

[2] Wiggins 1975–6.

like (*EN* X 5 1176a10–16).[3] The analogy is striking because it suggests that the good person has an intuitive sense of what is good and pleasant, which the bad person lacks. This suggestion may appear bolstered by Aristotle's comment that we should pay attention to "the undemonstrated remarks of experienced and older people or of intelligent people, no less than to demonstrations. For these people see correctly *because experience has given them their eye*" (*EN* VI 11 1143b11–14, my emphasis).[4]

It is, of course, a legacy of Hume that perceptual analogies in ethics are taken to herald a non-intellectualist or anti-rational picture of ethical deliberation. Not all of Hume's contemporaries shared his view, and Aristotle makes it plain that this is not how we are to take the analogy above. First, the analogy is meant to recall Protagoras's dictum that man, that is, each individual human being, is the measure of all things and to make the anti-Protagorean point that it is not just anybody but only the good person who is the measure of goods and pleasures. Second, later in Book VI, Aristotle points out an important disanalogy between the good person and the healthy person, when addressing the following puzzle: If there is no point in learning medicine if we are already healthy, what is the point of acquiring practical wisdom, the proper form of practical reasoning, if we already have the ethical virtues, the correct dispositions with regard to the emotions? Aristotle's answer, as we have seen in Chapters 5 and 8, is that we cannot have full ethical virtue unless we have practical wisdom. His answer reveals two disanalogies between ethical virtue and health. We can be healthy without learning medicine ourselves, and we can get better, when ill, simply by following the advice of a physician. By contrast, according to Aristotle, we cannot be good unless we have practical wisdom, and we cannot become good except by gaining practical wisdom ourselves. The analogy between the good person and the healthy person does not show that the good person needs as little knowledge of goodness as the healthy person needs knowledge of health. How much the good person needs to know, of course, depends on what exactly practical wisdom consists in, so I now turn to Aristotle's analogy between the good person and the physician.

---

[3] For present purposes, I am restricting my discussion to the *Nicomachean Ethics*, but Aristotle's *Eudemian Ethics* contains medical analogies as well.

[4] Translations are by Irwin 1985.

2. THE GOOD PERSON AND THE PHYSICIAN

At first sight, the analogy between the good person and the physician suggests that practical wisdom is analogous to medicine, in which case it might be thought that Aristotle is expecting the good person to have a great deal of knowledge. However, Aristotle's first mention of the physician comes among Aristotle's arguments against Plato's form of the good, and concerns what the physician does *not* need to know. "For what the doctor appears to consider is not even health [universally, let alone good universally], but human beings' health, and even more than that, presumably, this human being's health, since it is particular patients he treats" (*EN* I 6 1097a11–13). Clearly, Aristotle is arguing that the physician does not need to know Platonic metaphysics to be a good physician. He does not need to know Plato's form of the good. Nor does he need to know the universal health. He does not need to know what is healthy for all creatures. As Aristotle says elsewhere, "if there is no one medical science about all beings, there is no one science about the good of all animals, but a different science about each specific good" (*EN* VI 7 1141a31–3). In other words, physicians do not need to be veterinarians.

Does the physician need to know what is healthy for human beings in general? Aristotle later explains how individual moral education is best, "Moreover, education adapted to an individual is actually better than a common education for everyone, just as individualized medical treatment is better. For though generally a feverish patient benefits from rest and starvation, presumably some patient does not; nor does the boxing instructor impose the same way of fighting on everyone. Hence it seems that treatment in particular cases is more exactly right when each person gets special attention, since he then more often gets suitable treatment" (*EN* X 9 1180b7–13). The passage appears to support the interpretation of those who think that Aristotelian practical wisdom is only concerned with particulars, but Aristotle continues as follows: "Nonetheless," he says, "a doctor, a gymnastics trainer and everyone else will give the best individual attention if they also know what is universally [good] for all, or for these sorts" (*EN* X 9 1180b13–15). The physician, then, needs to know both what is beneficial for the individual and also what is beneficial for human beings or for human beings of a certain kind. It appears that one cannot have the one kind of knowledge without the other. If the physician does not know what is beneficial in general for human beings, he will not be able to tell what is beneficial for more than one individual, and if he is unable to tell what is beneficial for individuals, he will not be able to understand the more general principles.

So far, then, the analogy with the physician reveals an anti-Platonic strain in Aristotle's thought: the good person or the legislator (and this is one and the same person in Aristotle's preferred city-state), like the physician, has no need for Platonic forms and every need of experience of the particulars. However, Aristotle does not mean to deny that such a person will need knowledge of general principles as well.[5] My next question concerns the grounding of the general principles that such a person knows. Does the physician need to know biology or other sciences, and, if so, does the good person need to know other disciplines too?

3. THE GOOD PERSON AND PSYCHOLOGY

Aristotle writes:

> It is clear that the virtue we must examine is human virtue ... And by human virtue we mean virtue of the soul (*psuchē*) not of the body ... If this is so, then it is clear that the politician must acquire some knowledge about the soul, just as someone setting out to heal the eyes must acquire knowledge about the whole body as well. This is all the more true to the extent that political science is better and more honourable than medicine – and even among doctors the cultivated ones devote a lot of effort to acquiring knowledge about the body. Hence the politician as well must study the soul. (*EN* I 13 1102a13–23)[6]

---

[5] As Aristotle himself explains, these universals are only generalizations "for the most part".

[6] Irwin 1985, 30 cf. 1999, 16 translates, "this is all the more true to the extent that ... ". Ross has "and all the more since politics is more prized". What is all the more true, on my interpretation, is that the politician must study the whole soul, even if his primary interest is to educate the citizens in ethical virtue and practical wisdom, the second of which Aristotle describes as "the eye of the soul" (*EN* VI [=*EE* V] 12 1144a30).

Again, assuming that the good person in Aristotle's preferred city-state will take his turn making legislation and hence will also be a politician, these comments suggest that the good person will need to know something about human psychology, although Aristotle hastens to add only "as far as suffices for what he seeks". It is not completely clear how far that is, but perhaps Aristotle's claim that the "politician must acquire knowledge about the soul, just as someone setting out to heal the eyes must acquire knowledge about the whole body as well" shows that the politician cannot confine his sights to the rational part of the soul, but must also take into account those parts of the soul that have an affinity with the capacities of non-human animals and plants. He needs to have some understanding of human needs, capacities, and emotions. Indeed, this is borne out by the discussion of the soul that follows in the text.

At first sight, then, it looks as if the psychology in question need be no more complicated than what now goes by the name of folk psychology and which can be gained by experience and observation. (Indeed, some modern philosophers have complained that Aristotle's work pays too much attention to folk psychology.) But the psychology in question is broader than that, since, for example, the virtues themselves are dispositions of the psyche. Also, since Aristotle analyses the psyche in a different way from his predecessors, Socrates and Plato, as we saw in Chapters 3 and 5, the emotions and reason have different significance. For example, according to Aristotle, reasoning is not sufficient for ethical virtue, since the ethical virtues are dispositions of part of the non-rational part of the soul, and the good person is not someone who merely holds her emotions in check.

If, however, the good person needs to know the various components of human psychology, must he also know such claims as that each virtue is a state of character between two vices, one of excess and the other of deficiency? Thus described, it is unclear whether Aristotle's famous doctrine of the mean is a psychological or meta-ethical doctrine or both. Aristotle's work is often described as "moral psychology", a label that straddles both. Could the good person be a good person without knowing that each virtue is in a mean between two vices, assuming the doctrine of the mean to be true? According to Aristotle, the good person feels and exhibits the right amount of emotion on the right occasions and acts accordingly. On each occasion, it is possible to err in at least two directions, one of excess and one of deficiency. Must the good person know this, in order to be good? If the good person must know that certain actions fall under a particular virtue and others under the corresponding vices (i.e., the general principles I discussed in the previous section), it looks as if the doctrine of the mean must at least be implicit in the good person's understanding, otherwise the good person's judgments about feelings and conduct would surely go awry. For example, as I argued earlier, someone with a dyadic conception of virtue and vice might think that it is always good to be self-effacing or to forgo all pleasures. It appears, then, that the good person's knowledge of psychology is bound up with knowledge of more general Aristotelian ethical theses. Furthermore, it may not be possible to learn these very easily if one does not already live in an Aristotelian good society.

Be that as it may, it looks as if Aristotle's good person does need to know some general principles, some human psychology, and, with it, some more general Aristotelian doctrine – many of the things that are described in theoretical terms in the *Nicomachean Ethics*.

4. THE GOOD PERSON AND METAPHYSICS

I now turn to the question of metaphysics. In his *Nicomachean Ethics*, Aristotle is well aware when his discussion is taking him into realms that are not relevant to the ethical discussion at hand. For example, in the middle of his arguments against Plato, he says, "Presumably, we should leave these questions for now, since their exact treatment is more appropriate (*oikeioteron*) for another [branch] of Philosophy. And the same is true about the Form" (*EN* I 6 1096b30–2). Similarly, at the beginning of his discussion of friendship, Aristotle dismisses the view that like attracts like with the comments:

> On these questions some people inquire at a higher level, more proper to natural science (*phusikōteron*). Euripides says that when earth gets dry it longs passionately for rain, and the holy heaven when filled with rain longs passionately to fall into the earth; and Heracleitus says that the opponent cooperates, the finest harmony arises from discordant elements, and all things come to be in struggle ... Let us leave aside the puzzles proper to natural

science (*ta phusika*), since they are not proper to the present examination; and
let us examine the puzzles that concern human [nature] and bear on characters and feelings. (*EN* VIII 2 1155b1–10)

Here, I am assuming that if Aristotle leaves certain discussions out
of his *Nicomachean Ethics*, *a fortiori* they are not something the good
person needs to know. But one might object that it is other people's
metaphysical views that Aristotle thinks are irrelevant to the subject at
hand. The more difficult question is whether the good person needs to
know any Aristotelian metaphysics. True, Aristotle may not yet have
distinguished a separate discipline of metaphysics or first philosophy at
the time of composing his lectures in ethics, but the question is worth
posing nonetheless.

Aristotle's official distinction between theoretical and practical reasoning suggests that the good person need not know metaphysics.
Theoretical reasoning, according to Aristotle, concerns things that cannot be otherwise and necessary truths, whereas practical reasoning concerns contingent matters. Their subject matter does not overlap. At first
sight, Aristotle's own *Nicomachean Ethics* appears to be a counterexample
to Aristotle's own distinction, for it appears to contain nothing but theoretical discussion of practical matters, happiness, and the virtuous life.[7]
However, Aristotle says that his *Nicomachean Ethics* "does not aim, as our
other [inquirie]s do, at study; for the purpose of our examination is not
to know what virtue is, but to become good, since otherwise the inquiry
would be of no benefit to us" (*EN* II 2 1103b26–9 cf. I 3 1095a5–6
"the aim is not knowledge (*gnōsis*) but action (*praxis*)"). This suggests
that the work falls under the intellectual virtue of *practical* wisdom
(*phronēsis*), the intellectual virtue of the good person, since that is the
only intellectual virtue whose goal is (good) action. But many arguments
in the *Nicomachean Ethics* undoubtedly rely on Aristotelian metaphysical notions, for example, those of goal (*telos*), function (*ergon*), activity
(*energeia*), and process (*kinēsis*). Also, as we have seen, the very analogies
between the good person and the healthy person and between the good
person and the physician, which Aristotle presents in the *Nicomachean
Ethics*, are intended to locate Aristotelian metaphysics between that of

---

[7] For an attempt to blur the distinction between practical wisdom and wisdom,
see Winter 1997.

Plato and Protagoras; Platonic forms and the Protagorean standpoint are equally objectionable.

To make use of Aristotle's medical analogy, if one compares Aristotle's *Nicomachean Ethics* with a Hippocratic treatise, one will note that the Hippocratic treatises contain descriptions of different healthy and unhealthy states, just as Aristotle's treatises contain descriptions of the virtues and vices and other conditions, but also contain a slew of Pre-Socratic metaphysics involving the elements, humours, mixtures, and the like. Must physicians and legislators be metaphysicians?

Significantly, Aristotle himself does not seem to consider the Pre-Socratic metaphysics essential to the physician's method, since he discards the former while keeping the latter. He retains the doctrine of the mean, while discarding its Anaxagorean basis in mixtures of certain proportions. I shall not assume that Aristotle's own metaphysics can be discarded so easily. Instead, I wish to draw a distinction between what the good person's knowledge may ultimately be based on, and what the good person has to know. An analogy may be in order. In his *Posterior Analytics*, Aristotle explains how one science may be handmaiden to another without the practitioners of the first science knowing the second science. This is also true, he says, of sciences that are related but do not fall under one another. Aristotle's example, aptly, involves medicine: "it is for the physician to know that circular wounds heal more slowly and the geometer to know the reason why" (*A Post.* I 13 79a14–16). In other words, the physician needs to know that circular wounds heal more slowly so that he can give patients who have these wounds special treatment. A geometer, however, would be able to explain, presumably using a theorem, why circular wounds heal more slowly, but the physician does not need to know the theorem himself. Geometry and medicine are separate disciplines. Similarly, I think, *even if* the good person's knowledge is ultimately based on or related to Aristotelian metaphysics, it is unclear why the good person would have to be a metaphysician to be good, any more than the physician would have to be a geometer.

Aristotle's comment in his *Posterior Analytics* is consistent with his practice in the *Nicomachean Ethics*. Although Aristotle makes use of metaphysical conclusions from his own philosophy, he does not provide an extensive explanation of them in the *Nicomachean Ethics*. Some examples may be useful. First, in the famous function (*ergon*) argument of Book I, Aristotle very peremptorily introduces the idea that human beings have a function, and then goes from there. Second, in discussing pleasure, Aristotle makes use of his distinction between activity (*energeia*) and process (*kinēsis*) but does not provide arguments that it is correct. To complete the analogy, just as the physician needs to know that circular wounds heal more slowly but does not need a complete account of a circle and its geometrical properties that make that the case, so the good person may need to know, at least implicitly, that the virtues make people function well but not need to know a complete account of what a function is or how it relates to Aristotelian substance and essence. As Aristotle explains himself at the end of the argument from function, the degree of precision must fit the subject matter. The carpenter and geometer do not study the right-angle in the same way. The carpenter is interested in the right-angle's usefulness for his work, whereas the geometer is interested in what or in what sort of thing a right-angle is (*EN* I 7 1098a29–31). By analogy, the metaphysician and the ethicist may both be interested in human beings, but the metaphysician will be interested in what they are in relation to the first principles of metaphysics. If the good person knows anything of metaphysics, it need only be by induction and analogy, and not by demonstration. Hence, a further distinction between theoretical reasoning, which, according to Aristotle, relies on demonstration, and practical reasoning, which does not.[8]

Therefore, while Aristotle's analogy between the good person and healthy person is not supposed to show that the good person has no general knowledge at all, the analogy between the good person and the physician is not supposed to show that the good person needs to know Platonic or Aristotelian metaphysics.

5. THE GOOD PERSON AND THE GOOD STUDENT

I have so far been addressing the question of how much or what Aristotle's good person has to know. I should now like to see what light my answer throws on the related question of how much one needs to

---

[8] Here again, I am opposing the view of Winter 1997.

know in order to be a good student of Ethics, and what it is that the student will learn from reading the *Nicomachean Ethics*.

The question about the good student appears towards the end of a puzzling and controversial passage in Book I of the *Nicomachean Ethics*. At the beginning of the passage, Aristotle explains that we do not need to consider all the opinions, only sensible ones. Next, he notes that Plato was rightly puzzled about where to start because there are arguments to and from origins (*archai* – the Greek term covers first principles and starting-points) just as a race can be run from the starting line to the judges or the other way round. He then says that we must begin "from what is familiar", but that is ambiguous, meaning both "what is known to us" and "what is known without qualification". We need to begin from "what is known to us", Aristotle says, "This is why we need to have been brought up in fine habits if we are to be adequate students of what is fine and just, and of political questions generally. For the origin we begin from is the belief that something is the case, and if this is apparent enough to us we will not need the reason why it is true in addition; and if we have this good upbringing, we have the origins to begin from, or can easily acquire them" (*EN* I 4 1095b4–8).

The passage raises several problems. If the very beginning of the passage goes with the later part, why do we need to be well brought up to consider those opinions that have something to be said for them? Why can't anyone profitably study the ethical views that are current and/or those that have something to be said for them? Second, if "what is known to us" plays the role of the origin at one end of the stadium, we should expect that Aristotle is moving towards "what is known without qualification" as the origin at the other end of the stadium. But Aristotle says that the student does not need the reason why. Irwin accordingly amends the text to say that the student does not yet need the explanation.[9] True, Aristotle might be suggesting that we start and end at the same place, after a whole lap of the stadium, but the question still remains whether we gain anything new by making the whole lap, or whether we need to make the whole lap to grasp what we already knew. Third, Aristotle does not explain here which beliefs he has in mind and

---

[9] Irwin 1985, 6. Cf. Irwin 1999, 4, "if this is apparent enough to us, we can begin without also [knowing] why [it is true]".

what counts as the reason why. As Ackrill notes, "The contrast between fact and reason can of course be drawn at different levels".[10] Nor does Aristotle spell out what the origins are that the student has or can easily acquire.

It seems that if Aristotle's good student is the ethically virtuous person I have been describing, the beliefs he starts from cannot be ones of the form "this is the generous thing to do now", since, according to Aristotle, the good practical reasoner will know the reason why this is true, for example, that, for the most part, it is a good idea to be generous to one's friends. As we shall see, it is not clear that she could know that this is the generous thing to do now, as opposed to merely, "this looks like a nice thing to do", if she did not already have some general understanding.[11] If the beliefs in question are of a higher order – such as that generous people do not give away too much or too little money, an instance of the doctrine of the mean, then it is clear how the good person has or can easily acquire the origins, the psychological and ethical claims I discussed earlier on. Such a person does not need the reason why if this is a long rigmarole in metaphysics. On this account, then, Irwin does not need to add the phrase "at this stage" to the passage in question. Indeed, it would put the passage at odds with another passage a little further on in the same book where Aristotle comments, "Nor should we make the same demand for an explanation in all cases. Rather, in some cases it is enough to prove that something is true without explaining why it is true. This is so, e.g., with origins, where the fact that something is true is the first principle, i.e., the origin" (EN I 7 1098a34–b3).

Now, let us suppose that the good student is not the same as the ethically virtuous person but is reasonably well socialized. In that case, such a person might have some of the opinions about happiness that Aristotle mentions, for example, that it is a life of physical gratification or a life of fame and fortune. These origins would be one step removed from the virtuous person's so that learning the true nature of happiness would be an explanation for these people. It would be an explanation in a rather special sense, however, because the original views would not be ratified, but they would be shown to be false. However, Aristotle does

[10] Ackrill 1973, 242.

[11] Therefore Burnyeat's account of "the that" is too limited (Burnyeat 1980).

sometimes use the phrase "x to someone", as opposed to "x without qualification", for views that are false. For example, in his discussion of the Triballi he says "it is in some places honourable to sacrifice one's father, e.g., among the Triballi, whereas, without qualification, it is not honourable" (*Top.* II 12 115b22–4). In the Ethics, what is good to and for the good person is good without qualification. Perhaps it is also what is known without qualification in the present context.

I think that my account of what the good person has to know allows for the two possibilities described above. But these are not the only possibilities, and I should like to rule out some others.

5.1. The Ethically Virtuous Person versus the Person with Practical Wisdom?

It might be thought that the ethically virtuous person is the student, and the person with practical wisdom is the person who emerges from reading the *Nicomachean Ethics*. The author of the *Magna Moralia* gives the clearest account of such a two-stage process of moral education. He argues that first come the non-rational impulses in children, then comes the approval of practical wisdom. "It is not reason which is the origin (*archē*) of virtue, but the emotions. For first of all there must arise (as does arise) a non-rational impulse (*hormē*) towards the fine, and then reason must give its vote and verdict. This is seen in the case of children and other non-rational beings. For in these, [presumably, children] there are at first non-rational impulses of the emotions towards the fine, but later reason supervenes and by its approving vote makes them do fine actions" (*MM* II 3 1206b20–6). Since Aristotle defines ethical virtue as a state of the non-rational part of the soul relating to the emotions, the author of the *Magna Moralia* therefore seems to be suggesting that one can have ethical virtue first and then later gain the intellectual ability to go with it.

There are several problems with this idea. First, as we saw in Chapter 5, Aristotle explains that it is impossible to have ethical virtue fully without having practical wisdom (*EN* VI 13 1144b30–2). So it is impossible to have one's emotions in completely good order before one has the accompanying intellectual understanding of what one is doing. Second, in Book I itself, Aristotle says that youngsters and immature people are unsuitable students for Ethics, precisely because they are guided by their emotions and not by their reason (*EN* I 3 1095a2–9).

Therefore, if the Aristotelian student has ethical virtue, then he must at the same time have the practical wisdom that goes with it. Indeed, this supports the plausible view that successful Aristotelian habituation, as a way of becoming virtuous, is not a matter of merely repeating actions over and over again, a method that would be useless even for learning to ride a bicycle or playing the piano, but is a matter of paying attention to what one is doing, making improvements, and developing one's mental ability at the same time.[12] If that is so, there is no point where one has ethical virtue without any practical reasoning; the two develop hand in hand.

5.2. A More Sophisticated Two-stage Account

In his influential paper, "Aristotle on Learning to be Good", Myles Burnyeat draws attention to the way in which "morality comes in a series of stages with both cognitive and emotional dimensions",[13] but he still accepts a two-stage view, arguing that the Aristotelian learner may be brought up to enjoy performing good actions, but not yet understand the connection between what he is doing and happiness. Burnyeat denies that there are any general principles to be had on Aristotle's account, so "the fact" is simply which particular actions are fine and just. The reason "why" is the specification of happiness, to be provided by Aristotle's lectures. Burnyeat says, "The answer to Plato's question is that at this stage Aristotle is travelling dialectically toward a first principle or starting-point, namely, the specification of happiness, but in another sense his own inquiry must have its own starting points to proceed from".[14]

If the parallel between ethics and medicine holds good, there is no stage of enjoying the correct actions for their own sake independently of understanding why they are good in a more general way and having an implicit view of the kind of life they provide. Furthermore, if practical

[12] See too Sherman 1989.
[13] Burnyeat 1980, 70–1.
[14] Burnyeat 1980, 71.

wisdom requires a full specification of happiness, and full ethical virtue requires practical wisdom, as Aristotle says, it is not clear why Aristotle thinks that the explanation is not needed. Yet Burnyeat, unlike Irwin, does not amend the text. In addition, Burnyeat has to take "the that" of my second passage only to refer to happiness.

5.3. The Good Person versus the Ruler

On this account, there is a division of labour; the average good person does not need to know any metaphysics (or, depending on the exact version of the argument, any psychology etc.), but the ruler does, and Aristotle is addressing someone who has "the fact" of the ordinary good person, but not "the why" necessary for the ruler. It is certainly true that Aristotle says in the *Nicomachean Ethics* VIII 10, in the context of friendship and family life, that the best form of government is monarchy, which certainly would result in a very sharp division of labour between ruler and ruled, but in *EN* VI he describes the sort of intellectual virtues required in the more democratic society of Athens.[15] In the *Politics*, Aristotle's preferred system of government is Polity, where adult citizens are the rulers. In such a society, everyone would need to know as much as everyone else, to be good. There are no philosopher-kings as there are in Plato's *Republic*.

6. READING THE *NICOMACHEAN ETHICS*: THE GOOD PERSON AND THE IMMORALIST

As I have argued above, the good person is someone who knows what sorts of actions are generous, brave, magnanimous, and so on, and who has an implicit grasp of the doctrine of the mean and human psychology.[16] Accordingly, there are two possible sets of readers for Aristotle's *Nicomachean Ethics*: those who are socialized to a certain extent but have the wrong priorities, and those who are already good. Yet, Aristotle

---

[15] See Ch. 10.

[16] My general conclusion is similar to Burnet 1900, 17 and McDowell 1996, although I disagree with McDowell's account of "external ratification".

elsewhere sounds pessimistic about whether those with the wrong priorities can be swayed by rational argument (e.g., *EN* X 9). Therefore, modern commentators have often argued that Aristotle, unlike Plato, for example, has nothing to say to the immoralist. On the other hand, if the readers are already fully good and have practical wisdom, it may appear puzzling what they will gain from reading the *Nicomachean Ethics*. Aristotle's *Nicomachean Ethics* may appear to be a treatise without any suitable readers.

Not so. Aristotle's *Nicomachean Ethics* can be useful for the good person. Taking the parallel between ethics and medicine seriously, it is clear that the *Nicomachean Ethics* is to ethics what a Hippocratic treatise is to medicine. It is a theoretical presentation of the practical wisdom of the good person. It is not going to give the good person any new information; rather it usefully displays what he knows in perspicuous form.

If the good person can understand the *Nicomachean Ethics* because he already has some grasp of what it contains, it may now be even less clear how Aristotle can address an immoralist, someone who has been brought up in society but does not see the point in doing anything to benefit his fellow human beings.[17] Plato's *Republic*, on this view, is far superior. Socrates addresses Thrasymachus's contention that the just person is better off than the unjust person, and explains exactly how being just will always lead to a happier life than being unjust. While the interpretation of Plato's *Republic* remains controversial, certain aspects of the dialogue are not in doubt. For example, it is uncontroversial that in Plato's taxonomy of characters, based on his analysis of the human psyche, Thrasymachus has the psychological profile of a person not suited for a happy life, as well as the priorities of someone who has an immature view of what happiness really is. It is highly unlikely that Plato's analysis would persuade a Thrasymachean reader to alter his ways, even if Plato's analysis shows, to the non-Thrasymachean reader, what happens to one's psyche if one takes the Thrasymachean route. In this respect, Aristotle's analysis is no worse off than Plato's. In his taxonomy of mentalities developed in the doctrine of the mean, Aristotle

---

[17] Here, I am assuming that the arch-immoralist in Greek philosophy, Thrasymachus, has at least been socialized, but has the wrong priorities. Not even Plato is addressing a Cyclops, on which see Ch. 10.

shows clearly the unwelcome aspects of the Thrasymachean view of life. Thrasymachus may not appear as a protagonist in the *Nicomachean Ethics*, but the kind of person he represents is hardly presented in a favourable light.

In his *Metaphysics* IV, Aristotle argues that the principle of non-contradiction is an incontrovertible first principle. In explaining how the principle is necessary for rationality and for understanding the world in which we live, he is not going to persuade someone who is irrational, but that does not detract from the argument that shows what a rational person would be giving up if such a person gave up the principle. Similarly, even if Aristotle's account of the good person and the happy life is not guaranteed to persuade Thrasymachus himself, and Aristotle plausibly concedes that arguments alone are not going to do the trick, it does make clear why a human being should reject the Thrasymachean way of life, and that is the best that philosophical argumentation can do.

7. ARISTOTELIAN KNOWLEDGE

To conclude, the analogy between the good person and the healthy person is not supposed to show that the good person is merely instinctively good without any knowledge, for one cannot be good, according to Aristotle, unless one has practical wisdom, and practical wisdom involves some general knowledge, as I argued in Chapters 5 and 8. Nor is the analogy between the legislator and the physician supposed to show that the good person must know as much as Plato's guardians. Aristotelian knowledge is in a mean between merely instinctive knowledge and knowledge of metaphysics. I argued that experience and knowledge of particulars are important, as well as some human psychology and, at least implicitly, some more general theses like the doctrine of the mean. I also argued that even if the good person's knowledge is ultimately based on and uses conclusions from Aristotelian metaphysics, the good person need not be a metaphysician to be good, any more than a physician need be a geometer.

According to Aristotle, medicine, not mathematics, is the appropriate analogue to ethics. The *Nicomachean Ethics* is useful, even for the person who already has ethical virtue and practical wisdom, because it is to ethics as a Hippocratic treatise describing different medical conditions and the like is to medicine. It is also useful, given the taxonomy of different mentalities implicit in the third aspect of the doctrine of the mean, in showing what is wrong with the immoralist's life. Finally, Aristotle's use of medical analogies allows him to stake out a position between Protagoras and Plato, and hence between the early Utilitarians and Kant.[18] Aristotle is firmly in the tradition of virtue ethics.

According to Aristotle, however, a human being will be unable to attain the knowledge and emotional experience to become good, or, for that matter, bad, outside society. We saw the importance of friendship at the end of Chapter 7, and the way in which only good human beings can be true friends, but it is the polis that is essential for the development of ethical virtues. We are now in a position to understand how the various strands in Aristotle's ethic of virtue contribute in different and sometimes surprising ways to Aristotle's account of the best polis and the happy life. Chapter 10 addresses some long-standing puzzles in Aristotelian scholarship and weaves together the many threads of the previous chapters.

[18] On Kant's preference for Plato over Aristotle, see *KrV*, 311, where a view like Aristotle's is described as an "ambiguous monstrosity". Thanks to Christine Hendricks for the reference.

10   A Polis for Aristotle's Virtues

Aristotle's *Nicomachean Ethics* starts and ends with political concerns. At the beginning of his work, Aristotle says that the inquiry he is about to begin is a "sort of politics"; and at the end of the work, he suggests that the reader should complete the study of the humanities by studying different political systems. According to Aristotle, the political or social setting is crucial for the virtue and happiness of the citizens. In this chapter, then, I turn to the *Politics*, but my discussion, both of the polis and of Aristotelian happiness, is everywhere informed by the discussion of Aristotle's ethic of virtue that preceded it.

In previous chapters, I have argued that Aristotle's ethic of virtue is not susceptible to Millian or Kantian interpretations. In this chapter, I argue that Aristotle's view is also antithetical to the social contract tradition of ethics, most notably exemplified by Hobbes.[1] To that end, I explain why the polis is needed and why it is natural, according to Aristotle, and how the genesis and justification for the polis stems from Aristotle's objective view of the good for human beings. I also argue that Aristotle's account of the polis presupposes the non-remedial view of the virtues, as presented in Chapter 3 and explored in subsequent chapters.

I then consider the type of happiness that the polis aims at, according to Aristotle, and the point of the apparent ranking of two types of happiness in the final book of the *Nicomachean Ethics*. This is a crux

[1] Commentators on Aristotle pay particular attention to Hobbes. See Keyt 1991 and Miller 1995. Of course, the social contract tradition begins earlier, including, for example, Glaucon's account in *Republic* II.

in Aristotelian scholarship, and one of the puzzles presented in the introduction, but I approach the debate from a different angle from other commentators, being concerned with a prior puzzle about how the ranking can be consistent with the second aspect of the doctrine of the mean. As I go on to argue, the ranking has a political dimension, and the nameless virtues turn out to be most important in making the ranking.

Finally, I consider the role of justice in the polis, and the type of polis that is most suitable for the Aristotelian virtues, as these were described in earlier chapters. Here, I argue that the defence of such a polis depends on Aristotle's thesis about the unity of the virtues and his doctrine of the mean, two pillars of Aristotle's ethic of virtue.

1. THE NEED FOR A POLIS: A NON-REMEDIAL VIEW

Like Plato before him, Aristotle in his *Politics* argues that the polis develops because human beings are not self-sufficient, or rather because they need others in order to be self-sufficient. As he mentions in the *Nicomachean Ethics*, "By self-sufficient we do not mean what is sufficient for a human being living a solitary life, but for [a human being with] parents, children, wife, friends and fellow-citizens, since a human being is by nature suited to live in a polis (*politikos*)" (*EN* I 7 1097b8–11). According to Aristotle, the first unit of the polis is the household (*Pol.* I 2 1252b10). The children of one household may form new households, and those households together may form a village. Later, members of the village may leave the village and form other villages, and finally the villages together form a polis. Aristotle does not explain why these are the only stages in making a polis and why there could not be more. However, perhaps, again like Plato, he thinks that each stage fits the needs of a different part of the human psyche. An individual's basic needs of nutrition and reproduction are met by the household (a member of the opposite sex is necessary for procreation and the slave tills the land for food), less basic needs are met by the village, and finally the need to exercise reason in politics and the law is met by the polis. If this is true, not only are human beings naturally suited to live in a polis but the polis and its parts are naturally suited for human beings. When

Aristotle says that the polis exists "by nature", then, his aim is not to contrast it with what is artificial.[2] Rather, he means to contrast it with what is contrary to nature, just as, when discussing whether there is such a thing as natural slavery, the contrast is not between what is natural and what is artificial but between what is natural and what is contrary to nature, that is, between what is natural and what would be merely conventional and by force (*Pol.* I 5–6). Aristotle need not be contradicting himself, then, when he talks about the man who first established the polis as the greatest benefactor to human beings.[3] As the polis grows from one household, sends out shoots, and finally flowers into a polis, the founder can play the role of gardener in helping it along.[4]

Aristotle's discussion is an unusual mixture of analysis and genealogy. The household and groups of villages are described as early and more backward forms of community, the first populated by people living like Cyclopes, the one-eyed monsters of Greek myth, the second by Homeric kings. This enables Aristotle to point out that the polis is not to be modelled on the household where the husband rules over wife and slave, otherwise monarchy, a favoured form of rule among contemporary non-Greeks, would be the correct way to run the polis, which it is not. Aristotle nowhere considers that perhaps this shows that the arrangement in the original household was also unsatisfactory.

Be that as it may, Aristotle's polis is a far cry from a Hobbesian community. On Aristotle's account, it is human needs that bring the polis to fruition. According to Hobbes, it is fear that ultimately makes people want to leave the "solitary, poor, nasty, brutish and short" life they have in a state of nature and to agree to an artificial social contract so that they can live together in peace.[5] According to Hobbes, justice, mercy, and the like are contrary to our natural passions. Human beings naturally desire to better one another (the Aristotelian vice of injustice or greed, *pleonexia*), and fear and glory are overwhelming sources

---

[2] Aristotle's discussion of natural versus artificial objects in the *Physics* (*Ph.* II 1–2 and 8) is therefore beside the point here.

[3] For an influential statement of the view that this poses a contradiction at the very root of Aristotle's *Politics*, see Keyt 1991 esp. 118–120.

[4] For this view of the founder, see also Stalley's introduction in Barker 1995, xi and Kraut 2002, 245.

[5] Hobbes *Leviathan* I 13.

of motivation. In the state of nature, these desires have full reign. Any impingement on these desires must be contrary to nature, rather than in accordance with it. Where Aristotle argues that human beings' use of language and their ability to describe actions as just and unjust show that they are more political or social than bees, Hobbes uses the same considerations to argue that human beings are not naturally social animals like bees at all.[6]

Despite these differences, one might wonder whether Aristotle agrees with Hobbes that without the polis the kind of desires Hobbes describes will be exacerbated. It is tempting to think that human beings have natural defects that, according to Aristotle, the polis serves to correct. As Aristotle says, the polis is not just for living but for living well. However, just as it is a mistake to think of the virtues as remedial, as I argue in Chapter 3, so it is a mistake to think of the polis as remedying bad aspects of human nature. The person outside a polis, that is, someone who has never been touched by life in a society and can survive outside it, will be a beast or a god, according to Aristotle. As he explains elsewhere, a beast has neither virtue nor vice and neither does a god, but a beast's vice is outside the limits of ordinary vice, and a god's virtue is heroic (*EN* VII 1, 5). Neither human virtue nor human vice are possible without the polis. The polis enables humans to be both virtuous and vicious. Its aim is not to remedy pre-existing defects but to allow virtue and vice to develop. From Aristotle's standpoint, then, the whole project of basing society on an initial social contract in the way attempted by Hobbes looks misguided, for there is no-one outside the polis who could agree to such a contract except beasts and gods, none of whom can provide suitable models for the human beings who are to live in the polis itself. As Aristotle says, "a human being is by nature a political animal. He who is without a city, by reason of his own nature and not of some accident, is either base, or better than a human being" (*Pol.* I 2 1253a2–4). Aristotle goes on to quote Homer's description of the Cyclopes, pointing out that a human being who is like that by nature will be eager for war. The polis, according to Aristotle, is a peculiarly human institution, and so basing it on the motivation of the Cyclopes, as does Hobbes, is out of place.

[6] Hobbes *Leviathan* II, ch. 42.

Aristotle says that while the city comes into existence for the sake of mere life, it exists for the sake of living well (*Pol.* I 2 1252b29–30). The correct types of constitutions, according to Aristotle, have real happiness as their goal, the perverted types do not aim at the happiness of the citizens. According to Aristotle, everyone agrees that happiness is living well, but they disagree about what happiness consists in (*EN* I 4 1095a18–20). It is important, then, to find out what happiness really is, so that the legislators may arrange the polis accordingly.

2. A POLITICAL RANKING OF HAPPY LIVES, AND THE NAMELESS VIRTUES

At the beginning of his *Nicomachean Ethics*, Aristotle presented an argument to show that happiness is the activity of the rational part of the soul in accordance with virtue. Since there are two main virtues of the rational part of the soul, practical wisdom and wisdom, and the former requires and is required by the ethical virtues, the question remains whether the happy life: (a) involves the exercise of all the virtues; (b) involves the exercise of wisdom alone; or (c) involves the exercise of practical wisdom and the ethical virtues alone.[7] In the final book of the Ethics, Aristotle appears to be trying to rank these alternatives. On the face of it, he ranks (b) in first place, with the proviso that it would be impossible for a human being to live such a life without exercising practical wisdom and the ethical virtues to be found in (c), and (c) in second place, but the discussion goes back and forth, allowing puzzled commentators to attribute every possible combination to Aristotle as his number one choice, and to give different answers to the question whether Book X is consistent with Book I.[8]

---

[7] Some think that the question is already settled in Book I, but there still remains major disagreement about how it is settled, and whether the conclusion conflicts with the discussion in Book X. For example, Ackrill 1974 argues in favour of (a) in Book I but not in Book X.

[8] For example, Gauthier and Jolif 1958, Irwin e.g., 1985a, Devereux 1981, Keyt 1983, Whiting 1986, Cooper 1987, and Roche 1988 think that (a) holds in Books I and X. Cooper 1975, Kenny 1978, Kraut 1989, and Reeve 1992 think that (b) holds throughout. Others, for example, N. White 1988,

Aristotle's discussion is puzzling for many reasons, some of which I have already discussed in Chapter 3, but there is a prior problem concerning the whole project of ranking happy lives. First, a ranking of types of happiness makes no sense in terms of Aristotle's arguments about happiness in Book I. If there is something more choiceworthy than x, then x cannot be *happiness*, but if there is such a thing as *happiness* mark two, there can be something more choiceworthy than itself. Second, the whole project of ranking happy lives goes against the grain of Aristotle's own doctrine of the mean. If happiness is doing well, and what counts as doing well depends on one's particular circumstances and what is called for at the time, it makes no sense to give a ranking of happy lives in the abstract. What counts as a happy life depends on the particular human being who is living it, her particular abilities, and the very particular circumstances encountered in her life. Ranking happiness in the abstract, then, seems out of place. While a philosophical life might suit one person, it might be inappropriate for another, and so on. To find out the point of Aristotle's ranking, we must turn to Book VII of Aristotle's *Politics*.

Aristotle takes it as agreed that what happiness is for the city is the same as what it is for the individual. Someone who thinks that the happiness of an individual consists in wealth will think that the city as a whole is happy when it is wealthy. Similarly, those who rank the life of the tyrant as happy will rank the city with the largest empire as happy also (*Pol.* VII 2 1324a10–13). Thus, to rank types of happiness is not to rank the quality of individual lives as much as it is to rank the priorities that should govern the society in which individuals live. Those who rank the tyrant and empire-building life best will be making their first priority war. Aristotle is especially scathing about the Spartan way

Broadie 1991, and Lawrence 1997 argue that happiness is the *focus* of the best life, but the focal interpretation by itself does not solve the controversy, because one can dispute whether that focus contains one or more goods. N. White 1988 argues that the focus is simply contemplation. Lawrence 1997, 73 argues that the focus has more than one component. Kraut 1989 and Curzer 1991 think that the happy life aims at contemplation but includes ethical activity too. Richardson Lear 2004 argues that while contemplation is the final end, virtuous action is important and choiceworthy because it mimics contemplation.

of life. While the Spartan system was geared to war, it failed to prepare its citizenry for the aftermath of peace. In discussing the political versus contemplative life, Aristotle uses the parallel between the happiness of the individual and the happiness of the polis, to dispel objections to each (*Pol.* VII 3). Aristotle points out that not all political rule need be despotic, so objections to the political way of life from those who do not distinguish ruling freemen and ruling slaves fall to the ground. Similarly, objections to the contemplative life based on objections to a solitary life of inaction fall to the ground when the contemplative life is seen to be active, as is a solitary city when one looks at its inner life (*Pol.* VII 3). Aristotle concludes that one must be able to engage in work and war, and, even more, in leisure (time for study) and peace, so the legislator should not plan exclusively for war. While practical reasoning is necessary at all times, theoretical reasoning requires leisure, according to Aristotle.

The priorities of peace over war, ruling freemen over ruling despotically, being able to do fine acts over being able to do merely useful acts are for the legislator to implement via education. On this account, then, there is no clash with the doctrine of the mean. What counts as a happy life for a particular individual still depends on her particular circumstances and abilities, but Aristotle's ranking is first and foremost for the legislator who is arranging the city and its education to make a happy life for the citizens (*Pol.* VII 15 1333b27). If peace takes priority over war, the peace-time nameless virtues should also take priority in the "happy polis". The point is not that the virtues are remedial, but that while courage may be "more familiar to us", it is the nameless virtues that we need more.

3. JUSTICE IN THE POLIS

Given the non-remedial account of the polis, a bad polis can still be a polis. If that is the case, one might wonder whether the Aristotelian virtues are merely relative to the polis. Indeed, Aristotle sometimes talks as if this is so. For example, in discussing the appropriate qualifications for office, he says that what is needed is "virtue and justice, in relation to the political system (*politeia*). If what is just is not the same in all political systems, there must also be a difference in the quality of justice" (*Pol.* V 9 1309a36–9).[9] In Book V of the *Nicomachean Ethics*, Aristotle describes different types of distributive justice as if they are all equally correct. Nevertheless, Aristotle is also clear that there is such a thing as natural justice so that "the things that are just by human [enactment] and not by nature are not the same everywhere, since political systems are not [the same everywhere]; still, only one political system is by nature the best everywhere" (*EN* V 7 1135a3–5). Here, he draws an analogy with measures for wine and corn, which are larger in wholesale markets than in retail ones. The analogy is not quite exact, since there is nothing wrong with retail markets *vis-à-vis* wholesale ones, but presumably Aristotle's point is that a sub-optimal political system may still have laws that count as just relative to that system if they are suitable for the (sub-optimal) conditions of the polis. In that case, someone whose character accords with the laws will have the best character he can have in that situation. What is less clear is whether someone can count as just who has been brought up in accordance with a city whose laws cannot be justified by a sub-optimal situation, for example, a tyranny. Presumably, the just human being will work under the current laws while she tries to get new laws enacted for the better.[10] Aristotle certainly seems to envisage incremental change as the correct procedure to follow, as is clear from his discussion of how to bolster and improve different political systems in *Politics* V. In any case, natural justice – the justice enshrined in the laws of the very best state – would appear to be the standard that the good human being in any state should be working towards. The ethical virtue of equity would also appear to be especially important in an Aristotelian state, since, even in the best state, the laws may not exactly fit what is really just (*EN* V 10).

---

[9] In the *Politics*, "justice" usually covers the whole of virtue, as reflected in the laws of a just state. In the *Nicomachean Ethics*, this sort of justice is distinguished from particular justice, which is itself divided into rectificatory and distributive justice (*EN* V 1–4).

[10] More controversially, Richard Kraut interprets Aristotle's claim that the *good citizen* must preserve his state to mean that it is incumbent on the good citizen of any particular defective state to preserve the state by improving it and moderating its defects (Kraut 2002, 370–1).

4. A POLIS FOR THE ARISTOTELIAN VIRTUES

In his *Nicomachean Ethics*, Aristotle's ranking of different types of political system comes in the midst of a discussion of friendship, where Aristotle is explaining how every kind of community has some sort of justice and some sort of friendship at the same time (*EN* VIII 9–10). According to Aristotle, there are three correct types of political system: monarchy, aristocracy, and timocracy or polity; and three deviations: tyranny, oligarchy, and democracy. In the correct political systems, the rulers look out for the interest of their subjects; in the worst ones, they only look out for themselves. Aristotle says that the best type of system is monarchy. However, that is not his last word on the matter. In the very next chapter, Aristotle matches the different political systems with family relationships, noting that friendship appears in each of the political systems to the extent that justice appears too. Here, while the good king's friendship to his people is like a shepherd to his flock, polity is like the friendship of brothers; the citizens are equal and have the virtue of equity, taking turns ruling on equal terms. Democracy, Aristotle concludes, is the least bad of the deviations because the people are equal and have much in common. If this is a reason to prefer democracy over tyranny, it should also be a reason to prefer polity to monarchy. In addition, Aristotle has already said that friendship with a king is difficult, especially if the king is superior in virtue to his flock (*EN* VIII 7 1159a1). While Aristotle says that monarchy is best, then, there is another strand of his thought that points in a different direction. Indeed, if the virtues of thought that involve deliberation and judgment are important elements in the happy life, a more democratic society would appear to be preferable. As Mark Gifford argues, the virtues of thought of comprehension (*sunesis*) and sympathetic judgment (*gnōmē*), discussed by Aristotle (*EN* VI 10–11), were needed to discharge the civic duties of a member of the Athenian democracy. Comprehension was needed to be a good member of the assembly and council. Sympathetic judgment was required to be a good member of the jury, and even appears in the Athenian jurors' oath, as quoted by Demosthenes and Aristotle.[11] The exercise of such virtues would be very attenuated under a monarchy.

---

[11] Gifford 1995, esp. 58.

Aristotle's discussion in his *Politics* also treads a fine line between monarchy and polity, Aristotle's uncorrupted version of democracy. Even Kelsen 1937–8, who argues most vigorously that Aristotle's main aim is to present the hereditary monarchy of the Macedonians as the ideal political system, notes that Aristotle also wants to present polity as a worthy alternative. Yet, Aristotle's defence of monarchy has a strong proviso. The ruler, or ruling family, has to be of such superior merit that he or they deserve to rule over the others in the city (*Pol.* III 18 1288a15–19). In the previous chapter, Aristotle put the case against monarchy, arguing, among other points, that one superior king does not entail that others in his family will be as virtuous. As we have seen, Aristotle often attacks the militaristic and autocratic character of the Spartan state, which had two kings. Despite Kelsen's comments, then, it is not clear whether Aristotle's "defence" is meant to support the Macedonians, or to criticize their rule.[12] If monarchy is only defensible in principle and not in practice, polity would seem to be the better option, but it still needs to be defended against the third correct type of political system, aristocracy.

In the following, I shall argue that Aristotle's argument for polity over aristocracy is to be found in his ostensible defence of democracy in *Politics* III 11.[13] The gist of the argument is that the many may each have a share in virtue and practical wisdom, so that together they can surpass the judgment of one or a few good human beings, but in order for this to be possible, the political system in question must fit the requirements of Aristotle's polity. The argument, then, is not intended to be ironic.[14] Nor need Aristotle be disagreeing with the argument he puts forward.[15] Moreover, if the argument succeeds, it should work just

[12] Ober 1998, 342–4 argues convincingly that, according to Aristotle, which type of polis is best depends on the character of the citizen body.

[13] Simpson also argues that Aristotle is arguing in favour of polity here (Simpson 1998, 166–71).

[14] Here, I disagree with Winthrop who thinks that Aristotle is being ironic and is reducing to absurdity the view that democracy can be defended by any argument from collective wisdom and virtue (Winthrop 1978, 159–60). By contrast, see Josiah Ober, who agrees that the summation argument, discussed at the end of this chapter, is philo-democratic (Ober 1998, esp. 319).

[15] For such an interpretation, see MacKenzie 1989, esp. 153–59.

as well against monarchy as it does against aristocracy, and indeed, the analogies Aristotle uses to make his case sometimes refer to a single good human being and sometimes to a few.

5. DEMOCRACY AND POLITY

In his commentary on *Politics* III chapter 11, Richard Robinson states, "The chapter expounds an important consideration in favour of democracy, including our kind of democracy as well as Aristotle's", but it is in fact far from obvious what form of majority rule Aristotle means to defend.[16] According to Aristotle, there are two kinds of majority rule: democracy and polity, although Aristotle also points out that on the usual classification of forms of government into oligarchy and democracy, his polity would be classified as a democracy (*Pol*. IV 3 1290a17–18). Democracy, as Aristotle defines it, is a perverted form of government, which aims at liberty and in which the poor who are in the majority rule to their own advantage exclusively. Polity, according to Aristotle, is the correct form of government in which the majority, who are reasonably well-off, rule to the advantage of each and all.[17]

---

[16] Robinson 1962, 39. As I argue below, it is unclear whether Aristotle is defending *his* democracy. It is even less clear that what Aristotle is defending is Robinson's British parliamentary system. What Aristotle is defending is more democratic than modern-day "democracies" in that the people's will is not filtered through their representatives, or impeded by oligarchic interests, but it is less democratic in that women, slaves, and manual workers, excluding gentlemen farmers, have no say whatsoever. I do not think that Aristotle's general principles warrant these exclusions; in fact, the argument from collective practical wisdom and virtue suggests just the opposite. For different arguments to the same conclusion, see Irwin 1988, ch. 19, sections 220–2.

[17] Aristotle defines the genus *politeia* (a political system or constitution) as "an arrangement in the city in respect of the manner in which the offices are distributed, the sovereign element in the constitution and the aim of each community" (*Pol*. IV 1 1289a15–18 cf. *Pol*. III 6 1278b8–10). Good political systems, monarchy, aristocracy, and the species polity aim at the benefit of each and all (*to koinēi sumpheron*). As is clear from *Politics* III 6 1278b20–5, Aristotle does not think that *to koinēi sumpheron* is a "common good" in the sense of one

If Aristotle is advocating what he calls "democracy", there are two possibilities. Either he is defending the view that democracy is just as good or better at achieving the advantage of each and all than is the rule of a few good men (Aristotelian aristocracy), or he is defending the view that democratic government is better at achieving its aim, liberty, than aristocracy and monarchy are good at achieving their aim, the advantage of each and all. It would be extremely odd for Aristotle to be arguing that democracy is just as good or better at achieving the advantage of each and all than is aristocracy or monarchy, since by definition the good form of government rules in the interest of all, whereas any perverted form of government is bad precisely because it does not. Therefore, it might appear that Aristotle must be arguing instead that democratic government is just as good as or better at achieving its aim, liberty, than aristocracy is at achieving its aim, the advantage of each and all.[18]

In favour of the view that Aristotle means to be defending democracy, one might also point to the central section of the chapter in which he voices and responds to what sound like oligarchical objections to the idea that the poor (and hence, from an oligarchical standpoint, those who are not good at all) should have a say in government. However, the point of the section is to defend the idea that the majority should select and examine the magistrates, and in *Politics* IV Aristotle treats the selection of magistrates as a feature of oligarchy to be *contrasted* with the democratic practice of picking officials by lot (*Pol.* IV 9 1294b7–9). In fact, he there suggests combining oligarchic and democratic elements to achieve Aristotelian *polity*. In defending majority rule against aristocracy, it makes more sense to suppose that Aristotle is defending

that might or might not be the good of anyone in particular. Perverted political systems, tyranny, oligarchy (rule by the wealthy), and democracy (rule by a poor majority) only aim to benefit the rulers, and presumably do not attain real benefit even for them. On the classification of constitutions, see *Pol.* III 6, 7, IV 1, and for the classification of democracies into five types, *Pol.* IV 4. On liberty as the basis and aim of democracy, see *Pol.* IV 2 1317a40–1.

[18] Aristotle does not appear to consider a third possibility, that aiming at liberty might be a better way of securing the advantage of each and all than aiming at the advantage of each and all itself. However, perhaps he unwittingly concedes the point in his own tantalizingly brief description of the best form of democracy (*Pol.* IV 4 1291b30–9).

the sort of majority rule to be found in his polity. In that case, it is polity that is being defended over aristocracy and monarchy in the present discussion.

6. COLLECTIVE VIRTUE AND PRACTICAL WISDOM: AN ARGUMENT FROM THE UNITY OF VIRTUE AND THE DOCTRINE OF THE MEAN

Aristotle's defence of polity is very different from modern defences of democracy. Since Aristotle believes that there is such a thing as objective happiness and virtue, the argument cannot depend merely on what people happen to think or on their consent. It is not a social contract that makes a particular sort of political system good, on Aristotle's account, but whether its rulers are successful in aiming at the good of each and all. Aristotle therefore needs to show that the rulers in a polity can be as good as, or better than, those in an aristocracy or monarchy.

Aristotle presents several colourful analogies to show that there are recognizable cases in which the collective virtue and practical wisdom of many may equal or surpass that of one or a few good human beings. First, a potluck dinner is better than a meal provided by just one person.[19] Second, the many are better judges of music and poetry. Third, beautiful people differ from those who are not beautiful, and beautiful pictures from the objects themselves, by uniting together disparate features. People who are not beautiful may have one feature that is more beautiful than a beautiful painting overall. Fourth, the perceptions of many bad and a few good people may be beneficial in the way that a mixture of concentrated and other food is more beneficial than a little of the concentrated food alone.

Aristotle's argument is not that the collective virtue and practical wisdom of the majority will always equal or surpass that of one of a few good human beings, but that there are cases where it will.[20] The

[19] The analogy of the feast crops up again at *Pol*. III 15 1286a26–30.

[20] Aristotle concedes that not every populace will be superior to a few good men (*Pol*. III 11 1281b15–20 cf. 1282a15–16), and elsewhere he notes the importance of education in bringing up the populace correctly (e.g., *Pol*. V 9). Also, in Aristotle's polity, the middle class is to be as large as possible, presumably in

suggestion is in line with Aristotle's doctrine of the mean, according to which what should be done must fit the particular circumstances. It is not an objection, then, if counterexamples to the analogies can be found. The point is that there are cases where they hold true. Thus, it is easy to imagine a case where a potluck dinner is better than a meal provided by just one person, but if everyone contributes their best dish, the result may be better, more nutritious, and tastier than one person providing the meal, even if that person is a better chef overall.[21] Alternatively, Aristotle might be making a point about money, since he mentions the expense of the one person. If what is important is the expense, one would get more money from many people than from one, and so would be able to do more with the amount raised. In the case of judging music and poetry, each person may judge one part better than his peers, so that together they come to a good judgment about the music or poetry as a whole. In the case of beauty, Aristotle's analogy is supported by modern technology. Scientists have used computers to generate a beautiful face by combining many ordinary faces together. The result is often considered more beautiful overall, even though the individual faces on their own may be more ordinary and yet have particular features that are more beautiful than the composite. Finally, modern medicine supports the idea that a mixture of concentrated and other food is more beneficial than a little of the concentrated food alone. Eating vitamins by themselves is no recipe for health.

Even though Aristotle's examples are clearly recognizable, there still remains the question of how such examples occur. Aristotle says of the majority, "For each of these many may possess some share of virtue and practical wisdom, and when they get together, like a single human being with many feet and many hands and many senses, so it may be with their character and thought" (*Pol.* III 11 1281b4–7).[22] To those who are unimpressed by the analogy of the multiple human being

order to minimize the greed and envy that accompany great wealth and poverty and that promote injustice (*Pol.* IV 11).

[21] Also, given the preparation involved in an ancient Greek meal, one person would be unlikely to be able to provide the diverse and fresh food of many.

[22] The analogy of the multiple man reappears in an argument in favour of *aristocracy* over monarchy in *Pol.* III 16 1287b25–31.

and who think monarchy is best, Aristotle later presents an *ad hominem* argument on behalf of the anti-monarchists, which he never rebuts, using precisely this point. Even monarchs, the argument goes, think that many ears, eyes, hands, and feet are better than one and so need friends to help them carry out their policies (*Pol.* III 16 1287b25–32). Nevertheless, the original claim is puzzling. On the face of it, it conflicts with Aristotle's thesis about the unity of the virtues, that it is not possible to have any one ethical virtue fully without having all the rest. As we have seen, though, it is possible to have one natural virtue without having the others, that is, to have correct piecemeal information about how one should act in specific circumstances without having the correct synoptic understanding or reliable emotional responses in those circumstances. Therefore, Aristotle's defence of majority rule is compatible with the thesis about the unity of the virtues as presented in the *Nicomachean Ethics*.

One might wonder why one needs to have full virtue if one can be partially virtuous in the way I have described. The answer is that someone who is only partially virtuous will not reliably do the right thing. But this raises a further problem for Aristotle's defence of polity: Why suppose that a lot of unreliable individuals together will be just as or more reliable than a few good and hence reliable ones? Thomas Jefferson said that democracy is "the combined wisdom and folly of the people", but, on Aristotle's account, the folly appears to have dropped out. As Mulgan complains, "One cannot establish that the collective judgment of the group is superior without specifying some way in which the good qualities of each individual coalesce into a cohesive judgment while the bad qualities are rejected. This Aristotle fails to do".[23]

The solution can be found elsewhere in Aristotle's own work. First of all, in his *Nicomachean* (and *Eudemian*) *Ethics* Aristotle distinguishes several types of practical wisdom, and he sharply distinguishes legislative practical wisdom and judicial practical wisdom (*EN* VI [=*EE* V] 8 1141b24–33). The distinction is important because, in his *Politics*, Aristotle appears to be arguing that the kind of practical wisdom

---

[23] Mulgan 1977, 105 cf. Newman, "Aristotle forgets that bad qualities will be thrown into the common stock no less than good ones." (Newman 1881–1902 vol. 1, 256).

required from the people is political as opposed to legislative practical wisdom. Aristotle argues that the people are not to alter the basis of the constitution or its laws and that they are have only deliberative and judicial functions.[24] Also, the people are only supposed to decide matters on which the laws cannot possibly speak accurately because of their generality (*Pol*. III 11 1282b4–5). Here then, Aristotle clearly means to minimize the effects of the people's partial vices, and imperfect practical wisdom, by arguing that their decisions are circumscribed by correct law. Correct law, of course, according to Aristotle, aims at the happiness of the citizens (*Pol*. III 9).

If the laws are meant to filter out as many of people's bad desires and judgments as possible, it remains to explain how the people's good desires and judgments coalesce. Here, one might appeal to Aristotle's defence of his own philosophical method in ethics. He claims, for example, that "everyone has something of their own to contribute to the truth" (*EE* I 6 1216b31 cf. *EN* I 8 1098b27–9) and he argues that "all the facts harmonize with a true account, whereas the truth soon clashes with a false one" (*EN* I 8 1098b11–12). It may be reasonable to assume that Aristotle thinks that if the people meet in rational debate, the truth will emerge. As Barker comments, "The people at large have the merit of a good collective judgment not as a static mass, but when they are dynamic – in other words when they assemble, and when the process of debate begins".[25] But perhaps the best argument for the coalescing of a cohesive and correct decision on the part of the majority rests on the thesis of the unity of the virtues itself. According to Aristotle's account of the unity of the virtues and the third aspect of his doctrine of the mean, the vices are a disunited lot whereas only the virtues coalesce in a unified and coherent way. In fact, this suggests an argument for a far more radical form of government than Aristotle envisaged, for the more people are involved, the more various their partial vicious tendencies

[24] Aristotle elsewhere includes under the possible purview of deliberation decisions about war and peace, alliances, serious penalties, laws, and the selection of officials and their examination (*Pol*. IV 14 1298a3–9). Aristotle describes the different kinds of courts in *Pol*. IV 16.

[25] Barker 1946, 106 in footnote 1. Kraut also emphasizes debate (Kraut 2002, 404–6).

will be, and the more likely it will be that only their virtuous judgments will coalesce.[26]

In Part I of my book, I discussed and defended Aristotle's controversial doctrine of the mean, his nameless and named virtues, his view that the virtues are not remedial, and his claim that the virtues are unified. All of these aspects of Aristotle's ethics are key to understanding his arguments about why society is essential, and the sort of democratic society that will best allow the Aristotelian virtues to flourish. Even though, as I have argued, Aristotle presents an ethic of virtue, he is right to call his inquiry a "sort of politics", and it is therefore apt to end my discussion, as Aristotle himself does, on a political note.

---

[26] It might be suggested that the vices will always cancel out. Not so; in some cases, the excess vices of one group may reinforce the deficient vices of another and vice versa, and so this cannot be used as a general argument on Aristotle's behalf.

Conclusion

1. ARISTOTLE'S ETHIC OF VIRTUE

In the preface to the first edition of his classic work on Aristotle's ethical theory, W. F. R. Hardie wrote, "In the study of Aristotle familiarity can be an obstacle to understanding; we are prone to think we know what he means before we do".[1] In the preceding chapters, I have examined some familiar but puzzling Aristotelian theses, especially his much-maligned doctrine of the mean, from a less familiar perspective, arguing that Aristotle's ethics is primarily an ethic of virtue.

I have argued that the doctrine of the mean is of more interest and plays a larger role in Aristotle's ethics than has previously been thought. The doctrine of the mean combines three different aspects: (1) a doctrine of equilibrium, according to which the good human being has the emotions that are called for in a given situation; (2) a sophisticated view of the particulars of the situation; and (3) a triadic taxonomy of virtue and vices. The doctrine of the mean has substantive consequences. Aristotle's list of ethical virtues, including the important nameless ones, while quite controversial, is grounded in the doctrine of equilibrium. Moreover, the doctrine of equilibrium supports Aristotle's view that the ethical virtues are not essentially remedial, and is consistent with his claim that one cannot have one ethical virtue fully without having all the rest. The second aspect of Aristotle's doctrine of the mean enters into Aristotle's way of addressing moral dilemmas. Perhaps most surprisingly, the third aspect shows how Aristotle can reply to the

[1] The preface is reprinted in Hardie 1980.

immoralist, and it also contributes to Aristotle's views about democracy in the polis.

According to the first aspect of the doctrine of the mean, the good human being has appropriate emotions, at the appropriate times, in the appropriate way. Reason and emotions are so closely connected that one can have neither practical wisdom without the ethical virtues nor all the ethical virtues without having practical wisdom. I argued that Aristotle's rationale for this view is that ethical virtue "involves reason" (*meta logou*) and is not merely "in accordance with reason" (*kata logon*), and that this idea also lies behind Aristotle's discussion of motivation in important passages on bravery and friendship. The connection between practical wisdom and ethical virtue also explains the workings of the practical syllogism, and contributes to solving the puzzle about how much the good person needs to know.

In sum, I have argued that when familiar Aristotelian ideas, previously disparaged, are re-examined together, the result is a coherent ethic of virtue, drawn from a nexus of ideas and arguments that have often been misjudged when viewed separately. What is new and interesting about this approach can be seen in the solutions to the various puzzles I presented at the beginning of this book.

2. THE PUZZLES REVISITED

In the introduction, I pointed out that Aristotle thinks that the best way to become clear about a particular subject matter is by going through the puzzles (e.g., *EN* VII 1 1145b2–7). Following Aristotle's lead, and in order to clarify Aristotelian ethical virtue, I have addressed different puzzling questions about Aristotle's ethics in each chapter of my book. What does Aristotle mean by the claim that virtue is "in a mean relative to us"? An examination of particular virtues showed that the claim is more sophisticated than has been thought. I argued that while there are special factors about the agent that need to be taken into account apart from the agent's mere humanity, these factors are not relevant in all cases, and the same factors may or may not be at play in moral decisions affecting ourselves and others. What is the point of having triads of virtue and vices? On my interpretation, the triadic framework is far from vacuous. It captures the underlying psychology of three recognizable types of people, it can be used to diagnose the mistake of thinking that the Aristotelian vices are really virtues, and it also can be used to classify the mentality of the immoralist (Chapters 1, 4, and 9).

What are the nameless virtues, why are they included among the ethical virtues, and why are they nameless? The nameless virtues are the first five virtues on Aristotle's list. I argued that they may be more helpful than the others, especially in a societal context, and that their given names subtly miss capturing their true natures (Chapters 2 and 10). Do the ethical virtues presuppose that human beings are naturally good or bad or neither? Are the virtues remedial? I argued that, according to Aristotle, human beings are not naturally good or bad, and there are two ways in which the virtues are not remedial. Human emotions are not in themselves defects to be remedied, and the virtues' essential point is not to remedy defects in the world (Chapter 3).

How does Aristotle generate the ethical virtues on his list? Why does he include the ethical virtues he does, and not include other dispositions that have been considered virtues? Here, I argued that the different aspects of the doctrine of the mean are necessary in generating Aristotle's list. Justice is an exception, but equity, fitting the mean *par excellence*, is superior. Aristotle has a substantive account of virtue that rules out certain modern and other candidates for virtues, and rightfully so (Chapter 4).

What is the rationale for Aristotle's claim that it is not possible to have one ethical virtue fully without having all the rest? The answer concerns Aristotle's important and subtle distinction between being "in accordance with reason" and "involving reason" and the integration of reason and feeling (Chapter 5). What Aristotle says about the large-scale virtues confirms my account (Appendix).

Given his views about the doctrine of the mean and the unity of the virtues, what does Aristotle have to say about moral dilemmas, an important topic in both ancient and modern thought? Aristotle does have a relevant discussion, but his analysis is quite different from that of modern philosophers. I argued that his account depends on the second aspect of the doctrine of the mean, is consistent with his view about the unity of the virtues, and is ultimately more humane than recent accounts (Chapter 6).

How can Aristotle coherently hold that we can be motivated by some good both for its own sake and for the sake of something else? Can Aristotle explain how we can care for a friend for his or her own sake? I argued that Aristotle's claim that we can be motivated by some good both for its own sake and for the sake of something else should be taken at face value. We can be motivated by some good both for its own sake and for the sake of something else, provided that being motivated by the second good does not undermine being motivated by the first. Aristotle's account of cases of mock bravery support this interpretation and elucidate the incorrect, and therefore, the correct motivation on the part of the good person. One case of mock bravery, "civic bravery", turns out to be comparable to the civic disposition that Aristotle attributes to the warmongering Spartans, discussed further in Chapter 10. I also argued that Aristotle can explain how one good human being can care for another good human being for his or her own sake. Aristotle's example of mother and child is telling. Aristotle does not think that one cares for a friend merely derivatively from the friend's general character, and he is right not to do so, but a good friend needs to be someone of stable character and integrity, as explained in Aristotle's doctrine of the mean and his thesis about the unity of the virtues, in order to receive care for his or her own sake (Chapter 7).

How does the nameless virtue of truthfulness help explain the difference between practical wisdom and technical skill? Practical wisdom is not a skill. Whatever technical skills we have, practical wisdom involves having a proper view of those skills and abilities, as given by the Aristotelian nameless virtue of truthfulness, so that we are aware of when and what to do ourselves, and when to enlist the help of others. How can there be such a thing as a *practical* syllogism and how does it relate to Aristotle's account of ethical virtue? I argued that the key to answering this question is the neglected first part of the minor premiss, "I am (for example) a generous human being". This part of the syllogism refers to the salient ethical virtue, and the indexical "I" shows how the syllogism is *practical* (Chapter 8). As discussed in Chapter 5, practical wisdom and ethical virtue are inextricably linked. The practical syllogism makes the connection even more vivid.

How much does the good person have to know? Medical analogies and disanalogies show that the good person is not merely instinctively good, without any knowledge, for one cannot be good, according to Aristotle, unless one has practical wisdom, and practical wisdom involves some general knowledge. On the other hand, the good person need not know as much as Plato's guardians know, nor need she know all of Aristotle's metaphysics, whether or not Aristotle's metaphysics is related to his ethics. Aristotelian ethical knowledge is in a mean between merely instinctive knowledge and knowledge of metaphysics. It is meant to show how important experience and knowledge of particulars are, as well as general principles connected with human psychology. The *Nicomachean Ethics* is therefore analogous to a Hippocratic treatise (Chapter 9).

How should we understand Aristotle's claim that his inquiry in the *Nicomachean Ethics* is "a sort of Politics"? What sort of polis would be suitable for Aristotle's ethical virtues, and would that polis be democratic in any way? Can we make sense of Aristotle's ranking of different happy lives in *Nicomachean Ethics* X? One cannot be a virtuous person independently of society, and the best society in which the Aristotelian virtues, especially the nameless ones, will flourish is a democratic one. At first sight, Aristotle's ranking goes against the grain of his doctrine of the mean, but, considered as a political ranking, it makes more sense (Chapter 10).

Solving the puzzles required treating familiar Aristotelian views from a less familiar perspective, developing an ethic of virtue worth pursuing.

3. ALTERNATIVE APPROACHES

In arguing that Aristotle's ethics is an ethic of virtue, I have taken issue with alternative approaches, especially Kantian perspectives on Aristotle's ethics. I have argued that Kant misunderstood Aristotle's doctrine of the mean. I have also argued against the modern Kantian interpretation that would commit Aristotle to the false view that the ethical virtues are remedial, and against Kantian interpretations of Aristotle's more plausible account of ethical motivation and the correct attitude to take towards a friend.

Aristotle's account of practical reasoning is antithetical to the traditional Kantian view, according to which the reasoner identifies him or herself with a noumenal self instead of with a flesh-and-blood human being with emotions and intellectual capacities that are intimately connected. The Aristotelian practical reasoner is concerned with the here and now and "thisness" of things in a way inimical to the early Kant. Aristotle's list of ethical virtues also differs in important ways from Kant's. In particular, Aristotle omits self-control, but includes the nameless virtues of mildness, friendliness, and wit.

The original virtue ethicists of the 1960s presented their views as an alternative to Mill's Utilitarianism and Kantian theory. The Aristotle I have presented is firmly in that tradition.

4. FOREWORD TO ARISTOTLE

The Roman poet, Horace, called Aristotle's doctrine of the mean "golden". The doctrine has become somewhat tainted in recent times, but I hope to have restored its sheen by distinguishing and examining its three different aspects and showing how these relate to and throw light on other parts of Aristotle's ethics. I have also paid greater attention than is usual to Aristotle's particular ethical virtues; they help explain and are explained by the more abstract aspects of Aristotle's account, and they provide an important alternative to the deficiencies and excesses that all too often masquerade as virtues.

Throughout the book, I have shown how the good person's character and the way in which the good person thinks are intimately related. The good person has a certain mentality due to her character being in a mean, practical wisdom requires and is required by ethical virtue, and the sort of thought required to be a good person is both objective and also, as I argued in Chapter 9, not as rarefied as some think.

Therefore, in a modern ethic of virtue based on Aristotelian ideas, "*phronēsis*" (above translated as "practical wisdom") might better be rendered as "thoughtfulness". Virtue of character involves thought, and the two do not just run on parallel tracks. To coin some phrases, the good person has a metalog and not a mere katalog mentality. Thought and feeling are interwoven through and through, but the result, based on the doctrine of the mean, is in no way irrational. Medicine, as opposed to mathematics or formal logic, provides the appropriate analogies and disanalogies for understanding the intricacies of ethics.

On a practical note, Aristotle intends his discussion to help his readers become good, not just to know what virtue is (*EN* II 2 1103b26–9 cf. I 3 1095a5–6). While reading a book is no substitute for engaging in virtuous activity, working through puzzles and recognizing the different types of mentalities, motivations, and traits outlined in Aristotle's ethics can be as helpful as reading a book on medicine is to the physician.[2] While analysing moral dilemmas may be useful, eliminating the conditions for such difficult decisions is more important.[3] Here again, one part of Aristotle's non-remedial view of the virtues stresses preventative over merely rectificatory measures, and, as I argued in Chapter 10, Aristotle is well aware of the need for good, though not Utopian, societal arrangements, the importance of the nameless virtues, and the dangers of having the wrong priorities, both for individuals and for empires.

One virtue of Aristotle's ethics is that the parts of his theory examined here that have been maligned and neglected may be the most interesting and valuable of all. Here are only the seeds of a modern ethic of virtue based on Aristotle's thought, but, according to the ancient Greek proverb of which Aristotle is so fond, "the beginning is half the whole".

---

[2] Doris 2002 put forward the influential claim that ethical behaviour is caused, not by fixed traits of character, but by the context and the situation. I leave it to others to challenge Doris's controversial interpretation of the psychological and sociological data on which he relies. Suffice to say that Aristotle's complex doctrine of the mean and his view that motivation cannot be reduced to mere behaviour, presents a view of virtue orthogonal to the one that Doris decries.

[3] Thanks to Mark Lovas for his comments on this issue.

Appendix:
Uniting the "Large-scale" Virtues

As explained in Chapters 5 and 8, Aristotle does not think that it is possible to have any one ethical virtue fully without having all the others. Practical wisdom requires all the ethical virtues, and they require practical wisdom. While the thesis works especially well for the nameless virtues, it has often been objected that this requirement is too strong, because on Aristotle's own view, it seems possible to lack the wealth necessary for exercising magnificence or to lack the social milieu for exercising magnanimity, so that one can have some virtues without even being able to develop others. According to this argument, one can have the small-scale ethical virtues of generosity and the virtue concerning honour on a small scale without having the large-scale virtues of magnificence and magnanimity, although one cannot have the latter without having the former.

This problem has exercised philosophers at least since Aquinas, who is the first to finesse the issue with the suggestion that someone who is poor but has practical wisdom is "so disposed that he may become munificent [magnificent] when he has matter for the virtue".[1] But this goes against Aristotle's view that we need to practise the actions relevant to each particular virtue in order to attain the virtuous disposition itself. It also concedes that one can have practical wisdom without having all the ethical virtues.

Various solutions have been canvassed, restricting or re-describing the scope of Aristotle's thesis about the unity of the ethical virtues. For

---

[1] See Aquinas *CANE*, 405. The classic statement of the problem is by Irwin 1988b, with a response by Kraut 1988, and further comments by Irwin 1988c.

example, one option is to say that one cannot have practical wisdom without having at least one ethical virtue *in every area*, where magnanimity and the virtue concerning honour on a small scale belong to one area, and magnificence and generosity to another. Each of the other ethical virtues have their own areas.[2] Another solution rests on distinguishing two types of virtue: psychic – the frame of mind required to exercise the virtue; and proper – the successful exercising of the virtue itself. On this view, a person can therefore have the psychic virtues of magnificence and magnanimity without having the proper virtues themselves. Aristotle's thesis is to be restricted to all the *psychic* virtues.[3] Another option is to restrict Aristotle's claim about the unity of the virtues so that it applies only to those virtues other than magnanimity and magnificence.[4]

Here, one might take a step back and wonder whether it is right to assume that one *cannot* have all the virtues unless one is wealthy or of a certain status.[5] In his discussion of magnificence, Aristotle gives examples of exercising the virtue that do not require a huge amount of money, for example, putting on a tasteful wedding or buying a child an especially elegant toy. They still differ from acts of generosity because they have an aesthetic aspect that generous actions do not, as I explained in Chapter 4. In modern terms, a rich person might act magnificently in endowing a tastefully designed concert hall, whereas a poorer person might act magnificently in choosing to contribute to the matching funds for it rather than for the badly designed concert hall farther down the street. In the *Nicomachean Ethics*, Aristotle notes that it is not easy for a generous person to become rich (*EN* IV 1 1120b14–20). This comment should be a problem for any account that says that the good person can develop from having generosity to having magnificence. On the present account, this does not matter, since the generous person is

[2] This is the solution of Kraut 1988. Drefcinski 2006 achieves a similar result by distinguishing different genera. According to him, magnificence and generosity are two species of the same genus, and so are magnanimity and the virtue concerning honour on a small scale. On his view, practical wisdom requires having an ethical virtue in every genus.

[3] Halper 1999.

[4] Gardiner 2001 argues that the other virtues are virtues unconditionally, whereas magnificence and magnanimity are essentially relative.

[5] This is the strategy of Pakaluk 2002.

not thereby precluded from exercising magnificence or from having the same priorities and practical wisdom as his richer virtuous fellows.

While the problem about the unity of the virtues can be dispelled for the virtues of generosity and magnificence, in the case of magnanimity there are different possibilities that depend on different political arrangements.

As Aristotle explains in the *Eudemian Ethics*, magnanimity, though a separate virtue from the others, accompanies all the ethical virtues and they it (*EE* III 5 1232b24–7; 1232a35–8). Presumably, then, anyone who has all the other ethical virtues is thereby a suitable candidate for one of the great honours, for example, public office or public service, that he is worthy to put himself forward to accept. This is particularly plausible in the case of the nameless virtues that Aristotle includes in his *Nicomachean Ethics*, as described in Chapter 2. Being aware of his virtue and suitability for office, and caring about great honours, the magnanimous person will claim those honours that are his due. In a good society, such a person would readily be chosen to fill the appropriate office, or to fill it when his turn came, so the problem of having some virtues without being able to develop others should not arise for the virtuous person who lives in such a society.

Furthermore, the rationale I presented for the unity of the virtues would also apply. Someone who had the vices in the sphere of magnanimity would not have or be able to exercise the other virtues either. For example, the person who had the vice of thinking he deserved more than his due would also have the vice of stinginess in the sphere of generosity, as well as vices in the areas of the nameless virtues.[6] In order to have practical wisdom, all the ethical virtues would be needed and magnanimity would both accompany and be accompanied by the other ethical virtues. Aristotle assumes that a good person in a good society will be motivated to carry out his civic functions when he can. But what about a person who exercises all the other ethical virtues but is not interested in public office? I take it that Aristotle's discussion of the magnanimous person as disdaining "small" honours, wealth, and so on is his way of describing the perceived mentality of the magnanimous person who does not live in a good society, and who therefore views the

[6] See also Ch. 1 Section 4 for discussion of unity among the vices.

offices of his society as beneath his dignity. Aristotle is here describing the magnanimous person in a corrupt society. Such a person will be exercising magnanimity precisely by refusing to take part in the corrupt government of his city. If he claims those offices, he will be exercising the vice of vanity.

What about a person who has all the other ethical virtues but is ineligible to take part in running the city? As Aristotle notes in the *Eudemian Ethics*, there is a character who ought to count as virtuous even though he is ineligible for the great honours he deserves and so cannot claim them as his due, for example, if he is a resident alien (*EE* III 5 1233a28–9). According to Aristotle, such a person, unlike the pusillanimous person, "is disposed as reason bids. Also he is by nature the same as the magnanimous person, for both claim as their desert the things that they are worthy of. Indeed, he might become magnanimous, for he will claim as his worth the things that he is worthy of" (*EE* III 5 1233a22–5).[7] As I argued in Chapter 2, this is part of the reason Aristotle introduces the nameless virtue concerned with honour on a small scale in the *Nicomachean Ethics*.

This non-citizen is indeed the exception to Aristotle's claim that one cannot have any one virtue without having them all, but the rationale for the unity of the virtues explains why this person is the exception. Being ineligible to exercise the virtue of magnanimity, because he cannot claim any offices as his due, he also lacks the associated vices, and so the virtues he does have cannot be compromised. Can he have practical wisdom? If practical wisdom lets us discern which ethical virtue to exercise and on which occasions and relative to whom, as the doctrine of the mean implies, the resident alien can have practical wisdom. He can know when it is appropriate for him to exercise magnanimity and when not, even though he lacks the virtue himself.

The virtues of magnificence and generosity, then, pose no threat to Aristotle's thesis about the unity of the virtues. If magnanimity poses problems, these have less to do with Aristotle's thesis about the unity of the virtues than with deeper questions about the appropriate society for Aristotle's good person, a topic addressed in Chapter 10.

---

[7] The description is exactly parallel to Aquinas's comments on generosity and magnificence, *CANE*, 405.

Select Bibliography

References to the ancient Greek texts of Aristotle and Plato are to the most recent Oxford Classical Texts, unless otherwise stated. References to the Greek texts of Aristotle's *Historia Animalium*, *de Motu Animalium*, and the contested *Magna Moralia* are to the Loeb editions. I have also used the Oxford Classical Texts of the works of Aeschylus, Aristophanes, Pindar, Thucydides, and Xenophon.

Ackrill, J. L. 1963. *Aristotle's Categories and De Interpretatione.* Translation with notes and glossary. Oxford: Clarendon Press.

———. 1972. "Aristotle on 'Good' and the Categories." Reprinted in Barnes, Schofield, and Sorabji 1977 vol. 2, 17–24.

———. 1973. *Aristotle's Ethics.* Translation with notes. New York: Humanities Press.

———. 1974. "Aristotle on *Eudaimonia*." Reprinted in Rorty 1980, 15–33.

———. 1978. "Aristotle on Action." Reprinted in Rorty 1980, 93–101.

———. 1981. *Aristotle the Philosopher.* Oxford: Clarendon Press.

———. Ed. 1987. *A New Aristotle Reader.* Princeton: Princeton University Press.

———. 1997. *Essays on Plato and Aristotle.* Oxford: Oxford University Press.

Altham, J. E. J. and Harrison, R. Eds. 1995. *World, Mind, and Ethics: Essays on the Ethical Philosophy of Bernard Williams.* Cambridge: Cambridge University Press.

Annas, J. 1976. *Aristotle's Metaphysics Books M and N.* Translation, introduction, and commentary. Oxford: Clarendon Press.

———. 1993. *The Morality of Happiness.* Oxford; New York: Oxford University Press.

————. 1999. *Platonic Ethics, Old and New*. Ithaca: Cornell University Press.

Anscombe, G. E. M. 1957. *Intention*. Oxford: Blackwell.

————. 1958. "Modern Moral Philosophy." Reprinted in *Collected Philosophical Papers iii*, Minneapolis: University of Minnesota Press, 1981, 26–42.

————. 1965. "Thought and Action in Aristotle." In Bambrough 1965.

Anton, J. P. and Preus, A. Eds. 1983 and 1991. *Essays in Ancient Greek Philosophy*. vols. 2 and 4. Albany: State University of New York Press.

Aquinas. 1268–73. *Commentary on Aristotle's Nicomachean Ethics* (cited as "*CANE*"). Trans. C. I. Litzinger, O. P. Notre Dame: Dumb Ox Books, 1964, revised 1993.

Austin, J. L. 1956–7. "A Plea for Excuses." *Proceedings of the Aristotelian Society* 19: 1–30 (reprinted 1961 in *Philosophical Papers*. Oxford: Oxford University Press, 41–63).

Bambrough, R. Ed. 1965. *New Essays on Plato and Aristotle*. London: Routledge and Kegan Paul, New York: Humanities Press.

Barker, E. 1946. *The Politics of Aristotle*. Oxford: Clarendon Press.

————. 1995. *The Politics of Aristotle*. Translation of 1946 revised with an introduction and notes by R. F. Stalley. Oxford: Clarendon Press.

Barnes, J. 1975. "Aristotle's Theory of Demonstration." In Barnes, Schofield, and Sorabji 1975.

Barnes, J., Schofield, M., and Sorabji, R. Eds. 1975. *Articles on Aristotle*. vol. 1, London: Duckworth.

————. 1977. *Articles on Aristotle*. vol. 2, London: Duckworth.

————. 1984. *The Complete Works of Aristotle: The Revised Oxford Translation*. vols. 1 and 2, Princeton: Princeton University Press.

————. 1994. *Aristotle: Posterior Analytics*. Oxford: Clarendon Press.

Belfiore, E. 1985. "Pleasure, Tragedy and Aristotelian Psychology." *Classical Quarterly* ns 35: 349–61.

Bennett, W. J. 1993. *The Book of Virtues*. New York: Simon and Schuster.

Benson, H. Ed. 1992. *Essays on the Philosophy of Socrates*. New York; Oxford: Oxford University Press.

Bentham, J. 1789. *Introduction to the Principles of Morals and Legislation*. Oxford: Clarendon Press, 1907.

Brink, D. O. 1990. "Rational Egoism, Self and Others." In Rorty and Flanagan 1991.

Bosley, R., Shiner, R. A., and Sisson, J. D. Eds. 1995. *Aristotle, Virtue and the Mean. Apeiron* 25.4.

Bostock, D. 2000. *Aristotle's Ethics*. Oxford: Oxford University Press.

Boudouris, K. J. Ed. 1995. *Aristotelian Political Philosophy*. Athens, Greece: International Center for Greek Philosophy and Culture, vols. 1 and 2.

Broadie, S. 1991. *Ethics with Aristotle*. New York: Oxford University Press.

———. 2003. "Aristotelian Piety." *Phronesis* 48.1: 54–70.

———. and Rowe, C. Eds. 2002. *Aristotle's Nicomachean Ethics*. Translation and Commentary. Oxford: Oxford University Press.

Brown, L. 1997. "What Is 'the Mean Relative to Us' in Aristotle's Ethics?" *Phronesis* 42.1: 77–93.

Burnet, J. 1900. Ed. with introduction and notes. *The Ethics of Aristotle*. London: Methuen.

Burnyeat, M. F. 1971. "Virtues in Action." In *The Philosophy of Socrates*, ed. Vlastos, Garden City, New York: Anchor Books, 1971, 209–34.

———. 1980. "Aristotle on Learning to be Good." In Rorty 1980, 69–92.

———. 1984. "Platonism and Mathematics. A Prelude to Discussion." In *Mathematics and Metaphysics in Aristotle (Mathematik und Metaphysik bei Aristoteles)* Akten des 10. Symposium Aristotelicum Sigriswil, 6.–12. September 1984, ed. A. Graeser, Bern; Stuttgart: Haupt, 1987, 213–40.

Card, C. 1996. *The Unnatural Lottery: Character and Moral Luck*. Philadelphia: Temple University Press.

———. 1999. "Groping Through Gray Zones." In *On Feminist Ethics and Politics*, ed. Card, Kansas: University Press of Kansas, 3–26.

Charles, D. O. M. 1984. *Aristotle's Philosophy of Action*. Ithaca: Cornell University Press.

———. 1986. "Aristotle, Ontology and Moral Reasoning." *Oxford Studies in Ancient Philosophy* 4: 119–44.

———. 2000. *Aristotle on Meaning and Essence*. Oxford: Oxford University Press.

Clark, S. R. L. 1975. *Aristotle's Man: Speculations upon Aristotelian Anthropology*. Oxford: Clarendon Press.

Cooper, J. M. 1975. *Reason and Human Good in Aristotle*. Cambridge, Mass.: Harvard University Press.

———. 1987. "Contemplation and Happiness: A Reconsideration." *Synthèse* 72: 187–216.

———. 1996. "Reason, Moral Virtue, and Moral Value." In Frede and Striker 1996, 81–114.

———. with associate Hutchinson, D. S. Eds. 1997. *Plato: Complete Works*. Indianapolis: Hackett.

Cooper, N. 1989. "Aristotle's Crowning Virtue." *Apeiron* 22: 191–205.

Creed, J. L. 1973. "Moral Virtues in Thucydides' Time." *Classical Quarterly* 23: 213–31.

Crisp, R. Ed. 2000. *Aristotle's Nicomachean Ethics*. Translation and introduction. Cambridge: Cambridge University Press.

Curren, R. R. 2000. *Aristotle on the Necessity of Public Education*. Lanham; Boulder; New York; Oxford: Rowman and Littlefield.

Curzer, H. 1990. "A Great Philosopher's Not so Great Account of Great Virtue: Aristotle's Treatment of 'Greatness of Soul'." *Canadian Journal of Philosophy* 20.4: 517–38.

———. 1991. "The Supremely Happy Life in Aristotle's *Nicomachean Ethics*." *Apeiron* 24.1: 47–69.

———. 2005. "How Good People do Bad Things: Aristotle on the Misdeeds of the Virtuous." *Oxford Studies in Ancient Philosophy* 28: 233–56.

Dahl, N. O. 1984. *Practical Reason, Aristotle, and Weakness of the Will*. Minneapolis: University of Minnesota Press.

Davidson, D. 1980. *Essays on Actions and Events*. Oxford: Clarendon Press.

Dent, N. J. H. 1984. *The Moral Psychology of the Virtues*. Cambridge; New York: Cambridge University Press.

Deslauriers, M. 2002. "How to Distinguish Aristotle's Virtues." *Phronesis* 47.2: 101–26.

Detel, W. 1997. "Why All Animals Have a Stomach. Demonstration and Axiomatization in Aristotle's *Parts of Animals*." In Kullman und Föllinger 1997, 63–84.

Devereux, D. T. 1981. "Aristotle on the Essence of Happiness." In *Studies in Aristotle*, ed. D. J. O'Meara, Washington D.C.: Catholic University of America Press, 247–60.

———. 1992. "The Unity of the Virtues in Plato's *Protagoras and Laches*." *Philosophical Review* 101.4: 765–89.

Doris, J. 2002. *Lack of Character: Personality and Moral Behavior*. Cambridge: Cambridge University Press.

Dover, K. J. 1974. *Greek Popular Morality in the Time of Plato and Aristotle*. Oxford: Clarendon Press.

Drefcinski, S. 1996. "Aristotle's Fallible Phronimos." *Ancient Philosophy* 16: 139–53.

———. 2006. "A Different Solution to an Alleged Contradiction in Aristotle's *Nicomachean Ethics*." *Oxford Studies in Ancient Philosophy* 30: 201–10.

Driver, J. 2001. *Uneasy Virtue*. Cambridge; New York: Cambridge University Press.

Düring, I. 1961. *Aristotle's Protrepticus: An Attempt at Reconstruction*. Studia Graeca et Latina Gothoburgensia 12, Göteborg: Elanders Bokytryckeri Aktiebolag.

Engberg-Pedersen, T. 1983. *Aristotle's Theory of Moral Insight*. Oxford: Clarendon Press.

Engstrom, S. and Whiting, J. Eds. 1996. *Aristotle, Kant and the Stoics: Rethinking Happiness and Duty*. Cambridge: Cambridge University Press.

Ferejohn, M. T. 1982. "The Unity of the Virtues and the Objects of Socratic Inquiry." *Journal of the History of Philosophy* 20: 1–21.

———. 1984. "Socratic Thought-Experiments and the Unity of Virtue Paradox." *Phronesis* 29.2: 105–22.

Ferguson, J. 1958. *Moral Virtues in the Ancient World*. London: Methuen and Co.

Fine, G. 1992. "Aristotle's Criticisms of Plato." In *Methods of Interpreting Plato and his Dialogues*, ed. J. C. Klagge and N. D. Smith, *Oxford Studies in Ancient Philosophy*, supplementary volume, 13–41.

Flashar, H. 1965. "Critique of Plato's Theory of Ideas in Aristotle's Ethics." Reprinted in Barnes, Schofield, and Sorabji 1977 vol. 2, ch. 2, 1–16.

Foot, P. 1978. "Virtues and Vices." In *Virtues and Vices and Other Essays in Moral Philosophy*. Berkeley: University of California Press, 1978.

———. 1983. "Moral Realism and Moral Dilemma." *Journal of Philosophy* 80.7: 379–98.

———. 1985. "Utilitarianism and the Virtues." *Mind* 94: 196–209.

———. 2001. *Natural Goodness*. Oxford: Oxford University Press.

Fortenbaugh, W. W. 1968. "Aristotle and the Questionable Mean-Dispositions." *Transactions of the American Philological Association* 99: 203–31.

———. 1975. *Aristotle on Emotion*. London: Duckworth.

Frede, M. 1987. "Categories in Aristotle." In *Essays in Ancient Philosophy*. Minneapolis: University of Minnesota Press, 29–48.

———. and Striker, G. Eds. 1996. *Rationality in Greek Thought*. Oxford: Oxford University Press.

French, P. A., Uehling, T. E., and Wettstein, H. K. Eds. 1988. *Midwest Studies in Philosophy 13: Ethical Theory: Character and Virtue*. Notre Dame: University of Notre Dame Press.

Furley, D. J. 1967. "Aristotle on the Voluntary." Reprinted in Barnes, Schofield, and Sorabji 1977, 47–60.

Gardiner, S. 2001. "Aristotle's Basic and Non-Basic Virtues." *Oxford Studies in Ancient Philosophy* 20: 261–96.

Gauthier, R. A. and Jolif, J. Y. 1958. *Aristote: L'Ethique à Nicomaque.* Translation with introduction and commentary. vols. 1 and 2, Paris; Louvain: Publications Universitaires.

Gifford, M. 1995. "Nobility of Mind: The Political Dimension of Aristotle's Theory of Intellectual Virtue." In Boudouris 1995, vol. 1, 51–60.

Gildin, H. 1970. "Aristotle and the Moral Square of Opposition." *Monist* 54: 100–5.

Gilligan, C. 1993. *In a Different Voice: Psychological Theory and Women's Development.* Cambridge, Mass.: Harvard University Press.

Gómez-Lobo, A. 1989. "The Ergon Inference." *Phronesis* 34.2: 170–84.

Gotthelf, A. 1987. "First Principles in Aristotle's *Parts of Animals.*" In Gotthelf and Lennox 1987a.

———. 1997. "The Elephant's Nose: Further Reflections on the Axiomatic Structure of Biological Explanation in Aristotle." In Kullman und Föllinger 1997, 85–95.

———. and Lennox, J. G. Eds. 1987a. *Philosophical Issues in Aristotle's Biology.* Cambridge; New York: Cambridge University Press.

Gottlieb, P. 1991. "Aristotle and Protagoras: The Good Human Being as the Measure of Goods." *Apeiron* 24.1: 25–45.

———. 1994. "Aristotle's 'Nameless' Virtues." *Apeiron* 27.1: 1–15.

———. 1994a. "Aristotle on Dividing the Soul and Uniting the Virtues." *Phronesis* 39.3: 275–90 (reprinted in *Aristotle: Critical Assessments* vol. 3 *Psychology, Ethics*, ed. L. P. Gerson, Routledge, 1999).

———. 1996. "Aristotle's Ethical Egoism." *Pacific Philosophical Quarterly* 77.1: 1–18.

———. 2001. "Are the Virtues Remedial?" *Journal of Value Inquiry* 35: 343–54.

———. 2001a. A book-length analysis of and commentary on Aristotle's *Nicomachean Ethics* Books I and II for *Project Archelogos* on the web at www.archelogos.com.

———. 2001b. "Translating Aristotle's Ethics." *Apeiron* 34.1: 91–9.

———. 2005. "Aristotle's *Nicomachean Ethics.*" In the *Central Works of Philosophy vol 1: Ancient and Medieval Philosophy*, ed. J. Shand, Bucks, UK: Acumen Publishing, 46–68.

———. 2006. "The Practical Syllogism." In Kraut 2006, 218–33.

Grant, A. 1874. *The Ethics of Aristotle.* London: Longmans, Green.

Grene, M. 1963. *A Portrait of Aristotle*. Chicago: University of Chicago Press.

Grube, G. M. A. Revised by Reeve, C. D. C. 1992. *Plato's Republic*. Indianapolis; Cambridge: Hackett.

Halper, E. 1999. "The Unity of the Virtues in Aristotle." *Oxford Studies in Ancient Philosophy* 17: 115–43.

Hamlyn D. W. 1993. *Aristotle's De Anima Books II, III*. Translation with introduction and notes by D. W. Hamlyn and with a report on recent work and a revised bibliography by C. Shields. Oxford: Clarendon Press.

Hardie, W. F. R. 1964–5. "Aristotle's Doctrine that Virtue is a 'Mean'." Reprinted in Barnes, Schofield, and Sorabji 1977, 33–46.

———. 1967. "The Final Good in Aristotle's Ethics." In Moravscik, 1967.

———. 1980. *Aristotle's Ethical Theory*. 2nd edition. Oxford: Clarendon Press.

Heinaman, R. 1988. "*Eudaimonia and Self-Sufficiency in the Nicomachean Ethics*." *Phronesis* 33.1: 31–53.

———. 1993. "Rationality, *Eudaimonia* and *Kakodaimonia* in Aristotle." *Phronesis* 38.1: 31–56.

Herman, B. 1993. *The Practice of Moral Judgment*. Cambridge, Mass.: Harvard University Press.

Hicks, R. D. 1907. *Aristotle: De Anima*. Translation and Commentary. Cambridge: Cambridge University Press.

Hippocrates. *Ancient Medicine* and other works. Trans. W. H. S. Jones, The Loeb Classical Library, Cambridge, Mass.: Harvard University Press, vol. 1, 1923.

Hobbes. 1651. *Leviathan*. London: Printed for Andrew Ckooke.

Homiak, M. L. 1981. "Virtue and Self-Love in Aristotle's Ethics." *Canadian Journal of Philosophy* 11: 111–35.

Hume. 1888. *A Treatise of Human Nature*. Ed. L. A. Selby-Bigge, Oxford: Clarendon Press, 1967.

Hunt, L. H. 1990. *Nietzsche and the Origin of Virtue*. London; New York: Routledge.

Hursthouse, R. 1980–1. "A False Doctrine of the Mean." *Proceedings of the Aristotelian Society* 81: 57–92.

———. 1984. "Acting and Feeling in Character: *Nicomachean Ethics* 3.i." *Phronesis* 29.3: 252–66.

———. 1999. *On Virtue Ethics*. Oxford: Oxford University Press.

Hutchinson, D. S. 1986. *The Virtues of Aristotle*. London; New York: Routledge and Kegan Paul in association with Methuen.

———. 1988. "Doctrines of the Mean and the Debate Concerning Skills in Fourth-Century Medicine, Rhetoric and Ethics." In *Method, Medicine and Metaphysics: Studies in the Philosophy of Ancient Science*, ed. R. J. Hankinson, *Apeiron* 21.2: 17–52.

Irwin, T. H. 1975. "Aristotle on Reason, Desire, and Virtue." *Journal of Philosophy* 72: 567–78.

———. 1977. *Plato's Moral Theory*. Oxford: Oxford University Press.

———. 1980. "The Metaphysical and Psychological Basis of Aristotle's Ethics." In Rorty 1980, 35–53.

———. 1985. *Aristotle's Nicomachean Ethics*. Translation and notes. Indianapolis: Hackett.

———. 1985a. "Permanent Happiness: Aristotle and Solon." *Oxford Studies in Ancient Philosophy* 3: 89–124.

———. 1985b. "Aristotle's Conception of Morality." *Boston Area Colloquium in Ancient Philosophy* 1: 115–43.

———. 1986. "Stoical and Aristotelian Conceptions of Happiness." In Schofield and Striker 1986, 205–70.

———. 1986a. "Aristotelian Actions." *Phronesis* 31.1: 68–89.

———. 1988. *Aristotle's First Principles*. Oxford: Clarendon Press (especially Part 3).

———. 1988a. "Some Rational Aspects of Incontinence." *The Southern Journal of Philosophy* 27, supplementary volume, 49–88.

———. 1988b. "Disunity in the Aristotelian Virtues." *Oxford Studies in Ancient Philosophy*, supplementary volume, 61–78.

———. 1988c. "Disunity in the Aristotelian Virtues: A Reply to Richard Kraut." *Oxford Studies in Ancient Philosophy*, supplementary volume, 87–90.

———. 1995. *Plato's Ethics*. New York; Oxford: Oxford University Press.

———. 1999. *Nicomachean Ethics*. Translation with introduction, notes, and glossary. 2nd edition. Indianapolis: Hackett.

———. and Fine, G. 1995. *Aristotle: Selections*. Translated with introduction, notes, and glossary by T. Irwin and G. Fine, Indianapolis; Cambridge: Hackett.

Isocrates. *To Demonicus, To Nicocles, Nicocles or the Cyprians, Panegyricus, To Philip, Archidamus*. Trans. G. Nolin, The Loeb Classical Library, Cambridge, Mass.: Harvard University Press, vol. 1, 1928.

———. *Evagoras, Helen, Busiris, Plataicus, Concerning the Team of Horses, Trapeziticus, Against Callimachus, Aegineticus, Against Lochites, Against Euthymus, Letters*. Trans. La Rue Van Hook, The Loeb Classical Library, Cambridge, Mass.: Harvard University Press, vol. 3, 1945.

Jaeger, W. W. 1923. *Aristotle.* 2nd edition of the Oxford translation. Oxford: Oxford University Press, 1948.

―――. 1957. "Aristotle's Use of Medicine as a Model of Method in his Ethics." *Journal of Hellenic Studies* 77: 54–61.

Jamieson, D. 2007. "When Utilitarians Should Be Virtue Theorists." *Utilitas* 19.2: 160–83.

Joachim, H. H. 1951. *Aristotle: The Nicomachean Ethics.* A commentary ed. D. A. Rees, Oxford: Clarendon Press.

Kahn, C. H. 1996. *Plato and the Socratic Dialogue: The Philosophical Use of a Literary Form.* Cambridge; New York: Cambridge University Press.

Kant. *Critique of Pure Reason* (cited as "*KrV*"). Trans. N. Kemp Smith. New York: St. Martin's Press, 1965.

―――. *Doctrine of Virtue* (cited as "*DOV*"). In *The Metaphysics of Morals.* Trans. and ed. M. Gregor with introduction by R. J. Sullivan. Cambridge: Cambridge University Press, 1996.

―――. *Lectures on Ethics* (cited as "*LE*"). Trans. L. Infield with introduction by L. White Beck. Indianapolis: Hackett, 1963.

Kelsen, H. 1937–8. "Aristotle and Hellenic-Macedonian Policy." In Barnes, Schofield, and Sorabji 1977, 170–94.

Kenny, A. 1965–6. "Aristotle on Happiness." In Barnes, Schofield, and Sorabji 1977, 25–32.

―――. 1973. "The Practical Syllogism and Incontinence." In *The Anatomy of the Soul: Historical Essays in the Philosophy of Mind.* Oxford: Blackwell, 1973, 28–50.

―――. 1978. *The Aristotelian Ethics: A Study of the Relationship between the Eudemian and the Nicomachean Ethics of Aristotle.* Oxford: Clarendon Press.

―――. 1979. *Aristotle's Theory of the Will.* London: Duckworth.

―――. 1992. *Aristotle on the Perfect Life.* Oxford: Clarendon Press.

Keyt, D. 1983. "Intellectualism in Aristotle." In Anton and Preus 1983, 364–87.

―――. 1991. "Three Basic Theorems in Aristotle's *Politics.*" In Keyt and Miller 1991, 118–41.

―――. and Miller, F. Eds. 1991. *A Companion to Aristotle's Politics.* Oxford; Cambridge, Mass.: Blackwell.

Korsgaard, C. M. 1986. "Aristotle and Kant on the Source of Value." *Ethics* 96: 486–505.

―――. 1986a. "Aristotle on Function and Virtue." *History of Philosophy Quarterly* 3.3: 259–79.

―――. 1996. *The Sources of Normativity.* Cambridge: Cambridge University Press.

Kosman, L. A. 1968. "Predicating the Good." *Phronesis* 13.2: 171–4.

———. 1980. "Being Properly Affected: Virtues and Feelings in Aristotle's Ethics." In Rorty 1980, 103–16.

Kraut, R. 1976. "Aristotle on Choosing Virtue for Itself." *Archiv für Geschichte der Philosophie* 58: 223–39.

———. 1984. *Socrates and the State*. Princeton: Princeton University Press.

———. 1988. "Comments on 'Disunity in the Aristotelian Virtues' by T. H. Irwin." *Oxford Studies in Ancient Philosophy*, supplementary volume, 79–86.

———. 1989. *Aristotle on the Human Good*. Princeton: Princeton University Press.

———. Ed. 1992. *The Cambridge Companion to Plato*. Cambridge: Cambridge University Press.

———. 1997. *Politics, Books VII and VIII*. Oxford: Oxford University Press.

———. 2002. *Aristotle: Political Philosophy*. Oxford; New York: Oxford University Press.

———. Ed. 2006. *The Blackwell Guide to Aristotle's Nicomachean Ethics*. Oxford: Blackwell.

Kullman, W. and Föllinger, S. 1997. *Aristotelische Biologie: Intentionen, Methoden, Ergebnisse:* Akten des Symposion über Aristoteles' Biologie vom 24.–28. Juli 1995 in der Werner-Reimers-Stiftung in Bad Homburg. Stuttgart: Franz Steiner Verlag.

Laks, A. and Rashed, M. Eds. 2004. *Aristote et le Mouvement des Animaux: Dix Études sur le De Motu Animalium*. Villeneuve d'Ascq: Presses Universitaires du Septentrion.

Lawrence, G. 1993. "Aristotle and the Ideal Life." *Philosophical Review* 102.1: 1–34.

———. 1997. "Nonaggregability, Inclusiveness, and the Theory of Focal Value: *Nicomachean Ethics* I. 7. 1097b16–20." *Phronesis* 42.1: 32–76.

———. and Quinn, W. Eds. 1995. *Virtues and Reasons: Philippa Foot and Moral Theory: Essays in Honour of Philippa Foot*. Oxford: Oxford University Press.

Leighton, S. 1982. "Aristotle and the Emotions." *Phronesis* 27.2: 144–74.

———. 1992. "Relativizing Moral Excellence in Aristotle." *Apeiron* 25: 49–66.

———. 1995. "The Mean Relative to Us." In Bosley, Shiner, and Sissons 1995, 67–78.

Lemoine, N. R. and Cooper, D. N. Eds. 1996. *Gene Therapy*. Oxford: Bios Publishers.

Lennox, J. G. 1987. "Divide and Explain: The *Posterior Analytics* in Practice." In Lennox 2001, 7–38 (reprinted from Gotthelf and Lennox 1987).

———. 2001. *Aristotle's Philosophy of Biology: Studies in the Origins of Life Science*. Cambridge; New York: Cambridge University Press.

Liddell H. G., Scott, R. revised by Jones, Sir H. S., McKenzie, R. et al., with supplement by P. G. W. Glare with A. A. Thompson. 1996. *A Greek-English Lexicon*. Oxford: Oxford University Press.

Lloyd. G. E. R. 1968. "The Role of Medical and Biological Analogies in Aristotle's Ethics." *Phronesis* 13.1: 68–83.

———. 1996. *Aristotelian Explorations*. Cambridge; New York: Cambridge University Press.

Lockwood, T. 2005. *A Topical Bibliography of Scholarship on Aristotle's Nicomachean Ethics: 1880 to 2004*. *Journal of Philosophical Research* 30: 1–116.

Long, A. A. 1991. "The Harmonics of Stoic Virtue." In *Aristotle and the Later Tradition*, ed. H. Blumenthal and H. Robinson, *Oxford Studies in Ancient Philosophy*, supplementary volume, 97–116.

———. and Sedley, D. N. *The Hellenistic Philosophers*. Cambridge: Cambridge University Press, 1987.

Losin, P. 1987. "Aristotle's Doctrine of the Mean." *History of Philosophy Quarterly* 4.3: 329–41.

Lottin, D. O. 1955. "Aristote et La Connexion des Vertus Morales." In *Autour d'Aristote*, ed. Mansion, Louvain: Publications Universitaires de Louvain, 1955, 343–64.

Louden, R. B. 1992. *Morality and Moral Theory*. Oxford: Oxford University Press.

MacIntyre, A. 1981. *After Virtue*. Notre Dame: Notre Dame University Press.

MacKenzie, M. M. 1989. "Aristotelian Authority." In *Images of Authority: Papers Presented to Joyce Reynold on the Occasion of her Seventieth Birthday*, ed. M. M. MacKenzie and C. Roueché, *Cambridge Philosophical Society*, supplementary volume, 16: 150–70.

McDowell, J. 1979. "Virtue and Reason." *Monist* 62: 331–50.

———. 1980. "The Role of *Eudaimonia* in Aristotle's Ethics." In Rorty 1980, 359–76.

———. 1995. "Might There Be External Reasons?" In Altham and Harrison 1995, 68–85.

———. 1995a. "Two Sorts of Naturalism." In Hursthouse, Lawrence, and Quinn 1995, 149–79.

———. 1996. *Mind and World*. Cambridge, Mass.: Harvard University Press.

———. 1998. *Mind, Value, and Reality*. Cambridge, Mass.: Harvard University Press.

McKeon, R. Ed. 1941. *The Basic Works of Aristotle*. New York: Random House.

Menn, S. 1995. "Metaphysics, Dialectic and the *Categories*." *Revue de Metaphysique et Morale* 100.3: 311–37.

Meyer, S. S. 1993. *Aristotle on Moral Responsibility: Character and Cause*. New York: Blackwell.

Mill, J. S. *Utilitarianism, On Liberty, Essay on Bentham and Selected Writings of Jeremy Bentham and John Austin*. Ed. with introduction by M. Warnock. Glasgow: Collins, 1962.

Miller, F. D. Jr. 1995. *Nature, Justice, and Rights in Aristotle's Politics*. Oxford: Clarendon Press; New York: Oxford University Press.

Moravscik, J. M. E. Ed. 1967. *Aristotle: A Collection of Critical Essays*. Garden City, New York: Doubleday.

Mulgan, R. J. 1977. *Aristotle's Political Theory*. Oxford: Clarendon Press.

Nagel, T. 1969. "Sexual Perversion." Reprinted in *Mortal Questions*. Cambridge: Cambridge University Press, 1979, 39–52.

———. 1976. "Moral Luck." Reprinted in *Mortal Questions*. Cambridge: Cambridge University Press, 1979, 24–38.

Natali, C. 2001. *The Wisdom of Aristotle*. Trans. G. Parks. Albany: State University of New York Press.

Newman, W. L. 1887–1902. *The Politics of Aristotle*. vols. 1–4, Oxford: Clarendon Press.

Noddings, N. 1984. *Caring: A Feminine Approach to Ethics and Moral Education*. Berkeley: University of California Press.

North, H. 1966. *Sophrosyne: Self-Knowledge and Self-Restraint in Greek Literature*. Ithaca: Cornell University Press.

Nussbaum, M. C. 1978. *Aristotle's de Motu Animalium*. Text with Translation and Interpretive Essays. Princeton: Princeton University Press.

———. 1986. *The Fragility of Goodness: Luck and Ethics in Greek Tragedy and Philosophy*. Cambridge: Cambridge University Press.

———. 1988. "Non-Relative Virtues: An Aristotelian Approach." In French, Uehling, and Wettstein 1988, 32–53.

———. 2000. *Women and Human Development: The Capabilities Approach*. Cambridge: Cambridge University Press.

Ober, J. 1998. *Political Dissent in Democratic Athens: Intellectual Critics of Popular Virtue.* Princeton: Princeton University Press.

O'Meara, D. J. Ed. 1981. *Studies in Aristotle.* Washington D.C.: Catholic University of America Press.

Pakaluk, M. 2002. "On an Alleged Contradiction in Aristotle's Ethics." *Oxford Studies in Ancient Philosophy* 22: 201–19.

Pears, D. 1980. "Courage as a Mean." In Rorty 1980, 171–87.

Pence, G. 1984. "Recent Work on Virtues." *American Philosophical Quarterly* 21: 281–97.

Penner, T. M. I. 1973. "The Unity of Virtue." *Philosophical Review* 82: 35–68 (reprinted in Benson 1992).

———. 1987. *The Ascent from Nominalism: Some Existence Arguments in Plato's Middle Dialogues.* Dordrecht, Holland: Reidel.

———. 1992. "What Laches and Nicias Miss – And Whether Socrates Thinks Courage Merely a Part of Virtue." *Ancient Philosophy* 12: 1–27.

———. 1992a. "Socrates and the Early Dialogues." In Kraut 1992, 121–69.

Perry, J. 1979. "The Problem of the Essential Indexical." *Nous* 13: 3–21.

Prichard, H. A. 1949. *Moral Obligation.* Oxford: Clarendon Press. Reprinted 1968.

———. 1967. "The Meaning of *agathon* in the Ethics of Aristotle." In J. M. Moravscik, 1967, 241–60.

Rackham, H. 1935. *Tr. Aristotle: The Athenian Constitution, The Eudemian Ethics and On Virtue and Vices.* The Loeb Classical Library. Cambridge, Mass.: Harvard University Press, revised 1952, reprinted 1982, vol. 20.

Rand, A. 1964. *The Virtue of Selfishness, a New Concept of Egoism.* New American Library, New York: Signet Books.

Reeve, C. D. C. 1992. *Practices of Reason.* Oxford: Oxford University Press.

———. 2004. *Plato's Republic.* Indianapolis; Cambridge: Hackett.

Roberts, J. 1989. "Political Animals in the Nicomachean Ethics." *Phronesis* 34.2: 185–204.

Richardson, H. S. 1994. *Practical Reasoning about Final Ends.* Cambridge, Mass.: Cambridge University Press.

Richardson Lear, G. 2004. *Happy Lives and the Highest Good: An Essay on Aristotle's Nicomachean Ethics.* Princeton: Princeton University Press.

Robinson, R. 1962. *Aristotle's Politics Books III and IV.* Translation with introduction and comments. Oxford: Clarendon Press.

———. 1995. *Aristotle's Politics Books III and IV.* Translation and commentary revised with supplementary essay by D. Keyt. Oxford: Clarendon Press.

Roche, T. D. 1988. "Ergon and Eudaimonia in Nicomachean Ethics I: Reconsidering the Intellectualist Interpretation." *Journal of the History of Philosophy* 26: 175–94.

———. 2004. Comments on Curzer's "How Good People Do Bad Things: Aristotle on the Misdeeds of the Virtuous," unpublished.

Rodier, G. Ed. 1900. *Aristote: Traité de L'âme.* Translation and Commentary. Paris: E. Leroux.

Rorty, A. O. Ed. 1980. *Essays on Aristotle's Ethics.* Berkeley and Los Angeles: University of California Press.

———. and Flanagan, O. Eds. 1991. *Identity, Character and Morality: Essays in Moral Psychology.* Cambridge, Mass.: MIT Press.

Ross, W. D. 1923. *Translation of Aristotle's Nicomachean Ethics.* Oxford: Clarendon Press (and on the web, for example, via www.episteme.links.com).

———. 1949. *Commentary on Aristotle's Prior and Posterior Analytics.* Oxford: Clarendon Press.

Russell, Bertrand. 1930. *The Conquest of Happiness.* New York: Liveright.

Ryle, Gilbert. 1958. "On Forgetting the Difference between Right and Wrong." In *Essays in Moral Philosophy*, ed. A. I. Melden, Seattle: University of Washington Press, 147–59.

Sachs, Joe. 2001. *Aristotle's Nicomachean Ethics.* Translation, glossary, and introductory essay. Newburyport, Mass.: Focus Publishing, R. Pullins Company.

Salkever, S. G. 1990. *Finding the Mean: Theory and Practice in Aristotelian Political Philosophy.* Princeton: Princeton University Press.

Santas, G. 1989. "Aristotle's Criticism of Plato's Form of the Good: Ethics without Metaphysics?" *Philosophical Quarterly* 18.2: 137–60.

———. 2001. *Goodness and Justice: Plato, Aristotle, and the Moderns.* Malden, Mass.: Blackwell.

Sartre, J.-P. 1946. "Existentialism Is a Humanism." In *Existentialism and the Human Emotions.* New York: The Philosophical Library, 1947.

Schofield, M. and Striker, G. Ed. 1986. *The Norms of Nature: Studies in Hellenistic Ethics.* Cambridge: Cambridge University Press.

Schollmeier, P. 1998. "Ancient Tragedy and Other Selves." *Revue de Métaphysique et de Morale* 103: 175–88.

Sherman, N. 1989. *The Fabric of Character: Aristotle's Theory of Virtue.* Oxford: Clarendon Press.

———. 1994. "The Role of Emotions in Aristotelian Virtue." *Boston Area Colloquium in Ancient Philosophy* 9: 1–33.

———. 1997. *Making a Necessity of Virtue: Aristotle and Kant on Virtue.* Cambridge: Cambridge University Press.

Shields, C. J. 1999. *Order in Multiplicity: Homonymy in the Philosophy of Aristotle.* Oxford: Oxford University Press.

Sidgwick, H. 1884. *The Methods of Ethics.* Foreword by J. Rawls. Reprinted 7th edition. Indianapolis: Hackett, 1981.

Sim, M. 2003. "Harmony and the Mean in the Nicomachean Ethics and the Zhongyong." *Dao: A Journal of Comparative Philosophy* 3.2: 253–80.

Simpson, P. 1998. *A Philosophical Commentary on the Politics of Aristotle.* Chapel Hill: University of North Carolina Press.

Singer, M. G. 1990–1. "Polar Terms and Interdependent Concepts." *Philosophical Exchange* 1990–1: 55–71.

Sivin, N. 1995. *Medicine, Philosophy and Religion in Ancient China: Researches and Reflections.* Aldershot, Hampshire, UK; Brookfield, Vermont: Ashgate Publishing.

Slote, M. 1992. *From Morality to Virtue.* Oxford: Oxford University Press.

Smith, J. A. 1920. "Aristotelica." *Classical Quarterly* 14: 16–22.

Smith, R. 1997. *Topics Books I and VIII.* Translation and Commentary. Oxford: Oxford University Press.

Sober, E. 1993. *Philosophy of Biology.* Boulder, Colorado: Westview Press.

Sorabji, R. 1973–4. "Aristotle on the Role of Intellect in Virtue." In Rorty 1980, 201–19.

Stampe, D. "The Will and the A Priori," unpublished.

Stewart, J. A. 1892. *Notes on the Nicomachean Ethics.* vols. 1 and 2, Oxford: Clarendon Press.

Stocker, M. 1990. *Plural and Conflicting Values.* Oxford: Oxford University Press.

Swanton, C. 2003. *Virtue Ethics.* New York: Oxford University Press.

Taylor, C. C. W. 1976. *Plato's Protagoras.* Oxford: Clarendon Press.

Telfer, E. 1989–90. "The Unity of the Moral Virtues in Aristotle's Nicomachean Ethics." *Proceedings of the Aristotelian Society* 91: 35–48.

Tessitore, A. 1996. *Reading Aristotle's Ethics: Virtue, Rhetoric and Political Philosophy.* Albany: State University of New York Press.

Theophrastus. *Characters.* Ed. and Trans. J. Rusten, I. C. Cunningham, and A. D. Knox, The Loeb Classical Library. Cambridge, Mass.: Harvard University Press, 1993.

Thomas, L. 1989. *Living Morally: A Psychology of Moral Character.* Philadelphia: Temple University Press.

Thomson, J. A. K. 1976. *Aristotle's Nicomachean Ethics*. Translation with appendices by H. Tredennick, and introduction and bibliography by Jonathan Barnes. Middlesex, England: Penguin.

Torstrik, A. Ed. 1862. *Aristotle De Anima Libri 3*. Berlin: Weidmann.

Tracy, T. J. 1969. *Physiological Theory and the Doctrine of the Mean in Plato and Aristotle*. Chicago: Loyola University Press.

Trianosky, G. 1990. "What is Virtue Ethics All About?" *American Philosophical Quarterly* 27.4: 335–44.

Tuozzo, T. M. 1991. "Aristotelian Deliberation Is Not of Ends." In Anton and Preus 1991, 193–212.

Urmson, J. O. 1973. "Aristotle's Doctrine of the Mean." Reprinted in Rorty 1980, 157–70.

————. 1988. *Aristotle's Ethics*. New York: Basil Blackwell.

Veltman, A. 2004. "Aristotle and Kant on Self-Disclosure in Friendship." *Journal of Value Inquiry* 38.2: 225–39.

Vlastos, G. 1972. "The Unity of the Virtues in the Protagoras." *Review of Metaphysics* 25: 415–58 (reprinted in *Platonic Studies*, Princeton: Princeton University Press, 1973, 221–69).

————. 1973. "The Individual as Object of Love in Plato." In *Platonic Studies*. Princeton: Princeton University Press, 1973, 3–42.

————. 1991. *Socrates: Ironist and Moral Philosopher*. Cambridge: Cambridge University Press.

Von Arnim, H. Ed. *Stoicorum Veterum Fragmenta*. Leipzig: Teubner, 1905, vols. 1–4.

Wallace, J. D. 1978. *Virtues and Vices*. Ithaca: Cornell University Press.

White, N. P. 1988. "Good as Goal." *The Southern Journal of Philosophy* 27, supplementary volume, 169–93.

————. 2002. *Individual and Conflict in Greek Ethics*. Oxford: Clarendon Press.

White, S. A. 1992. *Sovereign Virtue: Aristotle on the Relation between Happiness and Prosperity*. Stanford, California: Stanford University Press.

Whiting, J. E. 1986. "Human Nature and Intellectualism in Aristotle." *Archiv für Geschichte der Philosophie* 68: 70–95.

————. 1988. "Aristotle's Function Argument: A Defense." *Ancient Philosophy* 8.1: 33–48.

————. 1991. "Impersonal Friends." *Monist* 74.1: 3–29.

————. 1996. "Self-Love and Authoritative Virtues: Prolegomenon to a Kantian Reading of *Eudemian Ethics* viii 3." In Engstrom and Whiting 1996, 162–99.

Wiggins, D. 1975–6. "Deliberation and Practical Reasoning." In Rorty 1980, 221–40.

Williams, B. A. O. 1962. "Aristotle on the Good: A Formal Sketch." *Philosophical Quarterly* 12.49: 289–96.

———. 1980. "Justice as a Virtue." In Rorty 1980, 189–99.

———. 1981. *Moral Luck*. Cambridge: Cambridge University Press.

———. 1981a. "Internal and External Reasons." In Williams 1981, 101–13.

———. 1981b. "Moral Luck." In Williams 1981, 20–39.

———. 1985. *Ethics and the Limits of Philosophy*. Cambridge, Mass.: Harvard University Press.

———. 1993. *Shame and Necessity*. Berkeley and Los Angeles: California University Press.

———. 1995. *Making Sense of Humanity*. Cambridge: Cambridge University Press.

Wingo, A. H. 1998. "African Art and the Aesthetics of Hiding and Revealing." *British Journal of Aesthetics* 38.3: 251–64.

Winter, M. 1997. "Aristotle, *Hōs Epi to Polu* Relations, and a Demonstrative Science of Ethics." *Phronesis* 42.2: 163–89.

Winthrop, D. 1978. "Aristotle on Participatory Democracy." *Polity* 11.2: 151–71.

Woodruff, P. 1976. "Socrates on the Parts of Virtue." *Canadian Journal of Philosophy*, supplementary volume 2, 101–16.

Woods, M. J. 1992. *Aristotle's Eudemian Ethics Books I, II and VIII*. 2nd edition. Oxford: Clarendon Press.

Young, C. 1988. "Aristotle on Justice." Proceedings of the Spindel Conference, *Southern Journal of Philosophy* 27, supplementary volume, 233–49.

———. 1988. "Aristotle on Temperance." *Philosophical Review* 97: 521–42.

Yu, J. 2002. "The Aristotelian Mean and Confucian Mean." *Journal of Chinese Philosophy* 29.3: 337–54.

Zagzebski, L. T. 1996. *Virtues of the Mind. An Inquiry into the Nature of Virtue and the Ethical Foundations of Knowledge*. Cambridge: Cambridge University Press.

Index